# UNDERSTANDING PROPERTY: A GUIDE TO CANADA'S PROPERTY LAW

2ND EDITION

**Marjorie Lynne Benson**

**Marie-Ann Bowden**

**Dwight Newman**

A Cataloguing record for this publication is available from Library and Archives Canada.

ISBN: 978-0-7798-1366-7 (2008 edition)

One Corporate Plaza
2075 Kennedy Road
Toronto, Ontario
M1T 3V4

Customer Relations
Toronto 1-416-609-3800
Elsewhere in Canada/U.S. 1-800-387-5164
Fax 1-416-298-5082
World Wide Web: http://www.carswell.com
E-mail: carswell.orders@thomson.com

# PREFACE

This work arose out of our teaching. Our task has been to try to simplify and synthesize the many layers of property law to provide a meaningful guide to students through first year real and personal property and Aboriginal title. The book reflects our ongoing journey to distill foundational understandings with fidelity to history, doctrine, and principle. This second edition incorporates eleven additional years of study since the first. New cases and statutes from across Canada highlight intervening changes in the law. Examples, language, style, and format have been updated. Chapters have been re-ordered and subjects combined, and the historical development of real property, including future interests, presented to reflect the building block approach taken by the common law. The Aboriginal Title section has been substantially expanded. Our goal throughout has been clarity and cohesiveness in understanding property law.

Three property regimes are recognized in Canadian law: the civil law system in Quebec, the common law system in nine provinces and the Territories, and *sui generis* Aboriginal title. Quebec civil law property doctrines are beyond our expertise. Within common law, current doctrines are more a product of history than logic, reflecting layers of Roman law, Norman feudalism, English common law and equity, Canadian constitutional law, federal, provincial, and municipal statutes.

Land and possessions are such an integral part of human identity that a society's property laws reveal much about its social structure, and each generation has worked out new property laws to reflect changes in its social reality. Common law precedents abstract rules from their geography of origin, universalize them across space, and continue to apply them long after the circumstances that gave rise to the rule have passed away. As words and concepts acquire new meanings, as rules interact and combine yet continue, common law doctrine becomes a rich study of history and the human condition as well as a jumble of rules and practices. The book attempts to provide road maps through the history and precedents, outline a conceptual structure that relates fundamental categories to one another, and describe elements of the present doctrines. With respect to Aboriginal title, the book attempts to provide an up-to-date guide to history and case law, a set of fundamental principles, and an accessible path through the case law to understand how the history and those principles work together in the Supreme Court of Canada and in trial decisions.

# Preface

The work is a starting point rather than an end point of research. It offers readers basic understandings and a framework within which to develop a detailed strategy for research in specialized treatises, statutes, and cases.

The work is divided into four parts. Parts I, II, and III on real and personal property were revised by Benson and Bowden, and Part IV on Aboriginal title by Newman. Part I provides definitions and sources of Canadian property law. Part II addresses personal property and its attendant legal relationships. Part III addresses real property, including a historical framework, common law doctrines, and conveyancing systems. Part IV addresses Aboriginal title, offering a historical introduction, principles of, and introductions to, the emerging case law, and comments on future issues.

The book offers a detailed table of contents and index, but it is not possible to comprehensively footnote each treatise writer from whom we have come to understand the history, sources, and boundaries of individual doctrines. Cases are fully cited within the textual material when first mentioned. The book's linguistic convention is to use the past tense and male pronoun in historical sections, and the present tense and alternate male and female pronouns when addressing current doctrine.

Any work of this nature is built on the shoulders of those who have come before. We thank the many teachers and authors from whom we have learned property law. We thank our colleagues and students who have supported us and constantly challenged us to be clearer, as well as Leah Howie and Sarah Burningham for research assistance and Michelle Halvorson for computer expertise.

This work is dedicated to those who recognize the connection between property law and the land and who seek rules and practices that sustain and nourish the earth.

With respect,
Marjorie L. Benson
Marie-Ann Bowden
Dwight Newman
University of Saskatchewan
Saskatoon, Saskatchewan
Spring, 2008

# TABLE OF CONTENTS

## Chapter 12 — Future Interests



## Chapter 13 — Co-ownership

# TABLE OF CASES

State of Ohio v. Shaw, 65 N.E. 875 (Ohio, 1902) ........ 3.1(a), 3.1(b)

Stein v. Van Eldik (2005), 16 E.T.R. (3d) 1 (Alta. Q.B.) ........ 5.0

Stewart v. Gustafson (1998), [1999] 4 W.W.R. 695 (Sask. Q.B.) ........ 3.2

Sutherland v. Canada (Attorney General), 2002 BCCA 416 (B.C. C.A.); additional reasons at (2003), 2003 CarswellBC 288 (B.C. C.A.); leave to appeal refused (2003), 2003 CarswellBC 1102 (S.C.C.) ........ 14.1(c)

Sutherland v. Vancouver Airport Authority ........ 14.3(d)

Syncrude Canada Ltd. v. Hunter Engineering Co., [1989] 1 S.C.R. 426 (S.C.C.) ........ 6.2(d)(iii)

Taku River Tlingit First Nation v. British Columbia (Project Assessment Director), [2004] 3 S.C.R. 550, 2004 SCC 74 (S.C.C.) ........ 18.3(e)

Tanenbaum v. W.J. Bell Paper Co., [1956] O.R. 278 (Ont. H.C.) ........ 6.3(a)(iii)

Taylor v. Scurry-Rainbow Oil (Sask) Ltd. (2001), [2001] S.J. No. 479, 2001 CarswellSask 539 (Sask. C.A.) ........ 12.8(c)

The Winkfield, [1900-3] All E.R. 346 (C.A.) ........ 6.3(a)(i)

Thomas v. Canada, 2006 ABQB 730 (Alta. Q.B.) ........ 4.0

Threatt v. Rushing, 361 So. 2d 329 (Miss., 1978) ........ 13.4(e)

Tilbury West Public School Board v. Hastie (1966), 55 D.L.R. (2d) 407 (Ont. H.C.); varied 57 D.L.R. (2d) 519 (Ont. H.C.) ........ 11.4(a)(i)

Trachuk v. Olinek (1995), [1996] 4 W.W.R. 137 (Alta. Q.B.) ........ 4.1

Tsilhqot'in Nation v. British Columbia, *see* Williams v. British Columbia

"Tubantia" (The), [1924] All E.R. Rep. 615 (Adm. Ct.) ........ 3.1(a)

Tulk. v. Moxhay (1848), 41 E.R. 1143 (Eng. Ch. Div.) ........ 15.4

Turta v. Canadian Pacific Railway, [1954] S.C.R. 427 (S.C.C.) ........ 16.3(d), 16.4(b)

# Part I

# Property Relationships

# CHAPTER 1 — DEFINITIONAL TERMS



## 1.1 — Holder-Right-*Res*-Enforceability

What is property law? Property is the Anglo-American phrase for the study of the legal relationships between people and the resources they use to live their lives and the relationships among various stakeholders in relation to those resources. The meaning of a property right, who can hold and enforce a property right, and against whom this can be done is historically based and changes over time. For example, women and slaves were once considered capable of being the subject matter of property; many natural resources were once not the subject of property, but now are; the moon is not now, but may in the future be the subject of a property interest. Property has shifted from being held communally to being held individually, although not all individuals have historically been seen as having the capacity to hold property. Property rights began with possession and now include many kinds of interests in addition to possession. The ability to enforce property rights has expanded from the person who has a right to possession against the person in possession to many parties against many other stakeholders.

In casual conversation, property is often a noun — a thing or a place. The thought is not just any thing or place but the particular thing or land that someone bought, inherited, or received as a gift. The thought is that he or she owns it, which means being able to do what one likes with it, generally excluding others, as well as deciding what happens to it when one no longer desires to keep it. The control of property might not be absolute. For example, with respect to land, a spouse's name might be on a land title as joint owner, the bank might have a mortgage on the land, or a utility company may have the right to cross the land with power lines. With respect to goods, an auto dealership may have a security interest in a car, the car can be loaned to a friend or taken to a garage for repairs, and although the mechanics may fix the car, they do not own it and may not use it to drive themselves around. Thus the (non-legal) idea of property is also an idea of rights, with different rights for different people. These rights become legal rights when a court of law recognizes certain behaviour with respect to property as being enforceable. Property law puts legal words and rules around these everyday relationships.

Property law requires care in the use of the word "own." Many different people can own the same property in different ways. In land law, the legal word is "holder" — one does not own land but rather holds a particular estate or interest in land. In moveable things, the law acknowledges a concept of ownership, but because several people can hold different rights in the same thing, it is always necessary to talk in terms of which portions of a bundle of rights one has to the particular property.

That which is the subject matter of a property right is called a *res* — Latin for thing. A property right is a particular right in a particular *res*, held by a particular holder, enforceable against particular persons. For ease of reference, we signify that relationship as holder-right-*res*-enforceability. The number of holder-right-*res*-enforceability relationships is infinite. There may be as many holders, rights, *res*, and enforceability variations as courts and legislatures are willing to recognize. Each relationship of holder-right-*res*-enforceability is governed by the rules applicable to that particular relationship as defined by legislation or judicial decisions applicable in that jurisdiction. For example, a holder who has title to a house may enforce it against anyone who cannot prove a better title but cannot enforce it against a mortgagee who obtains an order for foreclosure.

The rules governing each particular holder-right-*res*-enforceability relationship are the rules contained in the many fields relevant to property law. Analyzing a property problem requires determining each of the holder-right-*res*-enforceability relationships, selecting the rule that is relevant to the relationship, applying the respective rule to each unit of holder-right-*res*-enforceability in turn, and cumulating their effect to determine the legal outcome in the particular set of circumstances.

Canadian common law property rules descended from English property law. The categories of holder-right-*res*-enforceability and the rules governing them that developed in English law were the categories relevant to the society at the time they were formed. As societal requirements changed, new categories of property law developed to contain new rules governing the new types of holder-right-*res*-enforceability relationships. Many of the fundamental terms in English property law developed in pre-feudal times and can only be understood historically.

## 1.2 — Real and Personal Property

In pre-feudal England, communities farmed land in common. A community that lost possession of its land could not survive, and law provided a non-violent means to resolve disputes among communities over land. In terms of the holder-right-*res*-enforceability relationship, the holder of the rights was the community, possession was the right, and land was the *res*. This right of a community to land was enforceable against other communities that might try to dispossess an existing community of its land.

In this society, each family pastured cattle. A family that was dispossessed of its cattle raised a public hue and cry and followed the trail of the cattle to repossess them. Neighbours joined in the chase. When the cattle were located, the possessor was required to show why he had a better right to possess the cattle. In this case, families were the holders, the right was possession, the *res* were cattle, and the right was enforceable against anyone who dispossessed the family of its cattle.

The legal action that a community dispossessed of its land could take in a local court to recover its land was different from the legal action a family could take to recover cattle. In land, possession came to be called seisin. A holder who lost possession was disseised and could bring an action against the disseisor, the one who had taken over possession. Whoever could prove a better right to the land was put in possession of the land. Such an action decided the fate of the *res* — the land itself. Because of that, it was called a real action, and the recovery was called an *in rem* recovery — the land itself could be recovered.

In contrast, a family dispossessed of cattle was required to bring an action called detinue. A dispossessor had detained cattle and refused to return them on a demand to do so. If the action was successful the dispossessed cattle holder was not guaranteed the return of his cattle. The King might have already taken them under the King's right to the forfeiture of stolen property. The most that the family that had lost its cattle could achieve, even if successful, was an order for damages. The action was said to be *in personam*, meaning against the person of the dispossessor. The dispossessor would be required to pay damages.

If the courts permitted the thing itself to be recovered, the thing was called real property. Land was real property. Real property corresponded to the category that Roman law had called immoveables. If the courts would not order the return of the thing but only damages from a person, that thing came to be called personal property. Items of personal property were called chattels, after cattle, and came to include those things Roman law had called moveables.

## 1.3 — Tangible and Intangible Property

By the time English courts had developed the categories of real and personal property based on the kind of action taken to recover rights to possession, social structures had evolved so that different people were holding different rights in the same piece of land or the same cattle.

In real property, after William the Conqueror became King of England in 1066, he wished to claim an interest in all the lands of England in order to secure control and provide himself with a source of revenue. The solution offered by legal advisors was to declare all the land in England to be held of the King. Communities would no longer be full owners of land (allodial ownership), but rather they would hold of the King. The King would grant them tenure in the land (after the French word "tenir", meaning to hold). The King would grant an estate (derived from the word "status", meaning rank) to individual lords and barons. These grants were held in return for certain feudal dues. Lords in turn were permitted to grant portions of their land to lesser lords and impose their own additional dues. At the bottom of the feudal hierarchy, villeins had certain rights to go on the land to perform their duties as hewers of wood and drawers of water. Thus there was a need for a number of different rights in land that different people could hold. Many of these rights did not involve possession. The rights in land such as the King's underlying title, or the villein's right to go on the land to cultivate it, were rights that were not sensate. They were intangible. Yet they were property rights that courts enforced. Such rights came to be called incorporeal rights. They were rights, but they were intangible, as distinguished from corporeal rights — the right to possession of the land itself.

In personal property, the *res* was called a chose in possession. The right to recover the *res* was insensate, yet it was a right that the courts would enforce. Hence it was called a chose in action. This right was intangible personal property.

The result was that real property was subdivided into corporeal and incorporeal property. Corporeal was the tangible *res*; incorporeal was the intangible right. Personal property was also subdivided into choses in possession — the tangible *res*, and choses in action — intangible rights.

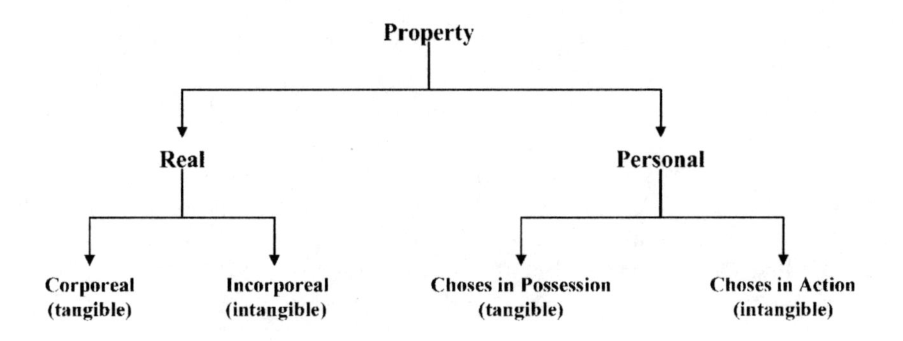


## 1.4 — Legal and Equitable Relationships

Property relationships also developed as either legal or equitable according to whether they arose through the Courts of Common Law (legal) or in the Courts of Equity (equitable).

Before 1066, disputes concerning the possession of land or chattels were resolved in local courts. After 1066, Norman Kings established royal courts that included the Court of Common Pleas to hear disputes among common people, the King's Court to hear disputes involving the King (including land granted by the King), and the Exchequer Court to handle sheriff's accounts.

No action could be initiated in the royal courts without permission from the King. This permission was given in the form of a writ authorizing a particular action. The Chancellor was the King's chief executive officer. As keeper of the Great Seal, the Chancellor issued the originating writs. Each writ permitted a very limited and narrow action. For example, if an inheriting son was dispossessed of land by a third party, he could request a *writ of mort d'ancestor* to take action against the disseisor. If he had inherited as a grandson, he needed a *writ of aiel*; if as a great grandson, a *writ of besaiel*. The wrong writ was fatal to his action.

The King, however, was the fount of all justice. A demandant — twelfth century name for a plaintiff — with a complaint not covered by an existing writ could appeal to the King for a new writ. Parliament was reluctant to allow the King to issue such writs, because it realized that the power to issue a new writ was the power to create new remedies, which was the power to make law. By 1258, the compromise was that the Chancellor could issue new writs, but only with the permission of Parliament.

In addition to being the King's chief executive officer, the Chancellor was the King's chief advisor. The Chancellor was usually a bishop trained in Roman and church law. If an action was brought against the King himself, the action was not a writ, but a petition for relief from the King. As the King's conscience, the Chancellor heard and advised the King's Council on such cases. The Chancellor also heard cases where a demandant did not believe that he had received justice in the Common Law courts.

When the Chancellor made a ruling, he insisted that he was not overruling the law made by the royal courts, but that he was providing only an equitable ruling, meaning justice on the case. His ruling was an order against a person in a particular situation, no more. His order required the person to do something (specific performance) or to stop doing something (injunction) on pain of going to jail. The Chancellor worked on the mind and body of the person. He based his ruling on principles from Roman Equity and Church canons, such as "no person should benefit from his own wrong", "equity looks to the intent rather than the form", and "equity will not suffer a wrong to be without a remedy".

Over time the number of cases being heard by the Chancellor increased and the Chancellor developed his own court staff, including clerks and a Master of the Rolls. They began to abide by their own previous rulings and became a court in their own right, known as the Court of Chancery or the Court of Equity. As the rulings of Equity became systematized, a new body of rights came into being known as equitable rights.

In the Courts of Common Law, the holder of the legal title held the entire interest in the property. The Courts of Equity, however, were prepared to recognize an equitable right to property that would defeat the legal title in certain situations. The equitable right became a property right.

While an equitable right was originally enforceable only against a particular person, over time the Courts of Equity expanded the persons against whom they would enforce the right. For example, Equity held that a purchaser of a legal estate who knew of a pre-existing equitable interest was bound, in conscience, to honour that interest. Eventually equitable interests became enforceable against all legal interests except those of a *bona fide* purchaser for value without notice. *Bona fide* meant in good faith. Purchase meant a transfer by an action of the parties rather than by a rule of law. For value meant having paid good consideration. Without notice meant no actual, constructive or implied notice. These terms will he explored in detail in the context of particular rules.

In 1873 in England, the *Judicature Act, 1873*, (U.K.), 36 & 37 Victoria, c. 66, merged the Courts of Common Law with the Courts of Equity into one court system called the Court of Queen's Bench, giving that new system authority to make decisions concerning both legal and equitable rights. Canada imported the English court system, and *Queen's Bench Acts* in each province give Canadian courts both legal and equitable jurisdiction. However, legal and equitable remain different species of property relationships reflected in modern law in subtle but important ways because legal and equitable rights are enforceable in different ways against different parties.

## 1.5 — Multiple Meanings of Terms

Clear thinking in property law requires close attention to context. Because historical evolution has given the same terms different meanings across time, it is easy to attribute meanings different from the ones intended. Three examples are offered: (a) common law; (b) *in rem* and *in personam*; and (c) chose in action.

### (a) — Common Law

Pre-1066, common law in England meant the law of the people or customary law. Post-1066, common law came to mean the law developed in the Courts of Common Law as opposed to the Courts of Equity. When the *Judicature Act, 1873* merged the Courts of Common Law and Equity, doctrines arising from both these Court systems came to be called common law to distinguish them from growing body of statutory law passed by legislators. Judge-made law from the courts became known as common law as opposed to statute law. In the twentieth century, common law has come to mean the legal system that developed in England as opposed to the legal system that developed in Continental Europe, which is called civil law.

### (b) — In Rem and In Personam

As noted, *in rem* was the name given to legal actions in which the *res* itself was recoverable. The category of real property emerged from this term. Real property consisted of land. In actions concerning land, the land itself was recoverable.

*In personam*, in contrast, referred to actions in which recovery of the thing itself was not guaranteed. An action for loss of possession could be taken in detinue or conversion but there was no assurance that the thing itself would be recovered (recall the King's power of forfeiture). The most the Common Law courts would assure a successful plaintiff was an order against the dispossessor to pay damages. Because recovery of the thing itself was not assured but action against the person was, the action was called *in personam*, and the property was called personal property. This rule applied to all moveable property.

When the Courts of Equity began to develop equitable rights to property, these were enforceable only *in personam* because the Courts of Equity acted only *in personam*. An injunction or an order for specific performance in the Court of Equity required a person to do, or not to do, something specific in relation to a thing, such as to stay off land or return a chattel. The effect was that in time an *in personam* order became an *in rem* right of recovery. The thing itself was protected. Further, once property rights became assignable by law, what was formerly only an *in personam* action became a right in the hands of a third party to sue.

The distinguishing feature of a property right is sometimes said to be that a property right is assignable and recoverable *in rem*, while a contract right is unassignable and recoverable *in personam*. What is accurate about this maxim with respect to property law is that a property right stays attached to the property itself, even if the property moves into new hands. But two things about the maxim are inaccurate. First, a property right is not automatically enforceable against the whole world as opposed to just the original person to the contract. Each property right is enforceable against different persons depending on the rules applying to the particular holder-right-*res* relationship. Second, not all property rights are assignable even today. For example, one cannot assign one's medical prescription to another.

### (c) — Choses in Action

As noted, choses in action were initially rights to recover real or personal property in a court of law. These rights to sue to recover possession were not at first considered *res*, or property. They were rights to recover property, but they were not property themselves. As Lord Fry said in *Colonial Bank v. Whinney* (1885), 30 Ch. D. 261 (Eng. Ch. Div.), at 282:

> As I understand it, the original idea was that a chose in action was not property in a particular class, but was no property at all. It was not that property was divided into choses in action and choses in possession, but that a chose in action was only a right to sue as distinguished from property.

However, chose in action had another meaning. If A and B had a contract by which A delivered goods to B in return for B's agreement to pay money, A had a right to sue B for the debt if he did not pay. Until B paid, what A had was insensate. B's agreement was intangible. Yet it was a valuable thing because A could take B's agreement to pay to the Common Law Courts and obtain an order for B to pay.

Courts recognized early that this right to sue was a property right. A was the holder of the right, and it was enforceable against B. The right was the right to sue. The *res* was B's agreement to pay. The *res*, however, could be realized into money only by an action in the court. Thus, courts called it a chose in action to distinguish it from a chose in possession, which was tangible. The chose in action was intangible personal property.

Once the Courts of Equity developed ways to make choses in action assignable, the types of intangible personal property increased exponentially. Assignment of intangible personal property was a catalyst for banking, negotiable instruments, and secured financing — features of a market economy.

The category of intangible personal property within choses in action has become so large that it has obscured the earlier, but still existing, meaning of choses in action as rights to recover real or personal property. In a modern market economy, the most frequent use of the term choses in action is in the context of one of the many forms of intangible personal property.

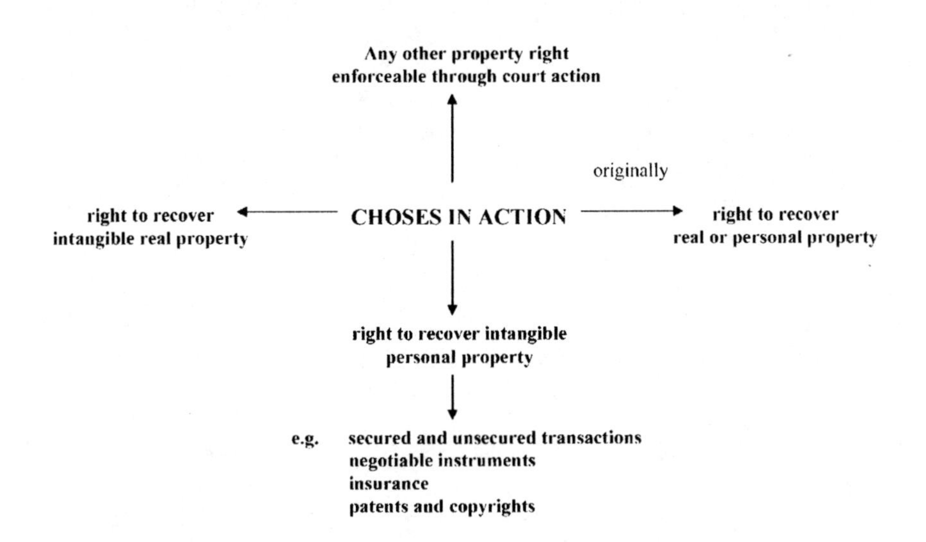


## 1.6 — Interaction of Property, Contract, and Tort Law

Property rights both arise out of other areas of law and ground rights in other areas of law, as illustrated by the complex interaction among property, contract, and tort.

Property rights may be a source of contract rights. For example, A holds certain property rights in a house and B holds certain property rights in a piano. A and B can voluntarily transfer to each other by mutual agreement whatever rights each has in each *res*. A may give B certain rights in her house in exchange for certain rights in B's piano. Contract law determines whether, or what portion of, the agreement between A and B is legally enforceable.

Contracts may also be a source of property rights. Once contract law has found a legally enforceable agreement, the subject matter enforceable by the court becomes a *res*. For example, if the court orders A to permit B to have possession of her house or B to permit A to have possession of the piano for certain periods of time, the house and the piano are the *res*. The right is the length of time and the terms and conditions on which each can have possession of the respective *res*. If the court orders damages rather than possession of the *res*, the damages become the *res*. A and B have a right to recover damages for non-performance of the contract. A's and B's rights to possession or damages, as the case may be, may or may not be assignable to other people depending on the assignability rules in these rights for these forms of *res*. The rules on assignability are property rules.

Similarly, property rights may be a source of tort rights and tort rights may be a source of property rights. In the above example, if A and B do not make an agreement but are neighbours, tort law will hold that A cannot use her house in a way that unreasonably interferes with B's use and enjoyment of his piano, and conversely, B cannot use his piano in ways that unreasonably interfere with A's use and enjoyment of her house. The tort is nuisance, held to be an offense against property. Both A and B have involuntarily lost the use and enjoyment of their property. Tort law decides when the courts will attach liability to actions in relation to property or persons. Once courts find liability, a new *res* is created, consisting of the right the court is willing to enforce. It may be an injunction to stop making the noise or it may include damages or compensation. The right to collect such damages becomes a chose in action. Such damages may or may not be assignable, depending on the rules of property law with respect to the particular right, *res*, and holder.

Property relationships, therefore, may be both a source and a result of relationships in other areas of law. A and B's property rights in the house and piano have been the source of rights held to be transferable by contract and the source of their tort right not to be interfered with in the use and enjoyment of the house and piano. Once the court finds an enforceable agreement between A and B, the right the court will enforce becomes a new property *res*, consisting of a particular right in the hands of a particular holder enforceable against particular people according to the rules of property law.

The development of terms is the particular challenge of property law, but is also the source of its flexibility and adaptability. Learning property law in its many branches and manifestations in other areas of law is the study of all the combinations and their evolution over time and by jurisdiction.

# Chapter 2 — Sources of Canadian Property Law by Jurisdiction



## 2.0 — Introduction

Because Canadian property law consists of layers of constitutionally mandated federal and provincial legislation, inherited English statutes, and common law doctrine, it is important to understand the individual sources in order to determine which doctrine or statute is applicable in a particular situation.

## 2.1 — Constitutional Division of Powers

In Canada, *The Constitution Act, 1867 (Constitution Act, 1867)*, 30 & 31 Vict., c. 3 (U.K.), R.S.C. 1985, Appendix II, No. 5, allocates jurisdiction over "property and civil rights" to the provinces (s. 92(13)). The federal government retains jurisdiction over several property-related matters, such as the public debt and federal Crown lands (s. 91(1A)), trade and commerce (s. 91(2)), taxation (s. 91(3)), fishing (s. 91(12)), bankruptcy and insolvency (s. 91(21)), Indians and lands reserved for Indians (s. 91(24)), and marriage and divorce (s. 92(26)).

During pre-Confederation constitutional negotiations, the four founding provinces insisted on control of the primary sources of wealth — land and natural resources. Section 108 of the *Constitution Act, 1867* transferred canals, ports, rivers, custom houses, post offices, and military property to the federal government, but s. 117 provided that the remaining public property was retained by the provinces. Section 109 provided that "all lands, mines, minerals and royalties belonging to the several provinces" should continue to belong to the provinces.

In the western provinces, however, the federal government initially retained varying degrees of control over natural resources and public lands for policy reasons relating to agricultural settlement and immigration. These provinces did not acquire jurisdiction over public lands and natural resources parallel to the founding provinces until the 1930 *Natural Resources Transfer Agreements* (embodied in the *Constitution Act, 1930*, 20-21 Geo. V, c. 26 (U.K.), R.S.C., Appendix H, No. 26). These agreements transferred the administration of public lands to Alberta, Saskatchewan, the expanded portion of Manitoba, and the parts of British Columbia that had been transferred to the federal government in the 1871 *Terms of Union*. This placed all ten provinces on an equal footing.

As a result of pre-1982 constitutional negotiations, the *Constitution Act*, 1982, 31 Eliz. II, c. II (U.K.), R.S.C. 1985, Appendix II, No. 44, assigned exclusive jurisdiction over specific aspects of non-renewable natural resources, forestry resources, and electrical energy to the provinces. Section 35 of the 1982 Act, which restricts both federal and provincial governments from abrogating Aboriginal and treaty rights, must also be considered (Part IV).

Depending on whether a property problem falls within federal or provincial jurisdiction, federal or provincial statutes may be the authoritative source of property law.

## 2.2 — Inherited English Law

The Canadian constitution and the laws of each province legally adopted and applied English law as of a certain date. For each province these dates were different. Received law included the English common law as of the adoption date as well as statutes passed in England before that date. In certain rare situations where Canadian law has not overruled it, that English law remains in force in Canada, thus requiring awareness of the dates of reception.

### (a) — Nova Scotia, New Brunswick, and Prince Edward Island

The *Treaty of Utrecht, 1713* transferred Nova Scotia from France to England. The Nova Scotia courts held in *Uniacke v. Dickson* (1848), 2 N.S.R. 287 (N.S. C.A.), that English law had been received as of 1758 when the first Nova Scotia legislative assembly was held. The case made no mention of the Peace and Friendship treaties with the M'kmaq in 1725 and 1752, which had specifically delegated jurisdiction over property matters in relation to European subjects to colonial governors.

The *Treaty of Paris, 1763* transferred New Brunswick, Cape Breton Island and Prince Edward Island from France to England. These lands were annexed to Nova Scotia, making them subject to the reception of English property law as of 1758. After Prince Edward Island separated in 1769, it held its first legislative assembly in 1773 without passing explicit legislation as to the date of reception. The same is true of New Brunswick's first legislative assembly in 1786 after it separated from Nova Scotia in 1784. New Brunswick courts have held 1660 as the date of reception of British laws, thus excluding the *Tenures Abolition Act, 1660*, (Chapter 10).

At Confederation, the *British North America Act, 1867 (Constitution Act, 1867)*, affirmed the application of the adopted property legislation as well as laws passed in Nova Scotia and New Brunswick in the intervening century.

In 1873, the *Prince Edward Island Terms of Union*, R.S.C. 1985, Appendix II, No. 12 creating the seventh province included s. 129 continuing laws in force at the time of union.

### (b) — Ontario and Quebec

*The Royal Proclamation, 1763* R.S.C. 1985, Appendix II, No. I, — the Imperial Order implementing the Treaty of Paris — provided for English property laws in the new colony of Quebec (as well as the Thirteen Colonies and Florida in the United States, and Grenada in the Caribbean). In 1774, the Imperial Parliament passed *The Quebec Act, 1774*, 14 Geo. III, c. 83 (U.K.), R.S.C. 1985, Appendix II, No. 2, restoring the pre-Proclamation French civil law in Quebec, with its origins in Roman civil law. *The Quebec Act, 1774* included much of what is now Ontario. In 1791, another Imperial Statute, *The Constitution Act*, 1791, 31 Geo. III, c. 31 (U.K.), R.S.C. 1985, Appendix II, No. 3, separated present-day Ontario and Quebec into Upper and Lower Canada. One of the first acts of the new assembly of Upper Canada was to pass a law adopting English laws as of 1792 (Stats. Upp. Can. 1792, 32 Geo. III). When the two Canadas were rejoined in *The Union Act, 1840*, 3-4 Vict., c. 35 (U.K.), R.S.C. 1985, Appendix 11, No. 4, the separate French and English property regimes were left in place. Section

129 of the *British North America Act, 1867* affirmed the laws existing in 1867 in these provinces.

### (c) — Manitoba

In 1868, the Imperial Crown purchased Rupert's Land from the Hudson's Bay Company, and joined it, along with the Northwest Territories, to Canada under the authority of s. 146 of the *British North America Act, 1867* in the *Rupert's Land Act, 1868*, 31-32 Vict., c. 105 (U.K.), R.S.C. 1985, Appendix II, No. 6. In 1870, an area in what is now the southern portion of Manitoba was carved out to become the fifth province of Canada (*The Manitoba Act, 1870*, 33 Vict., c. 3 (Canada), R.S.C. 1985, Appendix II, No. 8). The Manitoba legislature adopted English law as of July 15, 1870 (*The Queen's Bench Act*, S.M. 1874, c. 12, s. 5, supplemented by the Federal government's *The Manitoba Supplementary Provincial Act*, S.C. 1888, c. 33, s. 4). When Manitoba was expanded in 1905, reception was extended to the remainder of the province.

### (d) — British Columbia

In 1871, in the Terms of Union by which British Columbia joined Canada (*British Columbia Terms of Union*, R.S.C. 1985, Appendix El, No. 10), the existing laws of British Columbia were continued, which included an 1866 ordinance of the British Columbia legislative council adopting English laws as of 1858 (*The English Law Ordinance*, B.C. 1867, c. 7), which in turn continued a proclamation of the Governor of British Columbia of 1858.

### (e) — Saskatchewan, Alberta, Northwest Territories, Yukon, and Nunavut

In 1886, the federal government passed the *Northwest Territories Amendment Act*, S.C. 1886, c. 25, adopting English laws as of July 16, 1870 for the remainder of the Northwest Territories. Also in 1886, Parliament passed the *Territories Real Property Act, 1886*, 49 Vict. (Can.), c. 26, adopting the Torrens system of land registration throughout the Northwest Territories. The *Dominion Lands Act* of 1872, 35 Vict. (Can., c. 23) and the *Secretary of State Act*, S.C. 1868, c. 42, provided administrative systems for the management of public lands throughout the Northwest Territories and Indian lands throughout Canada.

In 1898, the Northwest Territories was divided into Yukon and the Northwest Territories to the north of the sixtieth parallel and Assiniboia to the south. The Act constituting Yukon specifically preserved the laws in force at the time of its creation (*Yukon Territory Act, 1898*, 61 Vict., c. 6 (Can.) R.S.C. 1985, Appendix II, No. 19). The *Nunavut Act*, S.C. 1993, c. 28, s. 29

stated that the laws of the Northwest Territories apply in Nunavut.

In 1905, when Assiniboia was divided into Alberta and Saskatchewan as well as an expanded Manitoba, the founding Acts continued the pre-existing property regime, including the reception of English law as of July 15, 1870, the *Territories Real Property Act*, the *Dominion Lands Act*, and the *Indian Act* (*Alberta Act*, 4-5 Edw. VII, c. 3 (Can.), R.S.C. 1985, Appendix II, No. 20; Saskatchewan Act, 4-5 Edw. VII, c. 42 (Can.), R.S.C. 1985, Appendix II, No. 21).

### (f) — Newfoundland

When Newfoundland joined Canada in 1949, its pre-1934 legislative provisions were continued in the *British North America Act, 1949*, which were taken to include the reception of English laws as of 1832 as outlined by the royal prerogative documents of that date (*Newfoundland Act*, 12-13 Geo. VI, c. 22 (U.K.), R.S.C. 1985, Appendix II, No. 32).

## 2.3 — Common Law Judicial Rulings

The background legal regime in all jurisdictions in Canada outside Quebec is the common law. This means that if no federal or provincial statute governs a particular situation, the common law provides the relevant law. The common law is also a guide where federal or provincial statutes apply but require interpretation by the courts. As noted, the common law is the body of judge-made law that grew up through the Courts of Common Law and the Courts of Equity in England from the twelfth century onward. The doctrines that arose in the Courts of Equity were called equitable doctrines. After these courts were merged in the *Judicature Act, 1873*, legal and equitable doctrines together came to be grouped under the umbrella term "the common law".

In Canada, the common law developed in tandem with English decisions until 1949 when the Supreme Court of Canada became the highest judicial authority. Hence, as of that date, the Supreme Court became the authoritative source of common law in Canada followed by the provincial courts of appeal and superior courts. Canadian courts may be influenced but are not bound by the common law as expressed in English cases, and may consider other Commonwealth and American jurisprudence in their deliberations.

# Part II

# Personal Property

# CHAPTER 3 — THE DOCTRINE OF POSSESSION



## 3.0 — Introduction

The adage that possession is nine-tenths of the law is accurate in the common law in that possession remains a powerful root of legal property rights and a defining aspect of the property relationships among individuals.

Possession, rather than ownership, is fundamental in personal property. In terms of establishing ownership of personal property, possession is such a large part of the bundle of rights that it is *prima facie* proof of ownership. An owner who seeks to defeat the claim of someone in possession bears the onus of establishing a prior possessory right. The law recognizes possession in situations other than ownership. For example, a finder retains possession until the true owner appears, a bailee has possession for as long as it takes to complete the specified purpose, and a salvor relinquishes possession to the true owner but is entitled to compensation.

The legal requirements of possession are context-specific and depend on factual and legal circumstances "[Canadian law] does not recognize the existence of a single concept of possession applicable for all purposes" (*Lifestyles Kitchens & Bath v. Danbury Sales Inc.* (1999), 1999 CarswellOnt 2594 (Ont. S.C.J.). The following guidelines offer a basis from which to assess those legal requirements.

## 3.1 — Establishing Possession at Law

In order to claim possessory rights, an individual must establish physical control over the *res* and the intention to possess (*animus possidendi*). It is possible to have control without an intention to possess — a legal relationship known as custody. It is also possible to have intention without the requisite control, such as a hunter who is unable to recover his felled quarry.

Proving possession exposes a tension in property law between a desire to award possession to those who actually have the *res* in their physical control and a desire to reward those who have established a prior claim by showing a pre-existing intention to control the *res* (*Popov v. Hayashi*, 2002 WL833731 (Cal. Super.)). Both of these tensions can be illustrated by examining possession of wild animals — *ferae naturae* — that according to the common law are not the subject of property rights.

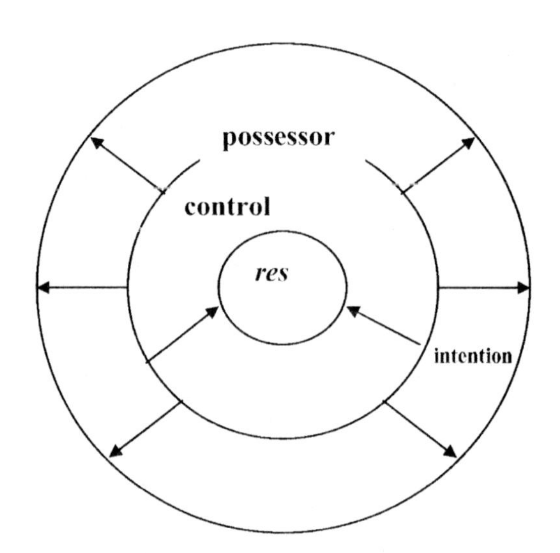


### (a) — Physical Control Over the *Res*

The courts have held that a high degree of physical control is required before any legal right of possession will be recognized. For example, in a dispute over a school of fish (*Young v. Hichens* (1844), 6 Q.B. 606), the court awarded possession not to the fishers who had surrounded and were preparing to enclose fish in their nets, but to other fishers who entered the enclosed area and actually netted the fish. The court held that all but reducing into possession is not the same as reducing into possession. The comparable American case is *Pierson v. Post*, 3 Cai. R. 175 (N.Y. Sup. Ct., 1805), in which the court awarded a fox to the hunter who actually killed it in preference to the hunter who was in pursuit.

The *ferae naturae* must be deprived of its natural liberty and subject to the unambiguous control of those who would claim possessory rights. Once established, control and intention must continue to be manifest; if the wild animal should recover its freedom, possessory rights will be lost (*Mullet v. Bradley*, 53 N.Y.S. 781 (N.Y. Sup. Ct., 1898)). There is an exception for wild animals such as bees and homing pigeons that by habit return to the possessor (*animus revertendi*; *Kearry v. Pattinson*, [1939] I All Eng. 65 (C.A.)) and certain rights may arise by virtue of ownership of the soil upon which wild animals are found — *rationae soli* (*Blades v. Higgs* (1865), 11 E.R. 1474 at 1478 (H.L.)).

Beyond *ferae narurae*, the degree of control requisite to establish possession is dependent upon the nature of the *res* in question. For example, the degree of control demanded to possess a bracelet lost in an airline passenger lounge (*Parker v. British Airways Bd.*, [1982] 1 All ER. 834 (C.A.)) would differ from the control necessary to claim possessory rights over a shipwreck lying on the bottom of the ocean floor (*"Tubantia" (The)*, [1924] All E.R. Rep. 615 (Adm. Ct.)). One must establish as much control as is practicable in the circumstances. The degree of control does not require the ability to physically ward off all those who might wrest the good from the possessor, but rather a degree of exclusivity such that others may not acquire it without committing wrongful interference.

A person who has actual physical control has a *prima facie* right to possession (*Young v. Hichens*). The claim of a prior possessor defeats such a *prima facie* case if the prior possessor can persuade the court that the intention to control was sufficiently manifest to have established possession at law. The argument was that he did all that was practical (*State of Ohio v. Shaw*) and that those engaged in the activity would recognize his efforts as sufficient to establish possession (*Ghen v. Rich*).

### (b) — Intention to Control

The contrary tension to physical control is the desire of the courts to award possession to the person who shows a sufficiently clear intention to control the *res* such that others should understand that someone has already claimed the *res* as her own. In these cases the courts decline to award possession to the person who actually has the *res* in physical control. In *State of Ohio v. Shaw*, 65 N.E. 875 (Ohio, 1902), the court denied fishers the fish they had taken from a net in a lake. The court held that the owners of the net had taken reasonable (as opposed to absolute) precautions to prevent the fish from escaping. In *Ghen v. Rich*, 8 F. 159 (Mass. Dist. Ct., 1881), the court awarded a beached whale not to the person who found it, but to the hunter who had harpooned it days before and awaited its appearance on shore. The argument in these cases was that those who are familiar with the custom should know that a fisher setting a net, or a hunter harpooning a whale, intends to control the netted fish or the beached whale. The intention to control required behaviour such that others familiar with the activity would understand the pursuer's intention to exclude others and to reduce the object to his own use and pleasure.

The policy tension is to reward the industry and labour of those who actually seek out and control, while at the same time rewarding those who have invested in the infrastructure sufficiently to set in motion the process of acquiring physical control to the extent possible at the given time. The courts retain flexibility to decide cases as they see fit within these tensions by saying that the degree of control necessary is that which is practical in the circumstances, and the requisite intention to control is that which is familiar in the custom of the particular activity.

As the following example illustrates, the time of acquisition of possessory rights is a continuum rather than a bright line. Sam is an avid archer. Armed with a provincially-issued licence, he actively pursues game throughout the hunting season. Last weekend Sam pursued a moose with a poison-tipped arrow. The fret on the arrow was unique to Sam and easily identified as his. The poison-tipped arrow struck the moose, but based on the location of the arrow and the size of the moose, it would be eight hours before the moose died. Four hours later, Sam was still pursuing the moose when a hunter stepped from the woods and felled it with a single rifle shot. Who gets the moose?

## 3.2 — Abandonment

One may choose to give up, (or be deemed at law to have given up), possessory rights and abandon the good by relinquishing both physical control and the intention to possess. The loss of physical control alone is not definitive; the intention of the individual involved must also be examined. Abandonment is a question of fact. It can be established through an express act or inferred from surrounding circumstances, including the passage of time, the nature of the transaction, the owner's conduct, and the nature and value of the property (*Stewart v. Gustafson* (1998), [1999] 4 W.W.R. 695 (Sask. Q.B.)). However, strong and convincing evidence is necessary to establish that prior rights have been surrendered (*Columbus America Discovery Group v. Atlantic Mutual Ins. Co.*, 974 F. 2d 450 (4th Cir., 1992)), and the onus to establish abandonment rests upon the party so claiming (*Simpson v. Gowers* (1981), 121 D.L.R. (3d) 709 (Ont. C.A.)).

In some circumstances, legislation sets a limit on the time wherein a claim to property can be made. Further, custom and usage have developed to establish standards relating to particular circumstances, such as goods lost at sea (Chapter 4).

Short of establishing abandonment a proprietor who becomes an involuntary custodian of another's chattel is not without legal options. He may protect the chattel and employ self help to abate a trespass or nuisance, providing adequate notice has been given (*Visscher v. Triple Broek Holdings Ltd.*, 2006 ABQB 259 (Alta. Q.B.)).

# CHAPTER 4 — FINDING



## 4.0 — Introduction

At common law, a finder discovers personal property owned by another and takes it into her possession. She demonstrates possession through physical control and manifest intent to control. The law excuses the taking because a finder is aware that the *res* is not abandoned but that their possession is for the benefit of the true owner. Courts have encouraged finders to come forward by allocating the finder better rights to the property than all others save the true owner (*Armory v. Delamirie* (1722), 93 E.R. 664 (Eng. K.B.)). Arguably, this recognition of the true owner's right to repossess the good serves public policy goals by encouraging finding, respecting possessory rights, and (at least in theory) enabling the person closest to the true owner to retain control until the good can be returned.

The rule is that a finder prevails against all but the true owner, but it is subject to qualification. Interest holders other than the true owner or the finder may assert a stronger right to the found object (*Thomas v. Canada*, 2006 ABQB 730 (Alta. Q.B.)). For example, the owners of the property on which the good is found argue that their rights to the chattel, although subordinate to those of the true owner, are superior to those of the finder. Employers of a finder claim a right by virtue of the employment relationship. At common law, a thief claims a better right to the good than the finder who recovers the stolen merchandise lost by the thief. The following explores the relative weight of these competing claims.

## 4.1 — Prior Possessory Interests

A finder's rights based on possession may be defeated by those who can establish a better right through prior possession (*Grafstein v. Holme*, [1958] O.R. 296 (Ont. C.A.)). The owner of the land upon which the object is found may be able to establish a better right to the good by virtue of his ownership of the real property (*Elwes v. Brigg Gas Co.* (1886), 33 Ch. D. 562 (Eng. Ch. Div.). Bare legal title to the property is not sufficient; the landowner must raise herself above the level of any other stranger by establishing the requisite intention and control over the real property (*Trachuk v. Olinek* (1995), [1996] 4 W.W.R. 137 (Alta. Q.B.)). A landlord who purchases and then rents property but never goes near it will be held not to have an intention to control things found on the property. A broach found in such a situation was awarded to the finder (*Hannah v. Peel*, [1945] 2 All E.R. 288 (Eng. K.B.)). The necessary degree of control is dependent upon the circumstances of each case. For example, the degree of control required for a private residence will differ from the requisite control over a quarter section of farmland.

A lessee in possession may have a superior claim to that of a finder and to a landowner if the landowner is unable to establish a prior possessory right. However, contractual obligations may force a lessee to surrender to the holder of bare legal title in accordance with terms of a lease. In *London (City) v. Appleyard*, [1963] 1 W.L.R. 982 (Eng. Q.B.), coins found hidden in a vault on leased property would have been awarded to the lessee but for a clause in the lease that reserved valuables to the landowner.

The actual location of the find — on, under, or attached to the land — can also impact on the success of those who claim prior possessory interests. If the *res* is under or attached to land already within the clear possession of the landowner, the claim of the landowner is superior whether he knows of the existence of the good or not (*Elwes v. Brigg Gas Co.*). If removal of the found good requires a trespass on the property by the finder, such a violation of property rights will not be sanctioned by the courts even if the control of the landowner is minimal.

The question of control becomes more problematic when the lost object is found resting on the property by an otherwise lawful finder. The owner of a shop where money was found on the floor (*Bridges v. Hawkesworth* (1851), 21 L.J.Q.B. 75 (Eng. Q.B.)) and an airline company that leased a lounge wherein a bracelet was found (*Parker v. British Airways Bd.* (1981), [1982] 1 All E.R. 834 (Eng. C.A.)) both lost to finders. Neither was held to have exercised sufficient control over the *locus in quo* — the place in which — nor over the objects within. Once again, control is dependent on the circumstances of each case; the line determining when the degree of control over the *locus in quo* is sufficient to defeat the possessory rights of the finder is a continuum. The greater the control over the *locus in quo*, the more likely the courts are to infer an intention to control things found on the real property.

## 4.2 — Finder as Employee

A finder's rights are further diminished by employers. A finder who finds during the scope of his employment finds on behalf of his employer (*McDowell v. Ulster Bank* (1899), 33 Irish L.T. 225). The more independent the employer-employee relationship, the more likely the courts are to permit the finder/employee to retain the goods rather than require him to turn them over to his employer. For example, an independent contractor might not have an obligation to the person with whom he contracted.

## 4.3 — Finder as Trespasser/Wrongdoer

A finder who is a trespasser will forfeit to the landowner any claim to objects found on the land. For example, a child who found money while trespassing on a neighbour's property would lose it to her neighbour. However, if the neighbour did not wish to claim the money, and someone else took it away from the child, the finder's rights would prevail over that subsequent wrongdoer (*Bird v. Fort Frances (Town)*, [1949] O.R. 292 (Ont. H.C.)). An unlawful possession, although frail, may prevail over a subsequent possessor who is not able to establish a better right (*Costello v. Chief Constable of Derbyshire Constabulary*, [2001] E.W.C.A. Civ. 381).

## 4.4 — Duties of a Finder

In addition to taking the good into her physical control and displaying an intention to maintain control, the finder is held to have a duty to conduct a reasonable search for the true owner. In doing so, the finder may demand proof from someone claiming a better right. If a reward has been offered, the finder may withhold the good until the reward is delivered.

The finder also has a duty to exercise reasonable care to preserve the good. A finder who expends money to preserve the found object, or to locate the owner, has no legal right to reimbursement, although legislation may require owners to reimburse finders for expenses incurred in caring for stray animals (e.g., *The Stray Animals Act*, R.S.S. 1978, c. S-60).

If the owner does not appear within a reasonable time to claim the good, the finder may try to establish that her possession has matured into ownership through abandonment. As noted, abandonment is established by evidence of loss of both control and intention to control. Lapse of time and non-use often supports such a conclusion, but may not be sufficient in and of itself.

## 4.5 — Salvage

In maritime law, a finder at sea is called a salvor. The rule is not that a finder's rights prevail against all but the true owner, but rather that a salvor is deemed to have taken the true owner's goods into his possession to conserve them in the face of danger. For his expenditure of time and labour, he is entitled to a salvor's fee, sometimes approaching the value of the goods, to encourage preservation of the property.

The salvor becomes owner only if the item is determined to have been abandoned by the true owner. Abandonment at sea requires considerably more than lapse of time and non-use. Before a salvor can claim ownership of goods found at sea, he must prove that the true owner intentionally gave up his claim to the goods, as evidenced by "clear and convincing evidence. . .such as an owner's express declaration abandoning title" (*Columbus America Discovery Group v. Atlantic Mutual Ins. Co.*, 974 F. 2d 450 at 464 (4th Cir., 1992)).

## 4.6 — Treasure Trove

A treasure trove, defined as hidden gold, silver, bullion, or coins is deemed to be the property of the Crown regardless of who finds it or where it is found (*Attorney General of the Duchy of Lancaster v. G.E. Overton (Farms) Ltd.* (1981), [1982] Ch. 277 (Eng. C.A.)). Legal rights with respect to museums and cultural property are an evolving area of the law.

# CHAPTER 5 — GIFTS



## 5.0 — Introduction

A gift is defined as a voluntary and intentional transfer of property from the owner to another, without consideration. The giver is called the donor and the recipient the donee. Because no consideration is involved, the donee is sometimes called a volunteer.

Courts on a policy basis do not favour gifts but rather require strict compliance with legal rules of giving in order to find a completed gift. The donor must have good title, as well as the capacity to have an informed intention to give (drunkenness or lack of mental capacity may defeat a gift). Once a gift is complete, a donor cannot revoke it, even if she changes her mind (*Standing v. Bowring* (1885), 31 Ch. D. 282 (Eng. C.A.)). Some gifts are prohibited by statute regardless of the desire or actions of the donor. For example, matrimonial property legislation prohibits gifting certain property to third parties as a way of avoiding spousal sharing. In addition, legislation may impose certain requirements in order to legally complete a gift (*Stein v. Van Eldik* (2005), 16 E.T.R. (3d) 1 (Alta. Q.B.)). A donee need not know of a gift at the time of giving but may reject it once aware. Acceptance will be assumed unless contrary evidence is advanced. Children may receive a gift subject to an option to reject once they come of age.

There are three types of gifts, each with different requirements for completion — testamentary gifts, *inter vivos* gifts, and *donatio mortis causa*.

## 5.1 — Testamentary Gifts

A testamentary gift transfers a donor's property to another effective at the donor's (testator's) death, recorded in a document known as a will. The rules governing such gifts are not governed by the common law, but rather by detailed legislation in each jurisdiction. Statutes also govern cases where a property owner dies intestate — without a will. There is little option but to consult the relevant statutes in each jurisdiction.

## 5.2 — *Inter Vivos* Gifts

*Inter vivos* gifts are gifts from one living person to another living person, literally between the living. *Inter vivos* gifts can be oral or by deed.

### (a) — Oral

The intention to gift must be unequivocal. If a donor's words or actions are equivocal or consistent with a possible intention to give or not to give, the courts will not infer a gift. The difference between a complete and an incomplete gift often turns on the use of specific words (*Jones v. Lock* (1865), LR 1 Ch App 25).

Delivery is not merely evidence of a gift being made. Courts demand full transfer of possession to complete an oral gift. The donor must put the good out of his control. A chattel still in the possession of a donor is not a valid gift (*Cochrane v. Moore* (1890), [1886–90] All E.R. 731 (CA.)). For example, a husband who held the household furniture in his name and said to his wife "This is all yours", and then continued to use and enjoy it with her would not be held to have given the furniture to her (*Cole, Re.*, [1963] 3 All E.R. 433 (C.A.)). If delivery is not present, the gift will fail, regardless of how clear the donor's words of intention. The courts will not "perfect an imperfect gift" (*Milroy v. Lord* (1862), 45 E.R. 1185 at 1189 (Eng. Ch. Div.)).

The change in possession can come before, during, or after the donor's words of intention to gift. For example, a father who owned the furniture in his daughter and son-in-law's house was held to have made a valid gift when he went into the house, uttered words of present gift to his daughter, and left the house (*Kilpin v. Ratley*, [1892] 1 Q.B. 582 (Eng. Q.B.)). Similarly, a son operating a barge for his father was held to have received a valid gift after his father uttered words of gifting and left the son in possession (*Winter v. Winter* (1861), 4 LT. 639 (Q.B.)).

If, due to size or location of the *res*, actual delivery is impossible, courts will accept constructive delivery providing there is an unambiguous transfer to the donee or her representative of the exclusive means of control. For example, delivery of all available sets of keys to a storage locker that contained the gift would be constructive delivery, while transfer of only one of several sets of keys would not.

When actual or constructive delivery is not possible, a donor may attempt symbolic delivery where she delivers a chattel representing the gift to the donee. For example, a donor may transfer one book of a collection as symbolic delivery of the whole. The concept of a change in dominion and control is uncertain in these cases; courts often find the gift suspect and rule it incomplete. Symbolic delivery should be viewed as a last alternative.

### (b) — By Deed

To make a gift by deed, the donor must deliver to the donee a sealed instrument in writing that states the intention to give and the subject of the gift. The seal is needed to corroborate the intent in the written document. The sealed instrument must be delivered out of the possession of the donor. It is now less clear how formal the instrument needs to be. While a sealed instrument may no longer be required, there must still be sufficient formality to corroborate an informed and considered intention to gift.

## 5.3 — *Donatio Mortis Causa*

Gifts made in contemplation of death contain elements of both *inter vivos* and testamentary gifts. The donor, contemplating imminent death, declares words of present gifting and delivers the gift to the donee or someone who clearly takes possession on behalf of the donee. The gift becomes effective at death but remains revocable until that time. If the anticipated death occurs, but not from the cause contemplated, the courts will examine the intention of the donor to determine if the actual cause of death will suffice (*Slagboom Estate v. Kirby* (1993), 48 E.T.R. 219 (B.C. S.C.)). The courts are more open in *donatio mortis causa* gifts than in *inter vivos* gifts to accepting constructive and symbolic delivery.

# CHAPTER 6 — BAILMENT



## 6.0 — Introduction

The word "bailment" is derived from the French word "bailler" — to keep in custody. In its simplest terms, bailment at law is the delivery of personal property by one party, the bailor, to another, the bailee, for a specific purpose (*Lesser v. Jones* (1920), 47 N.B.R. 318 (N.B. C.A.)). The bailee has a duty to care for the good and to safely return it when the purpose is completed (*Dorico Investments Ltd. v. Weyerhaeuser Canada Ltd./Weyerhaeuser Canada Ltée* (1999), [2000] 1 W.W.R. 334 (Alta. Q.B.)).

The doctrine of bailment developed in Roman law as a way to order the rights and responsibilities of someone in possession of the property of another, which was important in a legal system that had only unitary title and lacked the flexibility of legal and equitable rights developed in England. Nonetheless, the common law found bailment a useful way to regulate relationships of repair and rental.

Roman bailment law had specific standards of care for specific types of bailment; in English law these evolved to the standards associated with negligence law. Further, as the market developed, companies that habitually handled the goods of others, such as service, repair, and transportation companies, developed their own written contracts specifying the terms on which they agreed to hold goods. Thus elements of contract law increasingly entered bailment law.

While modern common law bailment includes elements of both negligence and contract law, it remains a property concept (*Lifestyles Kitchens & Bath v. Danbury Sales Inc.* (1999), 1999 CarswellOnt 2594 (Ont. S.C.J.)). A bailment is more than a mere licence (*Gobeil v. Elliot* (1996), 150 Sask. R. 285 (Sask. Q.B.). If the goods are damaged or destroyed, the bailor has a right not only to damages for breach of contract but also to the goods themselves and can sue in conversion. Further, an owner of bailed goods can sue not only the person with whom he has privity of contract, but also third parties who may have had possession of the bailed good for a specialized purpose or who are otherwise liable at law.

## 6.1 — Establishing Bailment — Bailor's Onus

To establish a claim in bailment, the bailor is required to prove three elements: delivery of personal property to a bailee for a specific purpose and the bailee's failure to redeliver the goods in conditions appropriate to the terms of bailment.

### (a) — Delivery

The onus lies on the bailor to establish a transfer of possession of the object to the bailee in terms of both physical control and intention to control. The transfer must be voluntary — a seizure is not a bailment (*Martyn v. Omega Developments Ltd.* (1980), 30 Nfld. & P.E.I.R. 13 (Nfld. Dist. Ct.)). Similarly, the bailee must receive voluntarily — one cannot be made a bailee without one's consent (*Herold v. Saskatchewan Wheat Pool* (1980), 6 Sask. R. 297 (Sask. Dist. Ct.)).

A series of decisions relating to parking lots illustrate the issues that typically arise in delivery. Parking lot companies often claim that they are not responsible for what happens to a vehicle on their lot because there is no bailment, only a licence. A licence permits that which would otherwise be a trespass, but brings into existence no special duty of care. An example of a licence would be parking at a city parking meter. Paying the meter only rents the space; the city will not protect the car while it is parked. At law, there is held to be no change of possession in a licence, that is no delivery. The driver retains the keys to her car parked at the meter; she does not turn them over to the city.

The courts determine whether a relationship with a parking lot is a licence or a bailment by looking at whether there has been a delivery of the vehicle: who has the physical control of the car and the intention to control during the time the car is parked. In searching for indicia of bailment pertinent questions are: Who has the keys? Is there a car attendant on duty? Did he ask for the keys? If so, what did he say, and where did he put them? Does the car owner have to surrender a ticket in order to receive the keys back? (*Palmer v. Toronto Medical Arts Bldg. Ltd.* (1959), [1960] O.R. 60 (Ont. C.A.)); *Martin v. Town N' Country Delicatessen Ltd.* (1963), 45 W.W.R. 413 (Man. C.A.); *Ashby v. Tolhurst*, [1937] 2 K.B. 242 (Eng. K.B.)). The courts will look at all the circumstances to determine the intention of the parties, based not on what a particular individual thought (i.e., subjective intention), but rather on what a reasonable person would conclude as to who had possession and control of the goods (i.e., objective intention) (*Lifestyles Kitchens & Bath v. Danbury Sales Inc.*).

### (b) — Purpose

The bailor must also establish the purpose for which the delivery was made. Often not all aspects of the bailment are explicitly discussed by the bailor and the bailee. The bailor must attempt to prove after the fact, that the agreement did or did not include, for example, starch in the shirt collar or the right to take the car rental out of the jurisdiction.

Courts use contract principles to interpret the agreement between the parties. To illustrate from the parking lot cases, courts will look at such evidence as signs and tickets, and attempt to determine whether a reasonable person would have understood that the purpose was for care of the vehicle or merely for space rental (*Brown v. Toronto Auto Parks Ltd.* (1954), [1955] 1 D.L.R. 461 (Ont. H.C.); varied [1955] 2 D.L.R. 525 (Ont. CA.); *Heffron v. Imperial Parking Co.* (1974), 46 D.L.R. (3d) 642 (Ont. CA.).

### (c) — Failure to Redeliver

Finally, the bailor must establish the safe condition of the goods when bailed and the failure to redeliver the good in an adequate condition at the end of the bailment. The end of the bailment coincides with the completion of the agreed purpose.

If a specific time for redelivery is agreed to, such as picking up dry-cleaning on Tuesday, the bailment is called "fixed term" and, barring specific circumstances such as deviance or another act inconsistent with the bailment relationship, the bailor cannot demand redelivery before that time. If there is no agreed time for redelivery, such as with a neighbour borrowing a shovel, the bailment is termed "at will" and the bailor can ask for his shovel back anytime.

If goods go missing during a time period that includes both a bailment and a licence, the bailor must prove that the loss occurred specifically during the bailment. If on the evidence, the loss may have occurred during the licence, the courts will not accept that the bailor has successfully proved a failure to redeliver at the end of the bailment period. The loss may equally likely have occurred when the bailee had no duty to care for the good (*Calgary Transport Services Ltd. v. Pyramid Management Ltd.*, [1976] 6 W.W.R. 631 (Alta. CA.); *Atlantic Furs Ltd. v. Moffatt Moving & Storage* (1985), 56 Nfld. & P.E.I.R. 19 (Nfld. Dist. Ct.)).

Often there are disputes about what exactly must be redelivered. Courts have held that the bailee must return any goods of which he had actual or constructive notice. Actual notice applies to those goods of which the bailee was aware; constructive notice applies to those goods that the reasonable person would have contemplated. For example, in the parking lot cases, did the bailment include only the vehicle or did it also include the radio, the CDs or the books that were inside the car (*Brown v. Toronto Auto Parks Ltd.*)?

## 6.2 — Bailee's Onus of Proof

Once the bailor establishes delivery of a good for a purpose, and a failure to redeliver, the onus shifts to the bailee to prove that he took due care of the bailed good.

### (a) — Duty of Care

As soon as the bailor proves delivery of safe, suitable, and non-defective goods, for a purpose, and failure to redeliver, the bailee's duty of care arises. In contrast, negligence principles would have required a plaintiff to establish a duty of care on the part of the defendant as a first step to establishing a negligence action. Negligence would also require the plaintiff to bring forward *prima facie* evidence of negligence on the part of the defendant. In bailment however, the bailor is permitted to remain silent and the onus shifts to the bailee to establish that he took all reasonable care. The policy behind this rule is that the bailee in possession of the good is the only one who can explain what she did to take reasonable care of the good.

### (b) — Standard of Care

Importing aspects of Roman law, *Coggs v. Bernard* (1703), 91 E.R. 25 (Eng. K.B.), set out specific standards of care for particular types of bailments. In a gratuitous bailment, where the bailee was taking care of something as a favour to the bailor, the bailee would be found not to have met the standard of care only if he was grossly negligent. At the other end of the spectrum, in a gratuitous bailment for the benefit of the bailee, such as borrowing a neighbour's lawn mower, the bailee would be found not to have met the standard of care if he was only slightly negligent. In between were four more categories with varying standards of care dependent upon the benefits and obligations between the parties.

Courts found fitting the "infinite variety of cases" into the six categories awkward, and taking a page from the evolving law of negligence, replaced the categories with a modern, flexible, negligence standard of "reasonable care under the circumstances" (*Houghland v. R.R. Low (Luxury Coaches) Ltd.*, [1962] 2 All E.R. 159 (Eng. C.A.)). Now the courts assess the bailment according to what a reasonable person would have done under all the circumstances, including such factors as:

- *the nature of the bailment* — Who benefits from the bailment? Was the bailment involuntary? Did the bailee receive compensation? Was there a benefit to the bailor? Was there a mutual benefit?
- *the value of the chattel* — The more valuable the chattel, the higher the standard of care expected.
- *conduct of the bailor* — For example, did the bailor inform the bailee that the good was of special importance, such as a family heirloom?
- *conduct of the bailee* — Was there a custom in the trade regarding care? Did the bailee hold herself out as an expert, and if so, did she act appropriately (*Gaudreau v. Belter*, 2001 ABQB 101 (Alta. Q.B.)?
- *understanding between the parties* — Was there an express contract for a certain level of care, and if so, was it met (*Grant v. Armour* (1893), 25 O.R. 7 (Ont. Q.B.)?

The bailee can satisfy the burden of proof either by showing that he knows how the loss was caused, and was not negligent, or by showing that he does not know how the loss was caused but took all reasonable care (*Coopers Payen Ltd. v. Southampton Container Terminal Ltd.*, [2003] EWCA Civ. 1223 (C.A.)).

If the bailee is unable to establish that he took all reasonable care under the circumstances, he will be liable in conversion to the bailor. On occasion the standard may be higher than reasonable care, such as if a bailee's regular practice establishes a higher standard (*Newman v. Bourne & Hollingsworth* (1915), 31 T.L.R. 209 (KB.)). In the case of involuntary bailment the bailee will only be liable if he was negligent.

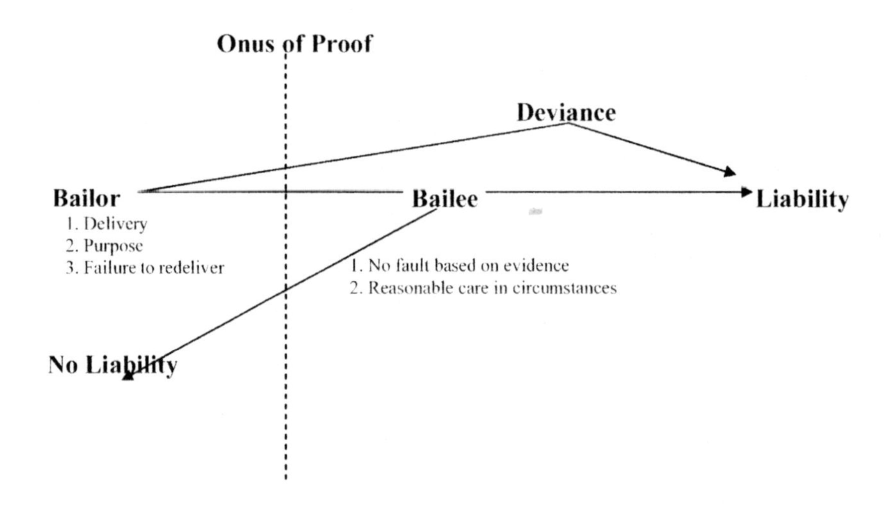


### *(i) — Deviance*

If a bailee uses a bailed good for a use other than the authorized purpose and damage occurs, the defence of having taken all reasonable care does not apply. He is deemed to have acted in an owner-like fashion with respect to the chattel by deviating from the bailment and is liable for the full value of the chattel in conversion, regardless of the cause of the damage (*England v. Heinbecker* (1977), 78 D.L.R. (3d) 117 (Sask. Dist. Ct.)).

### *(ii) — Wong Exception (Missing Goods, Missing Bailee)*

Normally the courts require a bailee to disprove negligence on the grounds that she has the best knowledge of what happened, and can either relate the exact circumstances that led to the failure to redeliver to show she was not negligent, or establish that she took reasonable care in the circumstances. In *Wong (National Trust Co. v. Wong Aviation Ltd.*, [1969] S.C.R. 481 (S.C.C.)), the Supreme Court of Canada held that it is unrealistic and inappropriate to ask the bailee's representative to meet the normal onus and disprove negligence when:

- the bailed goods and the bailee disappear together; and
- no one knows what happened.

The bailee is excused only if there is a complete lack of information as to what happened. In *Amo Containers Ltd. v. Mobil Oil Canada Ltd.* (1989), 62 D.L.R. (4th) 104 (Nfld. C.A.), the *Wong* exception was held not to apply, as evidence regarding the circumstances surrounding the loss was available in a Royal Commission investigation into the sinking of the relevant drilling unit (the "Ocean Ranger" disaster).

If the bailment is established, the goods and the bailee both disappear, and the bailor is not able to establish the bailee's negligence, then the doctrine of *res ipsa loquitur* — the thing speaks for itself — may apply. In these circumstances, there may be no reasonable explanation consistent with the facts other than the defendant's negligence. The court will look at the evidence as a whole and, in the absence of any direct evidence of negligence, may excuse the bailee, on condition his representative is able to provide a credible reason for the failure to redeliver that is consistent with no negligence on the part of the bailee.

### (c) — Bailee's Liability for Employees

Until the twentieth century, courts were unwilling to assign liability to employers for the negligence of their servants. However, since *Lloyd v. Grace, Smith & Co.*, [1912] A.C. 716 (U.K. H.L.), employers have been vicariously liable for their servant's treatment of bailed goods. If an employer delegates the care of a good to an employee, he is responsible for how that employee carries out her duties within the scope of her employment (*Morris v. C.W. Martin & Sons Ltd.* (1966), [1965] 2 All E.R. 725 (Eng. C.A.)). The question of what constitutes the course or scope of employment is sometimes confusing. For example, an employer is not liable if employment provides access to the good but the employee is not entrusted with the bailed good (*Frans Maas (UK) Ltd. v. Samsung Electronics (UK) Ltd.*, [2004] EWHC 1502 (Comm)). In contrast, an employer will be responsible to the bailor for an employee who damages an automobile joyriding while entrusted with possession (*Aitchison v. Page Motors Ltd.* (1935), 52 T.L.R. 137 (K.B.)). Similarly, an employer who hires employees without sufficiently inquiring into their character will be held vicariously liable for damage to bailed goods caused by such employees (*Van Geel v. Warrington*

(1928), 63 O.L.R. 143 (Ont. CA.)). If, however, the damage to the bailed good is caused by someone other than the delegated employee, the employer is required only to show that he took all reasonable care with respect to the goods.

### (d) — Exclusion Clauses

In a modern commercial context, bailees often seek to limit or avoid liability for damage to bailed goods through the use of exclusion or disclaimer clauses. Such clauses are contained in written-form contracts or business signs and typically disclaim liability for loss, or limit liability to a nominal amount. In such situations, courts import contract principles to interpret the understanding between the parties as to what was contained in the contract of bailment. The following guidelines apply.

#### *(i) — Notice*

Courts first examine the extent to which the bailor was aware of the liability disclaimer at the time of transferring possession of his property. Was the notice clear enough and direct enough that a reasonable person would have been aware of the bailee's intention to limit liability? Again, the parking cases are illustrative. Courts examine whether the lot signs are large enough and visible enough that all persons entering should read them. (*Brown v. Toronto Auto Parks*; *Bata v. City Parking Canada Ltd.* (1973), 43 D.L.R. (3d) 190 (Ont. CA.)).

#### *(ii) — Strict Construction*

If the courts find evidence of either actual or constructive notice of a limitation of liability on the part of the bailee, the courts will nonetheless construe the limitation narrowly, applying it only to the circumstances specifically outlined. The principle of *contra proferentem* applies — words (in this case exclusion clauses) are to be strictly construed against the interests of the party who drew the document. Assuming it is the bailee who proposed the clause, the tendency is to construe the clause and its effect in favour of the bailor. For example, a clause "not liable for loss however caused" has been held to be too wide to exempt a parking lot company for liability for damage caused by the negligence of a parking lot employee. If the company wished to disclaim liability for that particular circumstance, it should have specifically said so in the exclusion clause (*Judson Foods Ltd. v. Polar Quick Freezing Co.* (1979), 23 Nfld. & P.E.I.R. 92 (P.E.I. S.C.); *Falcon Lumber Ltd. v. Canada Wood Specialty Co.* (1978), 95 D.L.R. (3d) 503 (Ont. H.C.); *Spycher v. J.L. Coulter Ltd.* (1982), 40 A.R. 373 (Alta. C.A.)).

### *(iii) — Fundamental Breach*

Historically, even if an exclusion clause was clear, courts were unwilling to allow bailees to disclaim all liability for bailed goods. As the essence of a bailment is the duty to care for bailed goods, one could not create a bailment and at the same time deny all liability under the bailment. Courts struck down clauses that attempted to avoid all liability for the safety of the bailed goods as constituting a fundamental breach of the contract of bailment (*Heffron*).

In *Syncrude Canada Ltd. v. Hunter Engineering Co.*, [1989] 1 S.C.R. 426 (S.C.C.), the Supreme Court of Canada unanimously held, following the House of Lords in *Photo Production Ltd. v. Securicor Transport Ltd.*, [1980] 2 W.L.R. 283 (U.K. H.L.), that the doctrine of fundamental breach is no longer a rule of law but rather is a rule of construction. As a rule of construction, the exclusionary clause is examined to determine what the understanding of the parties was as to the purpose of the bailment. Courts will uphold clauses that exclude liability for fundamental breach providing the contract is not unconscionable, unfair, or unreasonable.

In that case, Dickson J. defined unconscionability as "over-arching by the stronger party", and held that the courts must determine if the contract was unconscionable at the time it was entered into. Questions involved include: Did the parties agree to and understand the limitation on liability? Was there equality of bargaining power? Did the bailor have a choice? In contrast, Wilson J. held that the courts must determine if enforcing the contract would be unfair or unreasonable, in light of subsequent events. To date there has been no clarification as to which approach will prevail.

## 6.3 — Sub-Bailment

In some situations, a bailee determines that he cannot perform the purpose of the bailment or the bailment is complete but another bailment of the good is necessary to achieve a different purpose. In the first situation, the bailor may suggest that the good be re-bailed to a different bailee who can fulfill the purpose of the bailment, and the bailee agrees to transfer the good to a new bailee as a courtesy to the bailor. The original bailee has no further involvement with the goods. A new contract of bailment is created between the bailor and a new bailee. This is called an attournment.

In the second situation, a bailee may deliver a bailor's good to a third party sub-bailee as part of the original bailment. This is called a sub-bailment. The delivery is with the express or implied permission of the bailor, now referred to as the original bailor. The bailee, now called the bailee/bailor, negotiates with the sub-bailee as to the purpose of sub-bailment. The sub-bailee knows that the goods are not owned by the bailer/bailor but by the original bailor. The duty of the sub-bailee is to care for the goods and return them to the bailee/bailor, who will return them to the original bailor (*P & O Nedlloyd B.V. v. Utaniko Ltd.*, [2003] EWCA Civ 83).

Establishing liability in a sub-bailment requires that the bailee/bailor prove delivery to the sub-bailee for a specific purpose and the failure to redeliver the goods in a safe condition. The bailee/bailor is also responsible for establishing that he had the original bailor's permission to sub-bail, and that the sub-bailee knew, or ought to have known, that the goods were not owned by the bailee/bailor but rather by an original bailor (*Pioneer Container, The*, [1994] 2 All E.R. 250 (P.C.), *Marq v. Christie, Manson & Woods Ltd.*, [2003] EWCA Civ 731). If these elements are proven, onus transfers to the sub-bailee to disprove negligence.

## (a) — Liability of Sub-Bailee

### *(i) — To Bailee/Bailor*

In early English law, the bailee/bailor was precluded from suing a sub-bailee or a third party wrongdoer on the grounds of *jus tertii* — the rights were in a third party. Only the owner could bring suit on behalf of his own goods. The goods were owned by the original bailor and thus the sub-bailee or third party wrongdoer was only responsible to him, not the bailee/bailor. In a growing market where goods were increasingly sub-bailed, it was often impractical for original bailors to take suit against the sub-bailee. In these circumstances, bailee/bailors argued that the sub-bailee was the one who knew what happened by virtue of his possession of the goods and therefore should be required to disprove negligence. In an admiralty case, *The Winkfield*, [1900-3] All E.R. 346 (CA.), the Court agreed, and held that a bailee/bailor could bring an action against a sub-bailee or third party wrongdoer for a failure to redeliver. The bailee/bailor may bring an action even if the sub-bailee has no direct bailment with the original bailor. Allowing the bailee/bailor to recover reinforces the importance of possessory rights and permits protection of goods that would otherwise be removed from protection of the law. However, courts reasoned that it would be unfair to allow a bailee/bailor to sue on behalf of goods she did not own unless she had permission from the original bailor to sub-bail the goods. Thus a bailee/bailor wishing to take action against a sub-bailee or wrongdoer has to prove that the goods were sub-bailed with the original bailor's permission.

### *(ii) — To Original Bailor*

Historically, there was another obstacle to the original bailor bringing suit against the sub-bailee — there was no privity of contract between the bailor and the sub-bailee. The original bailor was forced to recover for her loss from the bailee/bailor with whom she had the original bailment agreement. If a bailee/bailor became insolvent or was unwilling to take an action against a sub-bailee, the original bailor was often left without remedy (although there may have been an action in tort). This was changed in *Morris v. C.W Martin & Sons Ltd.*, [1965] 2 All E.R. 725 (Eng. C.A.), where the Court held that an original bailor could sue a sub-bailee. Again, courts reasoned that it would be unfair to impose a duty of care on the sub-bailee to the original bailor if the sub-bailee did not know that the goods belonged to someone other than the bailee/bailor. Thus, in an action by an original bailor against a sub-bailee, the original bailor with a right to possession must prove that the sub-bailee had actual or constructive knowledge that the goods in her possession were the goods of the original bailor.

### *(iii) — Scope*

The sub-bailee's duty to both the bailee/bailor and the original bailor is to take reasonable care under the circumstances. A sub-bailee may be sued by either the original bailor or the bailee/bailor but not both, and whichever one recovers must account to the other (*Eastern Construction Co. v. National Trust Co.*, [1914] A.C. 197 (P.C.); *Associates Discount Corporation v. Gillineau*, 78 N.E. 2d 192 (Mass. Sup. Ct., 1948)). The recovery can include economic damages for lost opportunity as well as the full value of the *res* (*Tanenbaum v. W.J. Bell Paper Co.*, [1956] O.R. 278 (Ont. H.C.)).

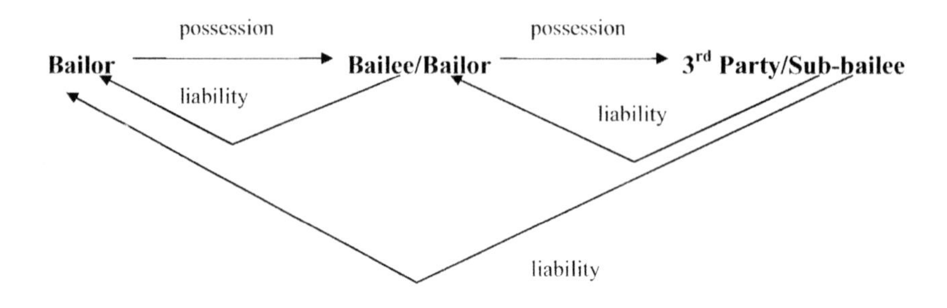


## (b) — Liability in a Chain of Sub-Bailments

Commercial transactions often involve a number of successive sub-bailments. Sorting out liability down the chain requires determining the duty of each successive sub-bailee to each of the previous bailee/bailors and original bailor (*Punch v. Savoy's Jewellers Ltd.* (1986), 26 D.L.R. (4th) 546 (Ont. C.A.)). This is done by checking, in relation to each successive sub-bailment:

- *whether each sub-bailment was explicitly or implicitly approved by each of the previous bailees in the chain* — If a bailee/bailor delivers goods to a successive sub-bailee without the explicit or implicit permission of the original bailor and any previous bailee/bailors, the offending bailee/bailor will be liable for negligence or deviance, depending on the extent to which the sub-bailment departs from the understanding of the previous parties. A bailee/bailor who delivers goods without permission of the original bailor and previous bailee/bailors will have, at best, an action against the party to whom he bailed the goods, but it will be on the basis of their immediate contract including any exclusion clauses. The offending bailee/bailor will remain liable to the original bailor and any previous bailee/bailors for conversion of the goods.
- *whether each successive sub-bailee knew or ought to have known that the goods belonged to someone other than the immediately previous bailee/bailor* — As noted, an original bailor who wishes to sue a sub-bailee must prove that the sub-bailee knew the goods were not owned by the bailee/bailor. Such knowledge must be proven at each succes-

sive stage of sub-bailment in order to find a duty on the part of the successive sub-bailee to anyone other than an immediate bailee/bailor.

If a successive sub-bailment is either without permission or without the sub-bailee's actual or constructive knowledge of the owners or other bailee/bailors, the previous duty of care does not extend to that successive sub-bailee, but exists only between the sub-bailee and the immediately previous bailee/bailor according to their particular understanding. Even if knowledge exists, a duty of care extends only to the terms of the original bailment. Thus, in both situations, a determination of the sub-bailee's liability to previous bailee/bailors and the original bailor requires an interpretation of the understandings among the original bailor and the respective bailee/bailors.

- *what the understanding was between the sub-bailee and each of the preceding bailee/bailors as to the terms of the bailment* — One must scrutinize not only the sub-bailee's understanding with her immediately preceding bailee/bailor, but also the understanding of each of the prior bailee/bailors as to the terms of a sub-bailment. Often, assumptions as to the nature of the bailment are not discussed in advance. Courts resolve this by holding the original bailor and previous bailee/bailors to have implicitly agreed to terms common in the trade, and beyond that, examining the facts of the specific case to determine explicit and implicit understandings throughout the chain. Often, exclusion clauses are involved.

### (c) — Exclusion Clauses in Sub-Bailment

Sub-bailees frequently introduce an exclusion clause to limit liability to the original bailor and bailee/bailors. Such clauses will bind the immediately preceding bailee/bailor who agreed to them, subject to the doctrines of notice and strict construction, and to the rule of construction of fundamental breach. They will, however, bind the original bailor and bailee/bailors in the chain only to the extent that each has implicitly or explicitly agreed to such clauses. If the exclusion clauses are common in the trade, the original bailor and previous bailee/bailor will be held to have agreed to them implicitly. However, terms in exclusion clauses to which the original bailor and the previous bailee/bailors have not agreed will be ineffective against them (*Punch v. Savoy's Jewellers Ltd.*).

Courts struggle with the balance between the rights of an original bailor and those of a sub-bailee who should not be held to a standard of care higher than the one to which she was willing to commit. Courts resolve this policy tension in a sub-bailment context by stringently requiring that each successive sub-bailment has been approved by the original bailor and previous bailee/bailors, and that the sub-bailee in each case knew of the original bailor or a previous bailee/bailor.

# CHAPTER 7 — PURCHASE AND SALE



## 7.0 — Introduction

The purchase and sale of choses in possession falls within the provincial jurisdiction over property and civil rights under s. 92(13) of the *Constitution Act, 1867*, and is governed in most jurisdictions by *Sale of Goods Acts* and *Factors Acts*. The Acts codify common law principles, and because they are conceptually consistent across jurisdictions are included in this chapter. However, these statutorily-enshrined common law principles are frequently altered by further statute. For example, *Personal Property Security Acts* significantly impact the rights of parties in commercial transactions in Canadian common law provinces. Specific reference must be made to these statutes to determine the interface.

## 7.1 — When Does Property Transfer?

The rights and obligations of the parties and third party outsiders are affected by who has property. The general rule is that when something goes wrong with the goods, the person who has property at that moment bears the risk of loss. Legislation determines who has property at any particular point in a sale transaction not by whether possession has been transferred nor by whether the goods have been paid for, but by the intention of the parties.

All *Sale of Goods Acts* state that once there is a contract for a sale of specific or ascertained goods, i.e., goods that are identified and agreed upon at the time the contract of sale is made, property passes when the parties so intend. If the contract is explicit as to when the property passes, that intention governs. In most cases that reach the courts however, the contract is not explicit and the intention between the parties as to when property would pass is not apparent. In such cases, the statutes direct courts to look at the intention of the parties as evidenced by the terms of the contract, the conduct of the parties, and the circumstances of the case. These factors are also applied in determining the intention as to when property passes for unascertained goods. Courts are asked to determine what a reasonable person would have concluded as to when the parties intended the property to pass.

If this does not reveal the intention of the parties, *Sale of Goods Acts* direct the property is deemed to have passed based on five default rules outlined in the legislation. The conceptual framework in the rules is that if the seller fulfils his contractual responsibility and the buyer is aware, then loss is at the buyer's risk. If however, the seller has yet to do something to make the goods ready for the buyer, then the seller retains the risk until he completes the task and notifies the buyer.

The first rule indicates that if the contract is for identifiable (specific) goods that are already in a deliverable state, property passes when the contract is made. Thus if a buyer concludes a contract to purchase a car, and before the car is delivered it is destroyed by fire on the seller's lot, the loss will be at the buyer's risk. The rule specifically states that it is irrelevant whether payment or delivery has yet been made. The buyer might still have an action in bailment against the seller because the Acts provide that a person in possession of goods in which the property has passed to another may be a bailee of those goods. If however, the car dealer meets the standard of care required by the bailment, the buyer's action fails and the buyer loses. This creates obvious difficulties for the buyer. Most commercial sellers have insurance to cover loss in such situations so as to not offend customers.

The second rule provides that if goods are not in a deliverable state, the property does not pass until the goods have been put in a deliverable state and the buyer has received notice thereof. Goods are deliverable when they are in such a state that the buyer under the contract would be bound to take delivery of them. Thus if the car that the buyer agrees to buy needs to have a battery installed, and the car burns before the battery is installed or before the dealer notifies the buyer of installation, then the property does not transfer to the buyer (*Jerome v. Clements Motor Sales Ltd.* (1958), 15 D.L.R. (2d) 689 (Ont. C.A.)).

The third rule, similar to the second, provides that if a seller has to do something to determine the price, such as to weigh, measure, or test the goods, property does not pass until the seller does this and notifies the buyer.

The fourth rule addresses goods that are delivered to the buyer on approval or "on sale or return" (the distinction remains unclear). Property passes to the buyer when she does any act adopting the transaction, or retains the goods beyond a fixed date or a reasonable time in light of the circumstances.

The fifth rule addresses unascertained or future goods by description. Unascertained goods include goods to be manufactured or grown by the seller, purely generic (fungible) goods, or an unidentified portion of a specified whole. Property passes when the goods are in a deliverable state and are unconditionally appropriated to the contract by either the buyer or seller with the assent of the other party. For example, once the length of silk requested by the buyer has been cut from the bolt, or the cookies baked and packaged (i.e., in a deliverable state), the property in the goods passes to the buyer. In a situation where these goods are delivered to a transportation company and are damaged before arriving at the destination, the buyer must pursue remedies against the transportation company.

The party who has property in the goods at a particular moment is said to have the general property, while the party who may have possession but not property is said to have a special property in the goods.

## 7.2 — *Nemo Dat Quod Non Habet*

The fundamental common law principle of *nemo dat quod non habet (nemo dat)* states that no one can give better title than she herself has. The unwitting purchaser who buys a stolen watch from a street corner vendor, or the bargain hunter at a garage sale who buys a set of dining room furniture for which the homeowner has not paid, can claim no better title to the goods than the thief or the homeowner. This occurs despite the fact that the purchaser is innocent, otherwise *bona fide*, and has paid value for the goods (*Clayton v. LeRoy*, [1911] 2 K.B. 1031 (Eng. K.B.); *Wilkinson v. King* (1809), 2 Cmp. 335 (C.P.)).

## 7.3 — Exceptions to *Nemo Dat*

Courts are concerned that the strict application of *nemo dat* is unfair to a third party who without wrongful intent and in the course of normal commercial transactions finds himself without title (*Dale Tingley Motors Ltd. v. Herbst* (1983), 27 Sask. R. 264 (Sask. Q.B.)). Equally innocent is the person whose watch was stolen by the vendor/thief or the furniture store owner who sold the dining room set in good faith on a money purchase plan. Why should he be forced to surrender title to the goods of which he is the true owner? If *nemo dat* was applied without exception, the titleholder would always prevail and there would be little freedom or safety in the field of commercial transactions. (*Bishopgate Motor Finance Corp. v. Transport Brakes Ltd.*, [1949] 1 All E.R. 37 (Eng. C.A.)). Common law and statutory exceptions developed to facilitate commercial transactions and allow a *bona fide* purchaser to prevail. Bear in mind that the principle of *nemo dat* remains, subject only to articulated exceptions which vary by province.

Provincial *Sale of Goods Acts* may include the following exceptions to *nemo dat*:

- a sale by a seller or buyer in possession of goods where the property has already passed
- a sale under a voidable title
- a sale by agent
- a sale in market overt (a legally chartered open public market)
- a sale under power of sale
- a sale meeting the requirements of the *Factors Acts*
- a situation involving estoppel.

In the market overt exception, the goods must be exposed and the purchase made during normal business hours, presumably to allow the true owner to recover the goods. There are no markets overt in Canada (*Mackenzie v. Blindman Valley Co-operative Assn.*, [1947] 4 D.L.R. 687 (Alta. T.D.)), despite this provision continuing in British Columbia (*Sale of Goods Act*, R.S.B.C. 1996, c. 410, s. 27). The common law exception of market overt may be relevant in some circumstances relating to international trade.

In addition, there are various other provisions unique to individual provinces. For example, the Saskatchewan, Alberta, and Manitoba *Sale of Goods Acts* (s. 25 in each of the Acts) provide that a *bona fide* purchaser for value will prevail in a sale to a licenced grain dealer.

### (a) — Sale by Agent

The general principle is that if goods are sold without the authority or consent of the owner, title does not pass. However, the rules of common law regarding principal and agent have been codified within *Sale of Goods Acts* to permit agents with actual, usual, or ostensible authority to bind the owner. An agent is an individual who is authorized to act on behalf of a principal. Actual authority is a specific understanding between the principal and agent. Usual authority is inferred from the nature of the office held by the agent in the custom of the trade. Ostensible authority is when the principal does or fails to do something that makes a reasonable third party believe that the agent has authority to act.

### (b) — *Factors Acts*

The *Factors Acts* protect the title of a *bona fide* purchaser for value without notice in purchases made from a consignment dealer providing that four conditions are met. First, the purchase must be made from a mercantile agent, defined in the Acts as an individual who in the customary course of business has authority to buy, sell, or take consigned goods, or raise money on security of goods, acting in his capacity as mercantile agent. For example, if an owner takes her car to a garage for repair, and the garage sells her car, the person who buys it does not receive good title, because the garage acted outside its capacity as garage. However, if an owner takes her car to a used car dealer for appraisal, and the dealer sells the car, the purchaser might get good title if all the other conditions of the *Factors Acts* are met because car sales are part of a car dealer's activity as a mercantile agent.

Second, the agent must be in possession of the goods with the consent of the owner. In the example above, the car dealer was indeed in possession with the consent of the owner, albeit only for appraisal. While the owner may lose her car to the purchaser, she still retains a right of action against the car dealer for breach of the understanding between them as to the purpose for which she left the car (*Alberta (Sheriff, Edmonton District) v. Kozak* (1965), 54 W.W.R. 677 (Alta. Dist. Ct.)). On the other hand, a purchaser who buys a stolen car from a used car dealer is not protected because the car dealer was not in possession of the car with the consent of the owner.

Third, the purchase must be during the normal course of business, that is, during normal business hours and under normal business conditions. It cannot, for example, be a black market transaction.

Fourth, the purchaser must be a *bona fide* purchaser for value without notice. The purchaser cannot encounter anything during the purchase that ought to raise her suspicions that the mercantile agent does not have good title or authority to sell.

### (c) — Estoppel

If an owner of goods behaves in such a way that others observing would believe that another party, the person in possession, is the owner of the goods, and a third party purchases the goods relying on the owner's actions, then the owner is estopped from claiming his title against that *bona fide* purchaser for value without notice. Estoppel may be by representation or negligence.

In estoppel by representation, the owner, by words or actions, allows a third party to reasonably believe that the person in possession of the goods is the owner. If the third party acts on that belief and as a *bona fide* purchaser buys the good, he is protected. For example, if a mortgagee attends a meeting between his debtor and a potential purchaser and says that the debtor owes him money but mentions nothing about having a mortgage on the goods, he will be estopped by representation from later claiming his title against that *bona fide* purchaser for value of those goods (*Pickard v. Sears* (1837), 112 E.R. 179 (Eng. K.B.)). Estoppel applies even if the owner has no intention to deceive or is not otherwise negligent so long as the representation is voluntary.

In estoppel by negligence, one has to first establish the owner of the good has a duty of care to the third party to do a particular thing, then prove that thing was not done. For example, in *McVicar v. Herman* (1958), 13 D.L.R. (2d) 419 (Sask. CA.), an owner of a car was held to have no duty to inform a third party purchaser, of whom he was unaware, that the person in possession of the vehicle had merely borrowed the car. Most purchasers' claims based on estoppel by negligence fail.

### (d) — Common Law or Statutory Powers of Sale and Court Ordered Sales

A final set of exceptions to *nemo dat* are powers developed at common law and codified by various statutes for certain classes of people to sell goods that they do not own. For example, sheriffs have power to sell goods seized under a writ of execution and buyers will acquire good title despite the lack of title in the sheriff. Similarly, innkeepers have the right to sell goods upon which they have a lien, as do pawn shop operators. Further, courts retain discretionary power to order sales.

# CHAPTER 8 — PERSONAL PROPERTY CROSS-OVERS



## 8.1 — Fixtures

A chattel that becomes affixed to land loses its designation as personal property and becomes part of the real property. The rule is contained in a Latin maxim *quicquid plantatur solo, solo credit* — that which is attached to the soil becomes part of the soil. A chattel owner loses her property in a good that meets the legal test of having become sufficiently affixed to the land.

Fixtures are of contemporary significance in a number of property-related matters such as whether household items (for example, a chandelier, kitchen appliances, or a garden shed) remain after a purchase of a house, and whether a financial institution with a security interest in a good can retain it against the owner of the real property to which it has now become attached. Courts determine whether something has become a fixture by looking at the intention of the parties. The intention of the parties is determined by a two-step test examining the degree of annexation and the object of annexation. The test is objective, i.e., the courts look to actions and evidence available to all and ask what a reasonable person would conclude in the circumstances rather than to the subjective intentions of the individual parties (*Stack v. T. Eaton Co.* (1902), 4 O.L.R. 335 (Ont. Div. Ct.)).

Parties often contract out of these common law rules by written agreement. For example, certain household goods such as blinds, appliances, entertainment units, and outdoor play sets, are often specifically addressed in real estate transactions. In situations involving financing or debt arrangements, attention must also be paid to *Personal Property Security Acts*.

### (a) — Degree of Annexation

At common law, courts first look to whether a chattel is resting on the land only by its own weight or whether it is attached. If it rests on its own weight, there is a *prima facie* presumption that it remains a chattel. Conversely, if the good is attached even slightly, the *prima facie* presumption is that it is a fixture. For example, a full length mirror in a house secured by screws would *prima facie* be a fixture because it is attached by more than its own weight. Conversely, a garage package resting only by its own weight on a cement pad would *prima facie* be a chattel.

The presumption emerging from the first step of the test determines the onus for the next step. The stronger the attachment, the stronger the presumption. The onus in the next step rests on the party claiming contrary to the *prima facie* case (*Holland v. Hodgson* (1872), L.R. 7 C.P. 328 (Eng. Ex. Ch.); *Ontario Wilderness Outposts Inc. v. Nishnawbe Aski Development Fund* (2006), 41 R.P.R. (4th) 286 (Ont. S.C.J.).

### (b) — Object of Annexation

A contrary intention is established by showing that a reasonable onlooker, familiar with the purpose of the good and customs of the time and place, would conclude that the parties intended the good to remain as a chattel or to become part of the real estate. The house purchaser would argue that a reasonable purchaser would expect that the suburban garage is part of the real estate, even if the garage is only resting on its own weight. The seller would argue that while the full length mirror has to be screwed into the wall in order not to fall and break, the custom of the time and place is that full length mirrors are attached for the personal use of the owners. They can be easily removed without damage to either the good or the real estate. Thus they remain personal property to be removed when they leave. Because the intention test focuses on the reasonable expectation of the parties, whether something is a chattel or a fixture may change over time. At the turn of the century bathtubs were considered chattels, while house purchasers now assume them to be fixtures.

One enunciation of the test — whether the affixation is for the better use of the chattel as chattel or for the better use of the property as property — is often ambiguous (*Royal Bank of Canada v. Maple Ridge Farmers Market Ltd.* (1995), 34 C.B.R. (3d) 270 (B.C. S.C. [In Chambers])). The answer to both questions may seem to be positive, as in the case of hotel carpets that were nailed to the floor not only for their use as carpets but also for the better and more effectual use of the hotel (*La Salle Recreations Ltd. v. Canadian Camdex Investments Ltd.* (1969), 4 D.L.R. (3d) 549 (B.C. C.A.)). In practice, the test tends to be whether the parties intend, based on their reasonable expectations, the objective purpose of the good, and on the custom of time and place, that a particular good become a fixture or remain a chattel.

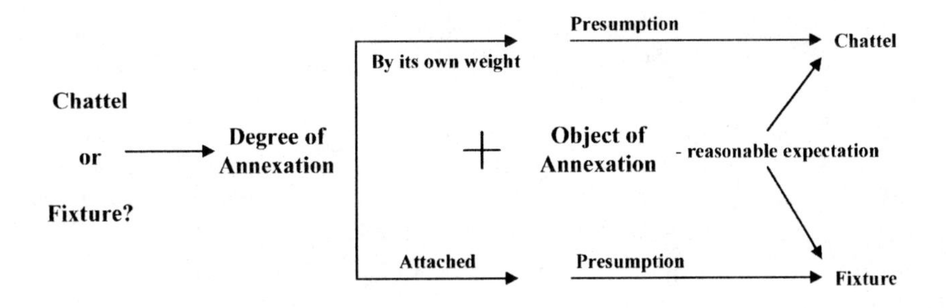


## (c) — Tenants' and Trade Fixtures

A long-standing exception to the above test is tenants' and trade fixtures (*Frank Georges Island Investments Ltd. v. Ocean Farmers Ltd.* (2000), 182 N.S.R. (2d) 201 (N.S. S.C. [In Chambers])). In the landlord/tenant relationship there is no intention on the part of the tenant to permanently affix chattels to improve the property for the landlord (the reversionary interest). Even though chattels such as display cases or area dividers are attached firmly to the real estate, tenants have historically been permitted to remove these. The policy argument is that tenants installed the chattels to improve their business (not to improve the landlord's property) and that to leave them would be a windfall to landlords and an economic disincentive to commercial leasing. This does not mean that the affixed items are not fixtures, but rather that the fixtures are removable. The only conditions fettering the tenant's rights are that the fixtures must be removed within a reasonable time depending upon the type of tenancy, without doing harm to the landlord's property, and without demolishing or losing the essential character of the items (*Hughes v. Towers* (1866), 16 U.C.C.P. 287 (U.C. C.P.)). In modern commercial properties, these matters are governed by leases, but the background common law rule remains.

## 8.2 — Accession

An accession occurs when two chattels become joined together as opposed to when a chattel affixes to real estate. The rule for accession is that when one chattel becomes sufficiently joined to a second chattel, the property in both accrues to the owner of the principal chattel. Simplistically, the principal chattel is often interpreted as meaning the chattel of greater monetary value. The issue is: When do the two chattels become sufficiently joined?

In the case of *Firestone Tire & Rubber Co. v. Industrial Acceptance Corp.* (1970), [1971] S.C.R. 357 (S.C.C.), a buyer had separately purchased a vehicle and four replacement tires. He had paid for neither the tires nor the vehicle. Both the tire company and the vehicle repossessor claimed the tires. The Supreme Court listed the previously-established tests for determining whether accession had taken place: (examples added)

- *injurious removal* — Can the two chattels be separated so as not to injure either? For example, floor mats might easily be removed from an automobile while stuffing might not so easily be removed from a sofa without injuring both.
- *separate existence* — Can the chattel still be separately identified? For example, paint adhered to a toy wagon loses its separate identity while a bell on a bicycle does not.
- *utility of the whole* — Would removal of the chattel destroy the utility of the whole? For example, removing the blade from a lawn mower would destroy the utility of the whole, while removing a bicycle rack from a van would not.
- *degree & object of annexation* — Similar to the fixture test, is a chattel resting on the second chattel by its own weight or is it attached to the second chattel? What are the expectations of the parties based on the custom of time and place. For example, people expect that appliances stay with a motor home when it is sold but do not expect that a propane tank is included with a new barbecue.

In *Firestone*, the lower court had awarded the tires to the vehicle repossessor on the basis that a vehicle could not operate without tires. The Supreme Court reversed the decision. It appears the Court relied on injurious removal (the tires could be removed without damage) and separate existence (the tires retained their identity). However, a closer look at Justice Laskin's (as he then was) reasons suggests that his decision was policy based. Laskin J. held that it is important to address underlying issues as well as precedent. In circumstances where accession has taken place and the attachment cannot be reversed one of the parties must prevail and gain title to the chattel. Laskin J. awarded the tires to the tire company because he held that it was commercially inappropriate for the vehicle repossessor to have a windfall benefit of the new tires that were not on its original vehicle. If the attachment is reversible, then the desire for fairness and the prevention of a windfall suggests that detachment be pursued to provide relief to both parties.

In most Canadian jurisdictions, *Personal Property Security Acts* have superseded the common law by establishing a statutory scheme with respect to priority of interests in financed property (e.g., *Personal Property Security Act*, R.S.A. 2000, c. P-7). Parties claiming a security interest in goods can register in a central personal property security register. This protects the registered party's interest in the goods regardless of accession.

## 8.3 — Intermixture

Intermixture occurs when two substances are combined and are no longer distinguishable nor separable. Examples are the inadvertent combining of two separate loads of wheat, the mixing of two booms of unmarked logs, or the unauthorized racking of wine into a common barrel. Historically, the circumstances surrounding the intermixture affected title in the new lot. For example, if a wrongdoer willfully combined his small amount of grain with a large shipment owned by another, title in the whole would be awarded to the latter. In contrast, an innocent intermixture led the courts to divide the goods between the parties on a proportional basis. In more recent cases, for example *Glencore International v. Metro Trading International Inc.*, [2001] 1 Lloyd's L.R. 284 (Q.B. (Comm. Ct.)) involving mixture of bulk fuel oil, the courts have moved away from the punitive approach in intermixture title disputes towards awarding shares in the whole according to the proportion each party can establish they have contributed.

## 8.4 — Alteration

Alteration occurs when, through the labour of a non-owner, a chattel loses its original identity and is changed into a new species. If alteration is complete — the grapes are now wine or the animal is now hamburger — title in the new *res* goes to the individual who transformed the good. The new title holder is responsible to the previous owner for the value of the goods that were converted. The question as to when alteration is complete is determined by the courts through the application of tests similar to those discussed in accession. If the original chattel is still identifiable or the process of alteration is reversible, after considering the other accession tests, the court may award title to the original owner.

# CHAPTER 9 — CHOSES IN ACTION



## 9.1 — Choses in Action are a Property Interest

As noted in the Chapter 1, choses in action originally referred to rights that could only be realized through an action of a court. If A loaned money to B, then A had a right to sue B for the recovery of the money. A's right to sue B was a chose in action. Medieval English law called A's right a chose in action to distinguish it from a tangible chose in possession.

The action at law to recover a chose in possession was detinue or conversion, both of which were claims of a denial of possession. Debts, however, could not be possessed in the same way. What A had was not a claim to possession, but a claim to have B fulfill his agreement to pay her. B's agreement was intangible. The agreement could only be turned into tangible money by taking an action in a court. The chose in action was property because B's agreement to pay A was a valuable thing to A. A could take his agreement to court and obtain an order to turn the agreement into money. It was enforceable only *in personam*, hence the courts classified it as personal rather than real property. The property was intangible, hence choses in action were intangible personal property.

In modern times, this meaning of choses in action continues. In the holder-right-*res*-enforceability relationship the right is the right to sue on an agreement. A is the holder of the right to sue, and it is enforceable against B. B's agreement to pay is a valuable thing, because it can be turned, through an action of the court, into money. In addition, the scope of choses in action has expanded beyond debt to include any assignable or assigned right such as corporate shares, trademarks, or patents.

## 9.2 — Choses in Action were Unassignable at Common Law

Assume that in addition to having loaned money to B, A also wished to borrow money from C, perhaps to start a new business. A did not have sufficient cash in her account to secure a loan from C. But A had something else. B owed her money. If B did not pay, A had a right to sue B in a form of action known as debt. A had a chose in action. If A could transfer that chose in action from herself to C as security for a loan from C, C could recover the money directly from B if A did not repay her own loan to C. C might find that right sufficient security to loan A the money.

With rare exceptions, the Courts of Common Law refused to recognize assignment of choses in action. The result was that if C attempted to realize on his security from A by collecting from B directly, he could not do so. Choses in action were not assignable at common law. A's security from B was worthless to C.

## 9.3 — Choses in Action Became Assignable in Equity

### (a) — Legal Choses in Action

While the Courts of Common Law insisted that choses in action were unassignable, the Courts of Equity applied their flexible jurisdiction to find a way to make them assignable in practice. In so doing they removed a legal barrier to the development of a market economy.

The Courts of Equity looked to the intent rather than the form, and assumed to be done that which ought to have been done. In our example, the Courts of Equity reasoned that if A assigned her right to sue B as security for her loan from C, then in conscience A was bound to allow C to realize on the security.

By its own maxim, Equity did not replace the law but only supplemented the law (in this case the Common Law). In the Courts of Common Law, A had a contract with B, and A had a contract with C, but there was no privity of contract between C and B. Further, Equity did not have jurisdiction in matters of debt. Equity's solution was to use its injunctive power against the person to order A to allow C to realize on his security by suing B in A's name in the Courts of Common Law. Equity ordered A to give power of attorney to C to sue on A's contract with B. To put legal names on the parties, A was the assignor, C the assignee, and B the account debtor.

In this way, Equity achieved several things. It remained true to its maxim of following the law by acknowledging that the contract to recover from B was a contract with A. It stayed within its jurisdiction by allowing the action in debt between A and B to be heard in the Courts of Common Law and by using its injunctive power. Yet it achieved justice on the case, looked to intent rather than form, and forced A to live up to her commitment in conscience.

With this, choses in action became assignable in Equity. Choses in action continued to be unassignable in the Courts of Common Law, but the Courts of Common Law enforced the solution that had been arrived at in the Courts of Equity. They allowed C to come into the Courts of Common Law as A's agent to sue B in A's name. Such pre-existing debts assignable in Equity came to be called legal choses in action, although the rule permitting their assignment had been developed in Equity.

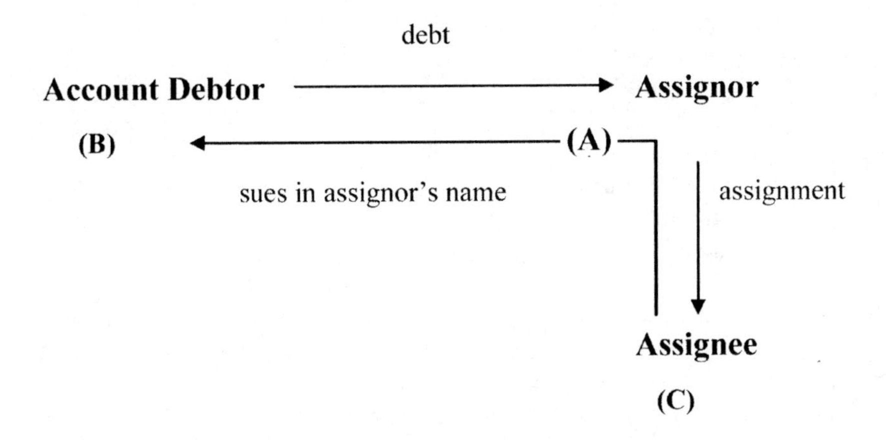


## (b) — Equitable Choses in Action

The right to assign intangible personal property to which the assignor already had title (B's existing debt to A) facilitated market transactions, but it was still limited to the transfer of existing wealth among parties. A had to have money or goods to loan or sell to B in order to create B's debt before A had anything to assign to C.

A market economy is premised not only on the transfer of existing wealth, but also on the creation of new wealth. Assume A wished to become a manufacturer. A needed supplies to begin her manufacturing process. But A had nothing to offer her suppliers as security. A needed to manufacture her product and sell it before she had any chose in action in the form of a purchaser's debt to assign as security to her supplier. Yet A could not manufacture her product to sell until she had the materials from her suppliers.

The economic solution was simple: allow A to assign the proceeds of the sales she intended to make in the future to her suppliers as security for the loan to obtain the supplies to get started. The problem was that at law, A had nothing that the courts recognized as property. A could assign nothing more than she had, and while her product remained unmanufactured, she had nothing.

Again, the Courts of Equity devised a practical solution to accommodate the market. In the landmark case of *Holroyd v. Marshall* (1862), 10 H.L.C. 191 (U.K. H.L.), a debtor had mortgaged machinery to a mortgagee as security for a loan to acquire inventory. The mortgage included not only the machinery he already had in the plant, but also, "all machinery, implements, and things which, during the continuance of this security, shall be fixed or placed in or about the said mill" (at 192). The mortgagor manufacturer acquired new equipment in the mill, but had not yet transferred legal title to the mortgagee creditor when another creditor obtained a judgment to seize all the mortgagor's machinery (execution creditor). In the Courts of Common Law, the execution creditor could have the new machinery seized since legal title was in the mortgagor manufacturer. The Courts of Equity, however, said that the mortgagor could not, in conscience, refuse to pass title to the new equipment to the mortgagee as he had agreed to do in the mortgage document. Equity assumed to be done that which ought to have been done, and said that each piece of new equipment that came into the plant passed in equity to the mortgagee creditor under the mortgage agreement. Although the mortgagee's title was only an equitable title, it prevailed over the execution creditor's right of seizure and sale. Thus the execution creditor could not seize the new equipment. *Nemo dat* applied: the execution creditor could not seize what the debtor did not have.

An interest in property not yet acquired is a future interest. In the Courts of Common Law, a future interest was not recognized. Yet future interests were potentially valuable items of property in an expanding market. A right to sue on a future interest was a chose in action. If that right to sue could be assigned, it would permit A to begin her manufacturing process, because she could assign the proceeds from the sales of the product she would be producing in the future to her suppliers as security for the material she needed.

It was a small step for the Courts of Equity to permit the assignment of choses in action in future property in the same way they had permitted the assignment of choses in action in existing property. Because future interests were recognized only in the Courts of Equity, the assignment was an assignment of an equitable chose in action rather than a legal chose in action.

Because the chose in action in future-acquired property was not recognized in the Courts of Common Law, Equity did not have to worry about following the law. The Courts of Equity developed their own rules on the assignment of equitable choses in action. Instead of requiring the assignee to sue as agent of the assignor in order to follow Common Law rules of privity, the Courts of Equity simply permitted the assignee to sue the account debtor in his own name. In our example, if A assigned proceeds of future sales to C, and later made a sale to B, C could sue B directly to recover the money without involving A as assignor.

Equity's pragmatic response of enforcing a property interest in future property became the foundation of modern secured financing. After *Holroyd v. Marshall* financiers and suppliers could provide the tools of wealth creation to entrepreneurs, and take property not yet acquired or created as security. At law, a property interest automatically arose in that property as soon as it was acquired or created.

Equity's approach was codified in 1873 by the *Judicature Act*. The procedures are also reflected in similar statutes in most Canadian provinces. The one exception is Saskatchewan, which retains a *Choses in Action Act*, R.S.S. 1978, c. C-11. Saskatchewan's legislation is a codification of both the substantive and procedural rules of Equity on assignment.

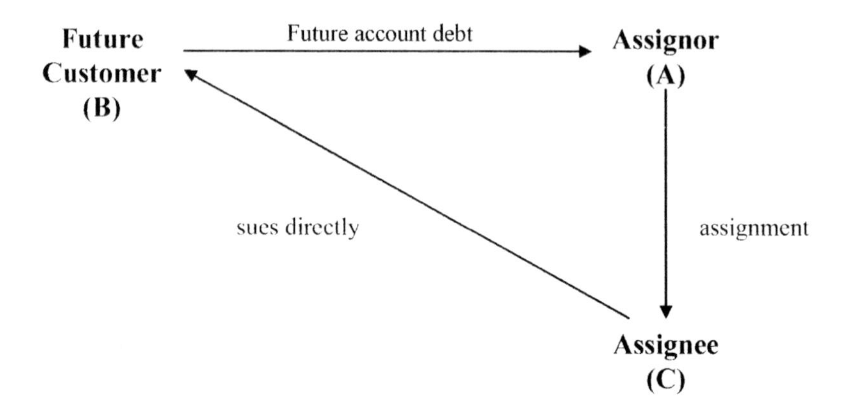


## 9.4 — Issues that Arise in Choses in Action

Once the Courts of Equity had developed a way to make choses in action assignable, they then had to determine the rules relating to assignability. Two issues arose: *nemo dat* and notice.

### (a) — *Nemo dat*

If the account debtor had defences against the assignor, were these defences valid against the assignee? For example, what if B's debt to A had arisen out of a sale of goods contract whereby A had sold B goods, and the goods turned out to be defective? C's action against B was in the Courts of Common Law. C was suing as agent of A. It stood to reason that C would be subject to whatever valid defences B had against A. Equity applied the *nemo dat* rule. A could not assign to C what she herself did not have. If A's right to sue B turned out to be an empty right because A had not fulfilled the terms of her contract with B, then all C got in the assignment was an empty right.

Thus the *nemo dat* rule governs assignment. An assignor can give an assignee no better title than she herself has.

### (b) — Notice

What if, subsequent to the assignment, the assignor A, entered into a new contract with the account debtor B, in which the assignor A, owed the account debtor? In any action by the assignor to collect on the former debt, the account debtor could claim what was called a set-off. Again, the assignee was taking action as agent for the assignor against the account debtor. The Courts of Common Law ruled that any set-off that B might have against A was enforceable against C.

Equity recognized that such arrangements by the assignor could seriously diminish the value of the security that the assignor had given the assignee, and therefore held that the assignor was bound from the moment of assignment not to diminish the value of the security by new arrangements creating a set-off.

Equity had already established that as of the moment of an assignment, the assignee had the right to give notice to the account debtor to pay the assignee directly. As soon as A assigned her right to collect from B on the debt to C, C had the right to give notice to B to pay him. Equity held that notice from the assignee to the account debtor ended the right to set-off. The assignee was subject to any set-offs existing at the time the assignee gave notice to the account debtor, but any set-offs arising after notice could not he enforced against the assignee.

The result remains a rule of assignment to this day. The assignee is subject to defences that arise out of the original contract or any set-offs that exist at the moment of assignment. However, following notice of the assignment to the debtor, the assignee is not subject to any subsequent arrangements that arise between the account debtor and the assignor.

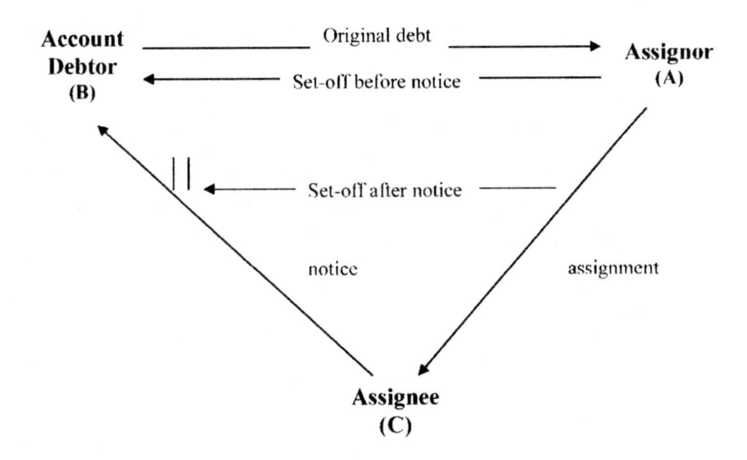

## 9.5 — *Personal Property Security Acts*

*Personal Property Security Acts* further codify the basic rules of Equity but also modify and expand them for commercial purposes. All Canadian common law jurisdictions now have legislation.

Thus, there is a richness of law in choses in action. The fundamental doctrines and rules governing assignability were worked out in Equity. These are still present in any areas not addressed by subsequent *Choses in Action* and *Personal Property Security Acts*. Together, they provide the certainty and predictability required by a market economy.

# Part III

# Real Property

# CHAPTER 10 — HISTORY OF ENGLISH REAL PROPERTY



## 10.1 — Landholding in England, Pre-1066

European land law into the fifth century was dominated by Roman law. Each household controlled an area of land known as an *allod*. Households consisted of blood descendants, adopted members, and those by the same name under the leadership or control (*dominium*) of a male head. The land was viewed not as being owned, but rather as an inseparable part of the household. The land was farmed by slaves (*coloni*) directed by the head of the household. Leadership of the household passed in solemn ceremonies dictated by custom and tradition. A failure to observe any aspect of the sacred ceremony of transition invalidated the leadership change and the transfer of land. When Roman Patricians acquired more land than their households could farm, they permitted slave gangs and free farmers (those unassociated with a household) to farm the land in return for a fixed rent or a share of the crop. In addition, soldiers on the border between the Roman and German empires were allowed to inhabit and farm land in return for guarding it and reporting for active military duty when called. The Roman jurists (*praetors*) viewed both kinds of tenants as having something akin to an equitable interest in land, which was inheritable. As long as tenants paid their rents, they could not be ejected. By the end of the Roman empire a form of double ownership known as *emphyteusis*, the conceptual predecessor of feudalism, had developed.

In the period from the fifth to the tenth century known as the Dark Ages, outside invaders buffeted land owners. Allodial family holders would grant their land to overlords in return for protection. The lords granted lands back in perpetual leases for which the tenants paid dues and services. As families granted their lands to the more powerful lords in return for protection, the control of land became concentrated in fewer hands. Families also granted land to the Church to avoid dues of reverence and respect while reserving for themselves life estates in the land.

In England, landholding was communal, governed by local customs. The practice of agriculture was common field — lands open for all to use. While the system of landholding had no particular name, it was later referred to as *folcland* or folkland. Local kings loaned out their land in return for services — *loenland*. They also granted land to bishops and earls under charters — *bocland* or bookland. *Bocland* was allodial in that it was not held of a superior but in the earl's or bishop's own right. Communal landholders began granting land upward to more powerful lords in return for protection. The lords would grant a perpetual lease known as *feu* to the occupants and offer protection against outside invaders in return for services and loyalty. Feudalism became the umbrella word for these double ownership arrangements.

## 10.2 — Landholding in England, Post-1066

By the time of the Norman Conquest in 1066, notions of granting and regranting land as a means of exchanging dues and services without disturbing occupation of the soil were familiar. Norman feudalism envisioned all land in the kingdom being held by a lord — *nulle terre sans seigneur*. The King would be the Lord Paramount and would grant all the land to barons who would become land lords throughout the kingdom.

But an obstacle stood between the granting up system of the pre-Norman feudalism and the granting down system envisioned by Norman kings. It might have been possible to persuade all the existing kings and lords of England to grant their land up to the King, but it would have been a cumbersome and uncertain process at best. The King's legal advisors avoided this problem by creating a legal fiction.

A legal fiction is defined as "a situation contrived by the law to permit a court to dispose of a matter" (*s.v.* Black's Law Dictionary). The Norman legal fiction was that the King was the original possessor of all the land in the kingdom. The legal fiction was contrary to fact. The King had never been in possession of the land. Rather, the King held what Roman law called *imperium* — control acquired through conquest or inheritance. This gave sovereignty over the territory, but not possession. *Imperium* was distinct from *dominium* — which was absolute ownership and control over land. The only lands over which the King had *dominium* were the lands on which his ancestors actually lived (*ancient demesne*). The legal fiction declared that the King had underlying title to all the land, and that anyone who held land held it, not allodially, but of the King. In return for the fictional grant, the King received an oath of fealty. In addition, the King demanded annual military, spiritual, personal, or pecuniary services as feudal dues. This system did not disturb occupancy of those living on the lands but created revenue to sustain the wants and needs of the King.

## 10.3 — Doctrine of Tenures and Estates

Each grant (tenement) was held on a certain set of conditions known as tenure, for a certain length of time known as an estate.

The 1500 barons granted land by the King were called tenants *in capitae* — chief tenants. The tenants *in capite* in turn carved lesser tenements from their holdings, and granted tenure to middle lords — *mesne* lords — in return for services. Each of the middle lords could again subinfeudate to lesser lords — *demesne* lords. The number of subinfeudations was in practice large and in theory infinite. This created a pyramid. At the bottom were the *villeins* — the hewers of wood and drawers of water who provided the agricultural and domestic labour that kept the tenement operating.

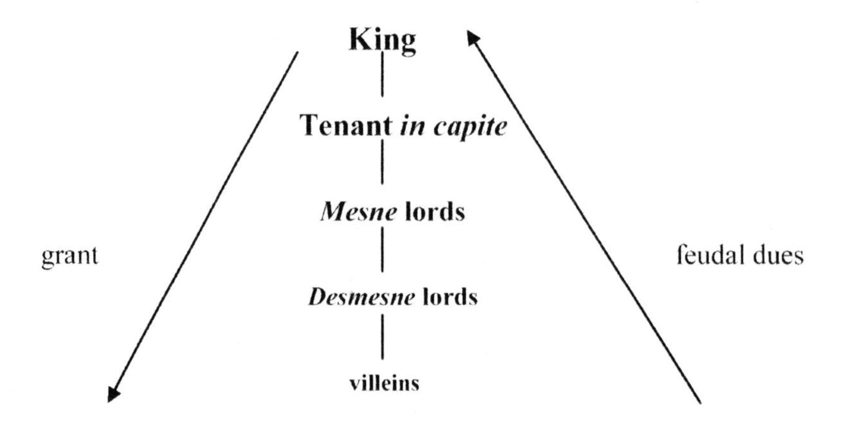


In feudal times, no system of recording transfers of real property existed. Rather, property was transferred openly and ceremoniously so that the lower tenants could identify the new lord to whom they owed service. The new lord in turn could acknowledge his responsibilities within the feudal pyramid and those in the upper reaches of the structure would know from whom they could expect services. The ceremonies required the transferor and transferee to attend at the property and in the presence of witnesses, pass a clump of earth, branch, or other symbolic representation of the land along with appropriate words of transfer (e.g., To X and his heirs). Upon completion of this livery of seisin, the landholder was said to be seised of the land, defined as the right to immediate possession according to the nature of the estate. Rights and obligations relating to real property were tied to the individual who was seised. The right to inherit, to transfer the land *inter vivos*, and to proceed with a real action were only available to the grantee seised of the land.

The King selected his tenants personally to ensure loyalty, and therefore wanted the land to return to him each generation to permit him to choose a new grantee. Thus the King granted land "to A" meaning "to A for life". At A's death the land would escheat, i.e. revert to the Crown.

The lords, however, did not take kindly to such an arrangement. They too had an interest in who controlled the land after they died. The pre-Norman traditions of land tenure had provided for continuity of occupation either communally or through Roman primogeniture — the eldest son inherited the family lands as the next head of the household. The barons demanded the Norman kings return to that pre-Norman system of inheritance. The

King yielded but in return imposed substantial inheritance taxes as one of the incidents of tenure. Every time the land passed by devolution from one generation to another, the King received a new round of inheritance taxes.

This resulted in a fundamental change in the duration of land holding. The interest granted was no longer a life estate but an inheritable estate. An estate described the duration of the interest, not the land itself. The form of the grant was "to A and his heirs" to distinguish it from the life time only grant "to A". The designation "to A and his heirs" became known as a fee simple estate.

## 10.4 — The Development of the Right to Devise Land

As noted, the system of inheritance that had existed prior to 1066 was the Roman primogeniture system. Land automatically devolved to the eldest son; daughters and other sons were disinherited. After 1066, primogeniture disappeared and life estates dominated. With the creation of the fee simple estate primogeniture re-emerged. Primogeniture was a rule of law, not a rule of construction — law dictated how land was to be inherited. Lords could not will land upon their death.

Land lords reacted by seeking ways to influence the devolution of land while still remaining technically within the law. Their legal advisors came up with two methods: *inter vivos* grants of entailed fees, and modified fees. Entailed fees limited who could inherit to a specified group, and modified fees applied conditions to the inheritance of a fee. In the thirteenth century, King Edward I attempted to eliminate entailed fees, but the land lords who controlled Parliament prevented it. The *Statute de Donis Conditionalibus, 1285*, 13 Ed. I, c. 1, enshrined entailed fees in statute.

## 10.5 — The Development of the Right to Alienate Land

Since the economy of feudal England was land based, the King's exclusive right to grant new tenancies was a strong incentive in the land lords to offer loyalty and continued service. In turn, those who held tenure were reluctant to surrender their interest and lose their most valuable asset. Since there was no limit on the number of intermittent steps between the King and the actual occupants of the real property, a lord could always create an additional tenure beneath his own. In so doing, a lord could retain the right to the provision of services from a lesser lord, meet the requirements of his own grantor, and provide sufficiently for himself — subinfeudation. As an alternative, with permission of his land lord, a tenant could substitute another tenant in his place for all or part of his estate holdings — substitution.

Subinfeudation and substitution led to both horizontal and vertical expansion of the pyramid. The system became complex, resulting in a loss of control over the revenue flow to the upper reaches of the pyramid.

The problems of subinfeudation and the desire to limit substitution were addressed in 1290 in the *Statute of Quia Emptores*, 18 Ed. 1, cc. 1, 2, which prohibited subinfeudation and provided, in effect, that every grantee was to hold directly or indirectly of the King. In technical terms, every grantee was to hold of the same lord as the grantor. The new name for the grantees was freemen.

With the exception of tenants *in capite*, who still required permission of the Crown to transfer land *inter vivos*, freemen were thenceforth permitted to alienate all or part of their tenement in fee simple without the consent of their immediate lord. Such transactions were required to take place during their lifetime, otherwise the tenement went to the tenant's heirs under the rules of inheritance. If a tenant chose to partially alienate the tenement, the services would be apportioned accordingly. The King retained the right to grant new lands and reconvey lands that had reverted back to the Crown.

With the *Statute of Quia Emptores* the feudal pyramid began to shrink. No new tenures in fee simple could be created by anyone except the Crown. Within that, freeman began to alienate (sell) *inter vivos* by agreement of the parties, and the new holder would hold the same tenure and estate. After 1290, the mesne and demesne steps gradually disappeared so that today, with rare exceptions, land in England is held directly of the Crown.

## 10.6 — The Development of Uses

The *Statute of Quia Emptores* served the King's interests in that all the inheritance taxes now accrued directly to him. As a consequence, lords turned to their legal advisors to find ways to avoid having to pay the incidents of tenure to the King. The legal mechanism developed was the use.

In Roman law, Franciscan monks had developed the practice of transferring land to an external body while retaining the right to use the land — a way to be true to their poverty vows while still having the benefits of the land. Further, during the thirteenth century Crusades, land lords, seeking a way to manage their land while they were out of the country, had transferred their land "to A for the use of B". A held the legal fee simple title and was known as the *feoffee to uses* (a *feoffee* is a person to whom a fee is conveyed). B received the benefits of the land and was known as the *cestui que use* (abbreviation of *cestui a que use le feoffment fuit fait*).

Land lords soon saw that conveying their lands to A for the use of B would allow them to control the destiny of that land and at the same time avoid inheritance taxes. Land held by a *feoffee to uses* could pass through several uses without ever becoming subject to inheritance taxes. Legal title remained in the *feoffee to uses*, avoiding the inheritance taxes that otherwise arose upon the devolution of legal title. The common law did not recognize the use as an interest. In the Courts of Common Law, the *feoffee to uses* was held to have the entire property interest in the land, while the *cestui que use* held no enforceable estate.

The initial disadvantage was that if the *feoffee to uses* proved untrustworthy, the *cestui que use* had no remedy. However, under Norman feudalism, the King was the fount of all justice in the land; therefore, the *cestui que use* appealed to the King personally. For reasons of conscience, the King's Chancellor was prepared to order the *feoffee to uses* to fulfill his obligation to the *cestui que use*. Not only was the Chancellor prepared to enforce the use against the *feoffee to uses*, but he was also prepared to allow the use to pass by inheritance to succeeding generations. Further, he was prepared to allow the grantor to change the orders to the *feoffee to uses* as to the nature and terms of the use. Over time, the use could be alienated, devised, or its terms changed by the grantor without altering the name of the legal title holder of the property.

The Chancellor's Courts of Equity were also prepared to hold successors in title to the *feoffee to uses* to the terms of the use if they had notice of the use. The Chancellor held that it would be against good conscience to require a purchaser of the legal estate who did not have notice of the beneficial interest to honour the use, but he was prepared to hold a successor in title to the use even if there was no notice if the successor had not paid money, but took as a volunteer by gift or inheritance.

The effect over time was that the use became enforceable against all but a *bona fide* purchaser for value of a legal estate without notice of the interest. Because the use arose in the Courts of Equity, it was called an equitable property interest. The use proved so attractive that by the beginning of the sixteenth century, land lords wishing to avoid feudal incidents, to devise land, to keep it in the family, or even to undertake certain frauds, readily deployed the use.

## 10.7 — Statute of Uses, 1535

The explosive growth of uses caused the King's revenues to plummet. Equitable land transactions were circumventing inheritance taxes at a time when King Henry VIII found himself facing increasing household costs. In 1535, the King forced the *Statute of Uses, 1535*, 27 Hen. VIII, c. 10, on an unwilling Parliament. The Statute was, on its face, a simple change in title.

It mandated that any land conveyed "to A to the use of B" was deemed to be held by B in legal fee simple. The Statute "executed" the use, transferring the legal estate from the *feoffee to use* to the *cestui que use*. As a legal fee simple holder, the *cestui que use* became subject to inheritance taxes.

## 10.8 — Statute of Wills, 1540

After the *Statute of Uses, 1535* the *cestui que use* held the legal estate. Legal estates, as noted, could not be devised. Land lords, unsurprisingly, reacted with disfavour at being precluded from controlling their property after death through the use. The reaction was sufficiently strong that Henry VIII agreed to compromise to avoid revolt and passed the *Statute of Wills, 1540*. 32 Hen. VIII, c. 1, providing that land could be devised by will without interference by the King.

## 10.9 — The Development of Future Interests

Land lords were not yet satisfied; they were unwilling to give up so valuable a legal tool as the use. Two types of uses were specifically exempted from the *Statute of Uses, 1535*: personal property, and active uses (where the *feoffee to uses* had duties to perform, such as collecting rents to pay them to the *cestui que use*). A third method, crafted by legal advisors was a use upon a use (where land was granted "to A to the use of B to the use of C"). Land lords began to utilize the use upon a use to create long strings of life estates, conditions, and entailed fees.

Controlling land long into the future raised conflicts among so many parties that it gave rise to a complex area of property law known as future interests. Chapter 12 is devoted specifically to these interests. For now, it is sufficient to summarize. For three centuries after the *Statute De Donis* in 1285, grantees had sought legal mechanisms to avoid restrictions on alienation. They gained the right to alienate land in the *Statute of Quia Emptores* in 1290 and the right to will land in the *Statute of Wills, 1540*. The new mechanisms actually threatened alienability by permitting interests that tied up land long into the future. In an attempt to balance control and alienability, grantees, legal advisors, and courts developed rules that limited grantor's long term control. The Rule in *Shelley's Case* (1581), I Co. Rep. 93 b., and the Rule Against Perpetuities as it was set out in the *Duke of Norfolk's Case* (1685), 3 Ch. Ca. I, remain today in Canada in relatively unchanged form to prevent controlling land too far into the future.

## 10.10 — *Tenures Abolition Act, 1660* and *Statute of Frauds, 1677*

By 1650, the feudal dues of military, personal, pecuniary, and spiritual services had almost universally been converted to monetary payments known as socage. When the Stuart dynasty was restored in 1660 after Oliver Cromwell, Charles II finally compromised with Parliament on feudal incidents. The *Tenures Abolition Act, 1660*, 12 Car. II, c. 24, converted all tenures to free and common socage. The only revenue-generating incidents that remained after the Act were escheat, whereby land returned to the Crown if a landholder died both intestate and heirless, and forfeiture, whereby land held by a grantee convicted of treason forfeited to the Crown.

The *Statute of Frauds, 1677*, 29 Car. II, c 3, required that all matters relating to land be in writing, creating a formality consistent with a serious and solemn transaction. This remains a central principle of land law to this day.

## 10.11 — Crossing the Atlantic

As explored in Part IV, before Europeans arrived in North America, the continent was inhabited by indigenous peoples whose understandings and rules with respect to property were much different. As European rulers claimed sovereignty over North America, they imposed European property regimes. By the end of the nineteenth century, these property regimes were the only ones recognized by the legislatures and courts as law in Canada, giving rise to legal conflicts which continue to this day.

# CHAPTER 11 — TENURES AND ESTATES



## 11.1 — The Doctrine of Tenures Today

The doctrine of tenure remains in Canadian common law jurisdictions in that the Crown claims the exclusive right to grant property and provides that all tenants hold land of the Crown either directly or indirectly. A tenure is a set of conditions upon which a tenant holds the land and all tenants hold on the basis of one of the various tenures. Land is held in free and common socage unless altered by statute (*Alberta (Attorney General) v. Huggard Assets Ltd.*, [1953] 3 D.L.R. 225 (Canada P.C.)).

## 11.2 — Historical Evolution of the Doctrine

Because the *Tenures Abolition Act, 1660* converted all tenures to free and common socage, the evolution of tenure prior to that time is only of historical interest, but nonetheless is important in understanding why the doctrine is a central tenet of English land law and how we arrived at land holders' current freedoms in devising, selling, and managing property.

In Normal feudalism, the conditions upon which tenants held tenements came to be classified according to the type of service rendered. The type of tenure paralleled the social status of the grantee's rank within the feudal pyramid. Tenures fell into two categories: free and unfree. The distinguishing feature of free tenures was that the duties were fixed and certain. Unfree tenures were subject to services on demand by the lord. Both free and unfree tenures carried additional obligations known as the incidents of tenure.

### (a) — Free Tenures

Free tenures were of three types:

- *Chivalry* — The tenants *in capite* held directly of the King and provided military support to the Crown in the form of knight service. Over time, monetary compensation known as socage became an acceptable substitute for the actual provision of men. Honourable personal services such as carrying the King's staff were known as grand serjeanty. This form of personal service was restricted to the upper echelons on the feudal pyramid.
- *Spiritual* — Frankalmoign and divine service involved the conveyancing of property to the church in return for religious services in support of the grantor. Frankalmoign only required prayers for the grantor's soul, while divine services required fealty as well as specific tasks such as the singing of masses and giving alms to the poor. By the thirteenth century the church was a major landholder.
- *Socage* — Petty serjeanty was a type of tenure satisfied by the performance of lesser services to a lesser lord, usually of a non-personal nature such as providing the straw for bedding. Common socage involved the provision of agricultural labour for a set number of days each year. A monetary payment was demanded from those not engaged in farming.

### (b) — Unfree Tenures

The unfree tenures, villeinage and customary freehold, had in common an uncertainty as to the type of service required of the tenants. Further, the holder of an unfree tenure could not avail himself of the protection of the King's Court. He had to rely solely on the manorial court of his lord. Land transfers of unfree tenures came to be completed by a form of registration noted in the lord's court upon the rolls. A copy of the transfer was made available to the transferee. Land transferred in this way became known as copyhold land and was common within England by the sixteenth century.

### (c) — Incidents of Tenure

The incidents of tenure, unlike the fixed services, depended on the value of the land. If the services were not performed, the holder defaulted and the lord was entitled to possession of the property. Although not all incidents were applicable to all forms of tenure, the more common incidents were:

- *Homage and Fealty* — This incident required the tenant to appear before his lord, attest to his loyalty, and swear to perform the feudal obligations required.
- *Forfeiture* — If a tenant breached his oath, otherwise failed to meet his feudal obligations, or committed treason, forfeiture was the penalty. In the latter case the property went to the Crown whether or not there was a *mesne* lord. Lords could also expressly reserve the right to forfeiture for breach of other feudal duties. Alternatively, the lord could seize chattels through an action known as distress until the duties were performed.
- *Wardship & Marriage* — If a minor inherited land, the lord was entitled to manage the land for his own profit until the minor came of age (21 for males, 14 for females). The incident of marriage provided the lord with some control over the marriage of wards (under the lord's care). If a ward refused a suitable spouse, a fee was due equivalent to the value of the marriage. If a ward married without the lord's consent, a fee double the value of the marriage was due.
- *Aids* — This incident included a number of payments that could be demanded by the lord to cover a variety of expenses associated with his status. Monies could be raised for matters such as paying a ransom, knighting an elder son, or raising a dowry for an elder daughter.
- *Relief & Primer Seisin* — These incidents were succession duties imposed upon heirs. In situations where the King was the immediate lord, an additional payment known as primer could be demanded wherein the Crown enjoyed the right to possess the land and its profits until relief and fealty were forthcoming. The level of payment was significant, often one year's income from the land in the case of relief and an additional year if inheritance was involved.

- *Escheat* — If a tenant died without heirs, the tenancy ended and possession of the land or rights reverted to the lord. This was known as escheat *propter defectum sanguinis*. Another form of escheat, *propter delirium tenentis*, occurred when a tenant was convicted of a felony and sentenced to death. The incident of escheat still exists in a modified statutory form entitling the provincial Crown to the real and personal property of any person who dies intestate and without heirs. The statute allows greater opportunity than the common law for claims based on moral right, but the Crown determines the extent to which the claim will be recognized (e.g., *Escheats Act*. R.S.S., 1978, c. E-11, ss. 3, 4).

## 11.3 — History of the Doctrine of Estates

While the doctrine of tenures described the allocation of land and obligations of the tenant holding the land (quality) the doctrine of estates described the duration of the land rights (quantity). In early Norman feudalism, the form of the tenure was of paramount importance. As the doctrine of tenures began to decline, the doctrine of estates came to define the terms on which land was held. The law recognized three types of freehold estates (fee simple, fee tail, and life estate) and three types of leasehold estates (leasehold for a fixed period of years, periodic tenancy, and tenancy at will).

## 11.4 — Freehold Estates

The freehold estates were considered the highest form of holding under the feudal system.

Freehold as it relates to estates has nothing to do with freehold tenure (socage). A freehold estate that is inheritable and continues indefinitely but not perpetually (i.e., it ends should the line of heirs end) is called a fee. The fee simple and the fee tail are freeholds that are also fees. The fee simple is the largest estate due to its longer possible duration. The life estate is a freehold but is not a fee, as it is not inheritable, lasting only for the life stipulated in the grant. This distinction is summarized in the statement "All fees are freeholds, but not all freeholds are fees".

All freeholds have three common characteristics. First, the duration of the estate is limited. Second, the actual term is uncertain but never perpetual — the estate can be determined by some future event. Third, freeholders are seised of the land, as opposed to leaseholders who have only possession of the land.

Historically, freehold estates were created by the use of appropriate words in either an *inter vivos* or testamentary document. Those words or phrases that identified the type of estate were referred to as words of limitation. Words of purchase identified the recipient of the interest. Courts reviewing *inter vivos* grants demanded strict adherence to recognized rules regarding words of limitation, while testamentary documents (after the *Wills Act, 1540*) were more flexibly interpreted to honour the intention of the testator.

## (a) — Fee Simple

The fee simple is the largest possible estate in our legal system. The fee simple absolute is what is being referred to most frequently in ordinary use of the term fee simple. It is the closest estate to absolute ownership known to the Anglo-American system of land holding. This estate lasts as long as the original tenant and his heirs survive. The words "and his heirs" were necessary to create the estate to differentiate it from the life estate created by the words "to A". Prior to 1290, "to A and his heirs" meant that the land devolved to his heirs by law, but the *Statute of Quia Emptores*, 1290, permitted grantees to alienate estates *inter vivos*, and the *Statute of Wills, 1540*, permitted grantees to specify the successor in title. After 1540, words of limitation set out the potential duration of the estate in the hands of the grantee as opposed to articulating a particular right in an heir apparent. A fee simple only escheats if it is neither alienated during the tenant's lifetime, nor bequested through a will, and there are no eligible recipients under intestacy rules.

In recognition of predominance of the fee simple, statutes often stipulate that in the absence of words of limitation to the contrary, a will or deed passes the greatest estate held by the transferor or testator (e.g., *Wills Act*, R.S.N.S. 1989, c. 505, s. 27; *Property Law Act*, R S.B.C. 1996, c. 377, s. 19). As a result, in the absence of words of limitation, the conveyance of land "to X" will convey a fee simple to X (if that is the estate held by the grantor). For certainty, most wills and deeds still include the words "and his heirs."

In addition to the fee simple absolute there are three types of qualified fee simple: the fee simple determinable, the fee simple subject to condition subsequent, and the fee simple subject to an executory limitation. These interests are defeasible in that the holder of the fee simple may lose her estate upon the happening of some event. They are still fees simple however, in that they are of uncertain though not perpetual duration, and are inheritable. They also create future interests (Chapter 12).

### *(i) — Fee Simple Determinable*

A fee simple determinable (sometimes called a fee simple subject to special limitation) is a defeasible estate that ends on the occurrence of a particular, though not inevitable, event. When or if the event happens, the estate reverts automatically to the grantor, his heirs, or assignees. In the meantime, the grantor has a vested future interest known as a possibility of reverter. The holder of the determinable estate may transfer or devise the estate but the limitation passes as well.

Specific language is required to create a fee simple determinable such as the words "to X as long as. . .", "to Y until. . .", or "to Z while. . .". The words limiting the duration are part of the description of the estate. As a result, if the limitation is void the entire estate fails and the grantee takes nothing (*Tilbury West Public School Board v. Hastie* (1966), 55 D.L.R. (2d) 407 (Ont. H.C.); varied 57 D.L.R. (2d) 519 (Ont. H.C.)).

### *(ii) — Fee Simple Subject to Condition Subsequent*

The fee simple subject to condition subsequent is a fee simple subject to termination on the occurrence of a specific event. Should the event occur, the estate can be ended by the grantor, his heirs, or assignees. However, unlike the determinable fee simple, the estate does not end automatically but continues until the grantor or his heirs exercise their right of re-entry. The estate is voidable at the breach and void at re-entry.

The language necessary to create a conditional estate is also specific, creating the fee simple then adding a proviso for divestment in certain circumstances. Phrases such as "to A provided that. . .", "to B, but if. . .", or "to C upon condition that. . .", have been found by courts to be acceptable word choices. Should the condition be found void, for reasons of public policy for example, the grantee takes an absolute fee simple.

The linguistic conventions necessary to distinguish between these two defeasible estates are artificial. Nonetheless, the legal consequences of creating one estate or the other differ. If the condition fails in a determinable fee simple, the entire estate is void, while if the condition fails in a fee with condition subsequent, the grantee takes absolutely. Circumstances in which a limitation or condition would be challenged include uncertainty, e.g. "to X as long as she resides in Canada", or restrictions contrary to public policy, such as a complete restraint upon marriage or stipulations that require breaking the law. As courts prefer to avoid forfeiture of estates, courts are more liberal in permitting determinable fees than fees with questionable conditions subsequent. Similarly, because the consequences of striking down a limitation are to make the grant void, courts prefer to characterize defeasible fees simple as being subject to conditions subsequent, rather than determinable in nature, so that the estate may remain in the grantee should the condition fail.

### (b) — Fee Tail

The fee tail or entailed fee was enshrined in the *Statute de Donis Conditionalibus* in 1285. From the French "tailler," meaning to cut, the fee tail limited or cut down the possible heirs of the estate. The estate continued as long as the original tenant or his lineal blood descendants survived. Collateral heirs (such as cousins) could not inherit the property. If the line failed, the land would revert to the holder of the fee simple (reversion), to the Crown if the original grant was a fee tail (escheat), or to a third party provided for in the original grant (remainder). As a freehold, its duration was limited, of indefinite length, and uncertain but not perpetual. As a fee, it was inheritable.

Unlike the fee simple, the tenant in fee tail could not completely alienate the estate. He could grant the estate to another for his lifetime but at his death the estate automatically descended according to the terms of the fee tail. Even after the *Statute of Wills, 1540*, the tenant could not alienate the property by will; the entailment superseded the desires of the individual tenant.

Historically, the estate was created *inter vivos* by using the word "heirs" plus words of procreation: "to X and the heirs of his body". Other words of limitation were acceptable providing that the word "heirs" was used in addition to a clear indication of an intention to limit inheritance to lineal blood heirs. Thus, phrases such as "to X and the heirs of his flesh" also created fees tail. To create a fee tail by will, no reference to heirs was necessary as long as a clear intention to bequeath such an estate was evident. Therefore phrases such as "to X and his seed" were acceptable.

Feudal law assumed that a fee tail estate descended to the oldest surviving male, the individual perceived to be in the best position to defend and maintain the real property. Over time, this was modified to permit other possible linear blood heirs to hold the fee tail. Four categories developed:

- *fee tail general* — passage through the lineal males, but if there were no male heirs, females could inherit. The children of any spouse were eligible.
- *fee tail male general* — passage only through males of any spouse
- *fee tail female general* — passage only through females of any spouse
- *special tail* — passage through a specified spouse (e.g., first wife only).

The greatest drawback associated with holding a fee tail was the restriction on alienability. Over time, legal techniques were developed to disentail land, converting the fee tail to a fee simple absolute. In Canada, statutes provide for either the abolition or disentailing of fees tail (e.g., *Property Act*, R.S.N.B. 1973, c. P-19, s. 19, *The Land Titles Act*, SK s. 157) but they may still be found in chains of title.

### (c) — Life Estate

Although not inheritable (and thus not a fee), the life estate is a freehold. It is of uncertain but limited duration, lasting for the lifetime of the person(s) named in the grant. The most commonly used words of limitation remain "to X for life", although in Norman feudalism the words "to X" alone also created a life estate since the grant contained no words of limitation to create a fee simple. Usually, the grantee is the measuring life or *cestui que vie* who determines the length of the estate, but it is possible to hold a life estate measured by the lifetime of an individual other than the tenant. So for example, a life estate can be created with the words "to X for the life of John Brown". A life estate of this type is termed *pur autre vie*. A life estate *pur autre vie* is also created when the holder of a life estate transfers his interest to a third party. The transferor remains the measuring life and the life estate ends at his death.

If a life estate is created in several persons, for example, "to the children of X for their lives", at the death of one of the measuring lives (the children) the estate continues to rest in the hands of the remaining life estate holder(s). It is only with the death of the final measuring life that the remainder or reversion becomes possessory.

The life estate remains a tool for limited intergenerational control of real property in Canada. Most often it arises in land-based, family-run businesses, such as the family farm. It is also used as a means of protecting property for particular family members to ensure either a source of income or lodging during their lifetime. Because of legislative presumptions favouring the fee simple, grantors or testators must be specific as to their intent to create a life estate. Although recognized in law, a life estate is not registrable in all provinces with Torrens systems.

### (d) — Dower & Curtesy

Social motives prompted the creation of certain life estates by operation of law. Most notably, dower and curtesy emerged to provide some protection for the spouses of property holders. Early English dower law provided that upon marriage, a wife acquired a life estate in one-third of all freehold inheritable estates of which her husband was seised during the marriage. She could only acquire a dower interest in property that was:

- a freehold, not a leasehold estate
- inheritable (only fees simple and fees tail qualified)
- seised in the husband during the marriage (i.e., no remainder interest nor equitable interest qualified)
- real, not personal, property.

During the lifetime of the husband, the dower remained a vested future interest in the wife. Dower rights could be avoided by the wife agreeing to bar her dower in any conveyance of the land by her husband. If she failed to do this, the conveyance could be completed but remained subject to her life interest at the death of her husband. This was a significant deterrent to would-be purchasers or mortgagees. If the husband predeceased the wife, her dower rights entitled her to a one-third life interest in the qualified attached properties. The interest survived remarriage.

Comparable, though not identical, to dower for wives was the common law interest for husbands known as curtesy. Widowers gained a life estate in all the deceased wife's inheritable legal estates of which she was seised, and all inheritable equitable interests in which she was entitled to possession There were two qualifications: the right arose only if there were children born of the marriage (the children need not necessarily have survive birth) and the right attached only to those estates that had not been alienated during her lifetime or devised by will. In other words, curtesy did not fetter alienability.

An alternative to dower and curtesy developed in the late nineteenth century in the prairie provinces and British Columbia. Homestead legislation required concurrence of the non-owning spouse in any dispositions of the home, provision for a life estate in the surviving non-owning spouse, and exemption of the home from seizure by creditors. The Saskatchewan statute states that dealings in homesteads made without spousal signature are void, and the spouse must have received independent legal advice (*Homesteads Act*, S.S. 1989-90, c. H-5.1, s. 7(3 & 4) [am. S.S. 1992. c. 27, s. 5j).

Additionally, common law curtesy and dower have been replaced in Canadian jurisdictions by statutes protecting spousal rights in property (Chapter 13).

## 11.5 — Leasehold Estates

The major difference between leaseholds and freeholds is that a freeholder is seised of the land while a leaseholder has only possession of the land.

The seised freeholder exercised control over the land and was correspondingly responsible to his lord. At common law, there could be no abeyance of seisin (Chapter 12). In this way the feudal lord knew who owed the feudal dues.

The first type of leasehold estate to be recognized at law was the tenancy at will, which gave only a personal action against the land lord and did not protect the tenant's possession. The lessee sued the lessor for damages; no action was available for recovery of the land itself. However courts recognized that every piece of real property was unique and that damages might be an inadequate remedy. As a result, leases became chattels real; the lessee could not only bring an action against the lessor himself, but also could recover the particular property. In this way, leases became rights to land. Leases expanded by the sixteenth century to include estates for a term of years. Leaseholders created their interest by an agreement and entry onto the land.

Even though the duration of one type of tenancy (the tenancy at will) is uncertain, leaseholds are unlike freeholds as all can be determined on a fixed date. The three types of leases are tenancy for fixed term, periodic tenancy and tenancy at will.

### (a) — Tenancy for Fixed Term

A fixed term tenancy, sometimes called a tenancy for years, is an estate of fixed term and certain duration determined by calendar reference. The term may be a stated number of days, weeks, months, or years as long as the termination date is fixed. Assuming no legislation in a jurisdiction to the contrary, a lease can be created granting a tenancy for as many years as the parties desire.

### (b) — Periodic Tenancy

A periodic tenancy is an estate of fixed term with the duration capable of being rendered certain. Month-to-month or year-to-year tenancies are examples of periodic tenancies in that the term is either a month or a year. The duration continues indefinitely until notice, often equivalent to the term of the tenancy, is given by either the lessor or lessee to determine the estate. Unlike a lease for years, which automatically ends at the conclusion of the stated period, the periodic tenancy continues subject to the same terms and conditions until ended by one of the parties.

### (c) — Tenancy at Will

A tenancy at will is an estate of uncertain term and uncertain duration, continuing indefinitely until determined by either the lessor or the lessee with notice.

# Chapter 12 — Future Interests



## 12.1 — Introduction

Future interests arose historically as a way to control land into the future. Grantors, including feudal kings and lords, wanted to grant land to a tenant for use in return for services but to have the land back at the end of the term in order to be able to re-grant it for new benefits to themselves. Grantees, for their part, wanted to control the land into the future for their own benefit in such ways as selling it or passing it by will to their families. These conflicting goals resulted in a legal tug-of-war in the development of Anglo-American land law that continues to this day.

The tension between the desire to control land into the future and the desire to keep it freely alienable to encourage market transactions unfolded within the Courts of Common Law, the Courts of Equity, and legislation. In the Common Law courts, the struggle manifested through the rules surrounding legal remainders; in Equity courts, around the rules regarding trusts; and in legislation, the rules surrounding legal executory remainders. The judge-made Rule Against Perpetuities, settled law by the nineteenth century, created an interpretive balance between control and alienability that continues to this day.

Understanding these developments requires distinguishing between certain legal terms, particularly estates and interests, vested and contingent interests, and remainders and reversions. It is also necessary to explore further the types of fees simple (absolute, determinable and conditional) and fees tail.

## 12.2 — Definitions

### (a) — Interests and Estates

Interest is a broad term used to describe a right or legal share in real property. Estates are but one of many possible types of interests. An interest describes the scope of the right, whereas an estate describes both the scope and the duration of the right. There are valuable interests in real property that are less than estates; for example, restrictive covenants, easements and mortgages (Chapter 15). Therefore, all estates are interests, but not all interests are estates. Furthermore, interests can be legal or equitable.

### (b) — Vested and Contingent Interests

In a vested interest, both the person who will take the interest and the event that will trigger the passing of the interest in the future are already known at the creation of the grant. For example, "to A for life then B for life", creates a vested interest in B because it is known at the moment of creation of the grant that B will take the interest at A's death.

With a contingent interest, some event which may or may not occur, or some condition precedent which may or may not be fulfilled, must happen before it can be known either in whom the interest will vest or when it will be vested. For example, "to the first of my children who marries so long as they are a non-smoker" creates a contingent interest because it is not known at the time of the grant which child will marry, when they will marry, or whether they will be smokers.

An interest need not be vested in possession in order to be vested in interest. To be vested in possession means that the transferee is already in possession of the interest. To be vested in interest means that, while the transferee may not yet have possession, it is known at the creation of the grant who the transferee will be and what event will trigger the transfer. Interests are therefore vested and certain, or contingent and uncertain.

### (c) — Reversions and Remainders

If a grantor retains an interest after granting a particular estate, that residual interest is called a reversion. Thus if A grants B a life estate, once B dies the estate reverts to A. On the other hand, if A wishes to convey the real property to C after B's death — "A to B for life, then C and her heirs" — A would have no reversionary interest. C's interest — that of a grantee subject to a prior particular estate — is called a remainder. In sum, a reversion reverts to the grantor, while a remainder remains away. All reversions are vested interests but remainders may be vested or contingent.

## 12.3 — Fees Simple: Absolute, Determinable, and Fee Simple with a Condition Subsequent

As noted, following open field communal property, the pre-1066 Roman system of landholding was primogeniture (Chapter 10). The Anglo-Saxons followed this system while also developing arrangements of *feus*, where landowners would grant land up to a higher lord in return for protection. Occupancy was not disturbed and the primogeniture system remained in place. Post-1066, when the Norman Kings developed the feudal pyramid, they granted estates to "to A" which meant for A's life, escheating at A's death to the Crown. The land lords resisted the loss of the old inheritance power so much that the king was forced grant land "to A and his heirs" meaning inheritable, marking a return of primogeniture.

Primogeniture required as a rule of law that all land pass to the eldest male heir upon the death of the fee simple holder. Fee simple holders balked at the restriction that they could not alienate land during their lifetime or pass it to whom they wished after death.

Legal advisors developed two types of fee simple that would avoid the primogeniture rules and the accompanying inheritance taxes. The first was the determinable fee. A determinable fee, still present today, includes in its grant words of limitation based on an event, such as "to A and his heirs until he marries". The words mark the end, or boundaries, of the estate. A has a determinable fee simple, i.e., a fee simple that will determine or end upon the happening of a specified event. The grantor has a possibility of reverter. Once A marries, his estate determines, i.e., has run its course, and the land reverts automatically to the grantor's estate. If the grantor wished the land to go to a third party when A marries, the grant would read "to A and his heirs until he marries, then to B and his heirs," giving B a remainder. If A marries, then B is immediately seised of the land. If A dies having never married, the determining event becomes impossible, and A and his heirs take absolutely. B takes nothing. Thus, an *inter vivos* grant of land by A "to B until he marries" would allow the grantor to decide both who got the benefit of his land, and retain for himself or his estate the right to have the land back should B marry.

A second way to avoid the primogeniture rules was for the grantor, again *inter vivos*, to grant a fee simple away but declare the grant subject to a condition subsequent such that if the condition happened, then the grantor had a right to re-enter and re-take the land. For example, "to A in fee simple unless he begins to smoke", grants A a fee simple estate, but if A begins to smoke the grantor can re-enter and take the land. Contrary to a determinable fee, the conditional fee does not automatically return the land to the grantor or pass it to a remainder person (if a third party is specified in the grant). Rather, the grantor has a right of re-entry. If this person chooses not to re-enter upon the happening of the stated event, the fee simple will remain with A. Thus if A dies without A beginning to smoke, or if A starts smoking but the grantor chooses not to exercise his right of re-entry, the fee simple will pass to A's heirs. A fee simple subject to a condition subsequent includes in the grant words of limitation which may cut short a fee simple on the occurrence of a particular event, i.e., the fee simple is defeasible.

Another form of condition simple is a fee simple subject to a condition precedent. This fee does not vest in possession until the condition is fulfilled. For example, a grant "to A providing he gives $1000 in alms to the church" gives the grantee a contingent interest. If the grant is otherwise valid and the grantee fulfills the condition precedent, he gets the land in fee simple absolute which causes the right of re-entry to disappear. If the condition is not fulfilled, the interest never vests in the grantee.

## 12.4 — Entailed Fees

The *Statute of De Donis, 1285* created a special form of conditional fee that allowed landholders to control who could inherit from *inter vivos* grantees.

Thus a transfer from A "to B and the female heirs of her body" allowed the grantor to alienate the fee simple during his lifetime to the party of his choice, B, and limit who could inherit from B to a restricted class of heirs. These entailed fees, though initially an outgrowth of the conditional fee (more precisely the transfer of fee simple subject to a condition subsequent), became so popular as to become classified as a species of fee in their own right.

*De Donis* was the intellectual forefather of the later *Statue of Wills, 1540. De Donis* gave precedence to the desires of the donor over the primogeniture rule of law. Entailed fees honoured the landholder's wish that his land descend only according to a particular line of descendants (all children, male, female, a particular spouse etc.). Regardless of what the first child to inherit might wish to do with the property, the donor's wishes governed to pass to the next lineal descendant, and so on, until the specified line ended and the property reverted to the grantor's estate. Thus the grantor always retained a reversionary interest, avoided the rule of law of primogeniture, and set the stage for the future development of testamentary rights at law.

## 12.5 — The Rules Regarding Legal Remainders in the Courts of Common Law

Over time, the use by grantors of determinable, conditional, and entailed fees tail to control land into the future limited conveyancing and left the King uncertain from whom to claim feudal dues. The King had, in his view, an imperative need to ensure that someone was always seised of the land in order to identify from whom he could collect dues. Landholders had an equally imperative sense of entitlement to security of tenure and estate, and to the ability to control land into the future or alienate it as they chose. The Courts of Common Law resolved this tension by articulating rules with respect to remainders.

Although complicated, these rules remain relevant today in discerning a future interest and are therefore important to understand. Different authors order and describe the rules governing legal remainders differently. Here, the four rules are classified through the lens of the competing tensions they represent.

To protect the King's interest, the Common Law Courts developed a foundational principle of English land law — no abeyance of seisen. To protect the land lords' interests the Courts developed a second foundational principle — no remainder after a fee simple or one that cut off a prior particular estate. Each principle gave rise to two of the four remainder rules.

### (a) — No Abeyance in Seisen

No abeyance of seisen meant that there could never be a moment during which someone was not seised of the land. As soon as one seised estate ended, another interest holder had to immediately become seised. This gave rise to two remainder rules. Remainders that took effect after a gap from the previously seised estate were invalid. Remainders that took effect out of no previously seised estate were also invalid.

#### *(i) — Rule 1. A remainder is void if it does not vest either prior to, or at the moment of, the ending of the previous estate*

Remainder holders must be ready and able to take immediately upon the expiration of the previous estate or there would be an offending gap in seisen and the grant would be void *ab initio*. Examples help illustrate the operation of the rule:

- *Void grant because clear abeyance of seisen* — The grant "to A for life, and one day later to B" creates a one-day gap in seisen and B's remainder is void *ab initio*.
- *Valid grant because no abeyance of seisen* — The grant "to A for life, then B" creates no abeyance of seisin because at the moment of A's death, B is immediately seised of the land.
- *Valid grant despite contingent remainder (wait and see)* — The grant "to A for life, with the remainder to B if he has reached the age of 21" creates a contingent remainder in B because it is not known at the creation of the grant whether B will have reached 21 at the time of A's death. However, at the moment of A's death, when the prior estate determines, B will either have reached age 21 or not. If B is 21, B immediately becomes seised of the land. If B is not 21, the land returns to the grantor. Thus the contingent remainder in the grant is valid because the land either goes to B or back to the grantor. There is no abeyance of seisen.

  The contingent remainder in this case is of the "wait and see" variety. It is not possible to know at the creation of the grant whether the contingent remainder is valid, but requires waiting and seeing whether the contingent remainder vests in time, either during the estate or immediately upon termination of the previous estate.

  The rule permits a wait and see form of contingent remainder to extend to a child *in utero*. For example, "to A for life, with remainder to his first son" creates, if A already has a first son, a vested remainder in that son. If A does not have a son at the creation of the grant, the remainder is contingent. If a son is born subsequent to the creation of the grant but during A's life, the remainder will vest at the moment of birth. If A dies with progeny *in utero*, a nine-month wait and see period follows before it can be known with certainty whether the contingent remainder is valid.

- *Grant invalid because theoretical possibility of an abeyance in seisen that "wait and see" won't solve* — The grant "to A for life, with the remainder to the first of A's sons to reach 21" creates a contingent remainder because it is not known at the creation of the grant whether any of A's sons will reach 21, and if so which son it will be. A may or may not have any sons at the creation of the grant. It is possible that at the time of A's death, A could have either no sons, or none that have yet reached 21. Nor is it possible to know at the moment of A's death whether any of A's underage sons will ever reach 21, or if so which one. Therefore it is theoretically possible that there would be an abeyance of seisen at A's death waiting for a first son to reach 21. If the contingent remainder could vest, even in theory, outside the period of the previous grant or beyond the moment the prior estate ends, it is void *ab initio*. This is known as destruction of the contingent remainder. Thus, a contingent remainder fails if it is not possible to identify at the creation of the grant both who will immediately take at the expiration of the previous estate, and that the remainder person meets the conditions to take at that same time.

#### *(ii) — Rule 2. A remainder is void, either vested or contingent, unless it is supported by a prior particular estate*

A remainder cannot arise out of nowhere. It must be tied to a prior particular estate at the time of creation so there will be no abeyance of seisen. For example, a grantor who has no children at the time of creating the grant cannot convey land "to my first born daughter and her heirs," because there is no one in existence at the creation of the grant to take seisen. Therefore the entire grant, consisting only of a remainder without a prior supporting estate, is void.

If the prior particular estate is a leasehold as opposed to a freehold, the grant is valid providing the remainder is vested and not contingent. For example, "to A for four years, remainder to B in fee simple" is a valid remainder because at the time of the grant, seisen will pass immediately to the remainder-person B, who will take it on behalf of the leaseholder.

On the other hand, if the prior estate is a leasehold and the remainder is contingent, the grant will be void. For example, a grant "to A in 2008 for four years, then to B if she completes law school by 2015" creates a contingent remainder in B that is void *ab initio* because it is possible that B will not graduate by 2012 when the leasehold expires.

### (b) — No Remainder After a Fee Simple

The second principle was designed to further the interests of the land lords and can be generally stated as no remainder after a fee simple. Two rules grew out of this principle: There can be no remainder after a fee simple; and a remainder that cuts short a prior particular estate is invalid.

#### *(i) — Rule 3. There can be no remainder after a fee simple*

The grant "to A and his heirs, then to B and his heirs" is void *ab initio* in relation to B. A grantee who receives a fee simple, in this case A, has the largest rights possible in that land and the grantor has no remainder to grant to a third party B. Hence any grant that purports to create an additional estate in a remainder person following a prior grant of a fee simple of the same land in the same instrument is void.

#### *(ii) — Rule 4. A remainder is void if it can, even in theory, take effect by cutting short a valid prior particular estate*

The grant "to A for life, but should he ever go to law school, then to B immediately" creates a remainder that is void *ab initio* in B because the condition in the remainder may reach back and cut off the life estate of A.

If the grant to A is a determinable particular estate, i.e., one that will automatically end upon the happening of a particular event, B has a valid remainder because A's estate expires upon the happening of the required event. For example, a grant "to A for life until A marries, then to B" creates a valid remainder in B because if A marries, the estate to A ends, i.e., the natural boundary of the estate is reached and B takes automatically.

On the other hand, a grant of conditional life estate, for example, "to A for life on condition that she never goes to law school, but if she does, then to B" creates a conditional life estate in A. If A does go to law school, under the rules of conditional fees the life estate will not automatically determine. B will have to enter and cut short the particular estate. A right of re-entry can only be held by a grantor or his devisee. Thus B's remainder is void.

The combined effect of the four rules developed by the courts of Common Law against legal remainders was to strike a workable balance between control and alienability. However, the solution was only interim. Equitable interests were not subject to the legal remainder rules, and with the growth of uses, the struggle between control and alienability re-emerged in the Courts of Equity.

## 12.6 — The Development of Uses in the Courts of Equity

As noted, grantees used equitable interests to avoid the incidents of tenure and inheritance taxes. The use, which conveyed legal title to a *feoffee to uses* for the benefit of a *cestui que use*, could pass through several *cestui qui uses* without a change in the *feoffee to uses*. As long as legal title remained in the same *feoffee to uses*, feudal incidents never came due. This provided an effective way to avoid feudal incidents, but did not offer the kind of long term control the landlords sought. Legal advisors again developed a solution. If by means of a use, seisin was vested in a *feoffee*, successive contingent remainders of uses could be strung together. Because they were not subject to the common law remainder rules, they were not required to vest within the lifetime of the previous holder. If one beneficial interest ended before another began, the Courts of Equity held that the *feoffee to uses* held the land on behalf of the grantor until the next remainder vested. This gave rise to uses that would "spring" and "shift" into the future.

In a springing use, land would be conveyed "to A and his heirs to the use of B and his heirs when B attains the age of 21". A would hold a legal estate. B would hold an equitable estate not exerciseable until he reached 21, at which point B would become the *cestui que use*. Until he did, A held a resulting trust in favour of the grantor. Thus A's legal estate was burdened by B's equitable interest, which would "spring" into existence when B became 21.

In a shifting use, land would be conveyed "to A and his heirs to the use of B, but if B begins to smoke, then to the use of C and his heirs". A would take the legal estate. B would be the equitable title holder, i.e., the *cestui que use*. However if B began to smoke, the equitable interest would shift to C. Thus A's legal estate was burdened by B's equitable estate, which was in turn subject to a shifting use that might arise in C.

## 12.7 — Legal Executory Interests

As also noted, uses became so prevalent in English land law that both the King's interests in knowing from whom he could claim feudal dues, and landowners' interests in security of title were in jeopardy. King Henry VIII addressed this problem by imposing on Parliament the *Statute of Uses, 1535* through which the legal title holder collapsed into the equitable title holder, making them one and the same, and therefore preserving for the King the right to inheritance dues. In response, the landholders extracted the *Statute of Wills, 1540* to secure their right to devise land according to their own wishes. Details of the statutes are needed to understand the ways land lords found to avoid the statutes.

### (a) — *Statute of Uses, 1535*

The *Statute of Uses, 1535* executed the first use, meaning that in a grant "to A to the use of B" the statute transferred the legal title from the *feoffee to uses*, A, to the *cestui que use*, B. Thus B became the legal and equitable title holder, feudal incidents were due, and the King hoped thereby to restore his lost source of revenue. Three types of uses avoided the statute, the first two by exemption through the statute and the third by virtue of lawyers' and land lords' creativity:

- *Active Uses* — If the *foeffee to uses* (a trustee post-Statute) had duties to perform, such as collecting rents for the *cestui que use* (a beneficiary post-Statute) the use was not executed. Known as *foeffee of an active use*, the trustee was allowed to remain to perform his duties.
- *Personalty* — The *Statute of Uses, 1535* applied only to uses on seised land, which meant that personal property was not affected. Because leases were at law personal rather than real property, personalty uses were not executed by the Statute. Land lords found it convenient to lease land "to A for 999 years to the use of B". The use was not executed and the equitable interest remained effective.
- *Use upon a use* — If land was granted "to A to the use of B to the use of C" the Statute executed the first use, vesting legal interest in B, and the equitable interest moved to C. Because the first execution exhausted the requirements of the Statute, the second use survived in Equity. Courts of Equity held a use upon a use to be valid. In *Sambach v. Daston* (1635), Toth. 188, the original *cestui que use* B, who by virtue of execution became a legal fee simple holder, was required to honour the use upon a use in C.

With the use upon the use, as well as personalty and active uses, land lords were again able both to avoid the inheritance taxes and to control land far into the future by stringing together long chains of future interests. Of the three, the use upon a use became the dominant means of avoiding the statute.

Springing uses and shifting uses re-entered the system as springing and shifting trusts. In a springing trust, land would be conveyed to "A and his heirs to the use of B and his heirs to the use of C and his heirs when C attains the age of 21". The Statute collapsed A's legal title into the first use B. B would become the legal title holder. Until C was ready to take, B held legal title subject to a springing interest in C that would come due at some time in the future, i.e., when C reached 21.

In a shifting trust, land would be conveyed "to A and his heirs to the use of B, but if B begins to smoke, then to the use of C and his heirs". The Statute would immediately execute the first use, making B the holder of the legal estate. The Statute ignored the second use. B's title was subject to an equitable contingent remainder in C. If B began to smoke, legal title would shift from B to C through C's equitable right. B's legal title was subject to a shifting interest that may arise in the future.

Equitable interests were not subject to the rules against legal remainders. A grant "to A and his heirs to the use of B for life and one day after B's death, to C", invalid under the common law legal remainder rules, was valid in Equity. Should a gap arise between successive holders of beneficial interests, the trustee was simply said to hold the land in trust for the grantor until the next beneficial interest vested.

Springing and shifting trusts were called legal executory interests. Executory meant not executed under the Statute. An executory interest is a future interest — a contingent interest capable of vesting at an uncertain time in the future. It was also called legal because the grant was one on which the law had operated. The Statute had collapsed the first legal and equitable interest. Combining the words created a class of interests known as "legal executory interests". They had been created by the operation of a legal statute but they survived as future interests that remained contingent until they vested.

### (b) — *Statute of Wills, 1540*

As noted, part of the tradeoff for the *Statute of Uses, 1535* was the King's promise to enact the *Statute of Wills, 1540* which enshrined land lords' right to devise land. Again land lords used the lessons they had learned through trusts to create conditions to avoid the common law rules against remainders. Through an executory devise, a testator willed land "to A and his heirs if A goes to law school". At death, the executors acquired the legal title in trust in favour of the grantor's estate until it was known whether or not A would go to law school. The "resulting trust" could last potentially until the end of A's life, at which point it would be known for certain whether A had gone to law school or not. If A did go to law school, the executors would convey the legal title. If not, it would be distributed according to the residual clause in the will.

Two practices developed in the Courts of Equity to interpret the *Statute of Wills, 1540* that, while seemingly insignificant at the time, had far reaching influence in the future. The first was to interpret words less literally than at common law. Similar to their practices under *De Donis, 1285*, the Equity

Courts favoured trying to honour the intention of the testator. For example, Common Law courts had always required particular language strictly interpreted to create a valid *inter vivos* grant. In testamentary dispositions, Equity courts attempted to honour the will of the testator, however imperfectly expressed. For example, any words of limitation consistent with an intention to create a fee simple were sufficient to pass a fee simple at death. Thus "my entire estate to C in fee simple" would succeed as a testamentary disposition where it would fail as an *inter vivos* conveyance because it lacked the words "and his heirs". The second practice was to favour early vesting. If a devise could be interpreted to vest either earlier or later, the courts would favour early vesting to protect security of title.

## 12.8 — The Rule Against Perpetuities

### (a) — Evolution and Content of the Rule

Over time, the combined weight of determinable, conditional, and entailed fees from the Common Law courts, uses from Equity court, and legal executory interests following the *Statute of Uses, 1535* and the *Statute of Wills, 1540*, created an ever-expanding body of future interests. Land lords found themselves hampered by their own practices. Complex litanies of conditions could endure long into the future, and interests could spring and shift, burdening the title and chilling the market on alienability.

Land lords began to challenge future interests not subject to the legal remainder rules, and Common Law and Equity turned their minds to ways to appropriately limit these interests, leading to the Rule Against Perpetuities. The evolution of the Rule was not a straight line conceptual development but took a number of twists and turns from the *Rule in Shelley's Case* (1581) through to the case of *Duke of Norfolk's Case* (1685) which is credited with the origin of the "modern" Rule. The 1890 case of *Whitby v. Mitchell* (1890), 44 Ch. D. 85 (Eng. C.A.), articulated what became known as the "old" Rule Against Perpetuities, which prohibited perpetual grants through the offspring of unborn children. Thus it took several centuries to create a seemingly stable equilibrium between control and alienability to address future interests. A completely judge-made rule, the "modern" Rule Against Perpetuities continues to limit remoteness of vesting. The Rule continues to be relevant, especially in assessing interests related to property rights in oil, gas, mineral, and other resource rights.

- *The Rule in Shelley's Case (1581)* — The first expression of the Rule arose in the context of entailed fees. Grantees began challenging complex strings of entailed fees used to control land devolution into the future. *The Rule in Shelley's Case* (1581), 1 Co. Rep. 93 b., stated that "whenever a limitation to A is followed by a limitation to heirs either general or special the limitation to the heirs are not words of purchase but rather words of limitation". The effect of the Rule was that if the same grantee (or heirs of a grantee) held two interests in a chain, the latter of which was an inheritable fee (simple or tail), then such grantees took a fee simple subject to intervening possessory interests. A grant "to A for life, then the heirs of the body of A" had created, without the Rule, a life estate in A followed by a remainder in A's heirs. Under the Rule, the heirs of A's body were viewed as words of limitation, and the interest merged with the life estate. Thus the grant became "to A and his heirs". If a grant read, "to A for life, then to B for life, then to the heirs of the body of A", under the Rule, "A for life" and "heirs of the body of A" merged so that A would take a fee tail. This interest was known at the moment of the grant, creating a vested rather than a contingent remainder. The fee tail was subject to the life estate of B. Because the Rule in Shelley's Case applies only if the interests are either both legal or both equitable, if the grant had been "to A for life, then to B for life with remainder to the use of the heirs of A's body", the Rule would not have applied to create a fee simple in A. Thus the Rule limited independent grants to an individual and then by way of remainder to the individual's heirs.

- *The Rule in Purefoy v. Rogers (1671)* — This Rule addressed a situation in legal executory interests parallel to the wait and see situation in the common law remainder no abeyance of seisen rules. If a grant of land contained a contingent remainder that could meet the common law rules (i.e., would vest prior to the ending of the prior estate) then the case of *Purefoy v. Rogers* (1671), 85 E.R. 1181 (Eng. K.B.), held that the grant must follow the common law rules on remainders. For example, a grant "to A to the use of B for life with remainder to the daughters of B" was valid under the common law rules. Because all of B's daughters would be born during B's life (or within nine months of B's death), the remainder could follow the common law rules and therefore survived. Their interest as remainder-persons could vest prior to the termination of the previous grant. In such a situation, all the common law rules on remainders were satisfied as there was no abeyance of seisin. On the other hand, in a grant "to A to the use of B for life, then C when she graduates from law school", the grant to C may be capable of complying with the legal wait and see rule (i.e., no abeyance of seisen at the time of creation) but it is not certain to do so. Even if the interest was created under a will or trust (not normally subject to the legal remainder rules), the courts of Equity applied the wait and see rules from the legal remainder rules because of *Purefoy v. Rogers*. Perversely therefore, the rule in *Purefoy v. Rogers* did not apply to contingent interests that would clearly not vest within the wait and see period.

- *The Rule in the Duke of Norfolk's Case (1685)* — In 1685, the Courts took on the issue of remoteness of vesting, which is why the case is credited as being the first expression of the "modern" Rule Against Perpetuities. The facts of the case involved a father attempting to provide for his family without allowing the property to go to an eldest son who was deemed insane. He created a life estate in the property for himself, then a life estate in his widow, after which the property would go to trustees for 200 years, with the remainder to his children still remaining. The Court held that this tied up the property for too long, and created a Rule Against Perpetuities, though it could more precisely be called a rule against remoteness of vesting. The Rule states "a future interest is void, ab initio, unless it must vest, if at all, within a period measured by lives in being plus a further period of twenty-one years". The core idea is that future interests are only permitted to endure as contingent interests for a certain period of time — the perpetuity period. If there is any possibility that they could vest outside that period, they are void *ab initio*. If it will be known who exactly will take, and that person will stand ready to take before the end of the perpetuity period, it is possible to wait and see if it happens within a period of 21 years plus an *in utero* period beyond a designated life (or class of lives) in being at the time of the grant. Complexities arise as to the calculation of the relevant perpetuity period, especially in defining the measuring lives. In situations of contemporary resource management leases, there is seldom a relevant life in being, in which case the perpetuity period is 21 years after the effective date of the instrument creating the interests.

If one holds in mind the core idea that the Rule Against Perpetuities is a rule against remote vesting, and that it declares a future interest is only valid if it necessarily must vest within 21 years of the beginning of the perpetuity period, then one can navigate the intricacies of the Rule.

### (b) — Application of the Rule

Consider an example. A grant "to my sons who are still alive 20 years after the death of the Rolling Stones". The grantor has two sons, ages 3 and 5, at the time of the grant.

- *future interest* — The first step is to determine whether the future interests are vested or contingent. Because it is not known at the moment of the grant which sons are going to meet the condition in the grant, the interests are contingent.

- *must vest, if at all* — If there is any possibility that the contingent interests may vest outside the perpetuity period, they will be void *ab initio*. However, the relevant perpetuity period must first be determined.
- *within the period measured by lives in being* — The perpetuity period is calculated by determining the class containing the measuring lives. Because it is an *inter vivos* grant, the relevant lives are the Rolling Stones alive and the grantor's sons alive at date of the instrument. If the instrument is testamentary, the relevant class is all the Rolling Stones members and the sons alive at the testator's death.
- *plus 21 years* — The perpetuity period runs until the last relevant band member dies, at which point 21 years is added plus an *in utero* period. The grant calls for the land to go to the sons alive 20 years after the death of the Rolling Stones. Therefore we will know at the time of the grant whether someone will be eligible to take within the perpetuity period, and if so who. The issue in the Rule is not what is likely to happen, but what is possible. Each of the sons will or will not be alive 20 years after the Rolling Stones die. So the interest must vest, if at all, within 21 years after the death of the last Rolling Stone. The contingent interest does not offend the Rule Against Perpetuities and is therefore valid.

### (c) — The Rule Against Perpetuities Today

In the three centuries following 1685, the Rule has been modified only slightly at common law, continuing today in Canada as the major limitation on the ability of landholders to control the destiny of their land into the future (*Robinson v. Adair*, 2004 SKQB 138 (Sask. Q.B.)). The depth and reach of the Rule can be seen in recent case law in relation to oil and gas leases: (*Scurry-Rainbow Oil Ltd. v. Galloway Estate*, [1993] 4 W.W.R. 454 (Alta. Q.B.); affirmed (1994), 1994 CarswellAlta 216 (Alta. C.A.); leave to appeal refused (1994), 26 Alta. L.R. (3d) 1 (note) (S.C.C.) and *Taylor v. Scurry-Rainbow Oil (Sask) Ltd.* (2001), [2001] S.J. No. 479, 2001 CarswellSask 539 (Sask. C.A.)).

# CHAPTER 13 — CO-OWNERSHIP



## 13.0 — Introduction

Just as it is possible to grant estates successively over time, such as a lease, followed by a life estate, followed by a fee simple, it is also possible to divide estates through co-tenancy or co-ownership. With co-ownership, two or more persons have simultaneous and concurrent rights, sharing the title, use, and enjoyment of the real property.

Several different forms of co-ownership evolved at common law, many of which were incorporated into statute. There are also newer forms of co-ownership that are wholly creatures of statute, such as matrimonial property, co-operative, and condominium ownership.

Three questions identify the type of co-ownership. How is it created? What are the rights and obligations among the parties? How can the relationship be changed or terminated?

## 13.1 — Common Law Regimes of Co-ownership

### (a) — Joint Tenancy

In Norman feudalism, a conveyance to two or more people — "to X and Y" — created a joint tenancy, imparting the property to them as a single owner. Joint tenancies may still be created in all provinces by specific words. As between themselves, joint tenants have separate rights and obligations, but vis-à-vis third parties, they are viewed as a single tenant. The joint tenancy is distinguished by two factors:

- *Right of Survivorship* (*jus accrescendi*) — On the death of one tenant, that tenant's interest passes automatically to the surviving tenant(s) to hold jointly until the estate is held by a sole tenant. The only way to defeat the right of survivorship is to sever the joint tenancy during the lifetime of the parties; *jus accrescendi* takes priority over a will or intestate succession rules (*Negrey v. Podesky*, 2004 ABQB 550 (Alta. Q.B.). The surviving joint tenant takes all. A joint tenancy is an option for couples, e.g., to avoid the need for probate or to permit same sex couples to ensure their partner takes the shared real property, and in trust situations where trustees may be named as joint tenants.
- *Four Unities* — The four unities reflect the feudal beginnings of joint tenancy. Unity of possession entitles each tenant to possession of any and all of the real property. Unity of interest provides that each tenant's interest is the same in terms of extent (share of the whole), nature (type of estate), and time (length). Each tenant must take under the same title, i.e., by the same instrument. Unity of time requires that the interest of each tenant vest at the same time.

Joint tenants have the same interest, established in a common title (document), commencing at the same time, held by all in undivided possession, with the right of survivorship: Possession + Interest + Time + Title + Survivorship = PITTS.

In Norman feudalism, a grant containing the four unities created a presumption of joint tenancy, unless specifically rebutted. Grantees, however, preferred to be able to freely devise their shares, something precluded by the *jus accrescendi*. Canadian statutes now reverse the presumption, specifying that a joint tenancy in real property does not exist unless intentionally created by the parties (e.g., *MacGregor Estate, Re*, 2001 NSSC 9 (N.S. S.C.), *Land Titles Act*, S.S. 2000, c. L-5.1, s. 34(3); *Real Property Act*, R.S.N.S. 1989, c. 385, s. 5(1)).

### (b) — Tenancy in Common

Unless specifically rebutted, statutes now presume a tenancy in common even if all the four unities are present. In a tenancy in common, two or more persons use and enjoy the property in undivided shares (unity of possession). Unlike a joint tenancy, none of the three remaining unities (title, interest, and time) need be present, nor is there a right of survivorship. For example, three individuals could be granted a tenancy in common as follows: two could be recipients of an estate in fee simple now and one of a life estate later (no unity of title); with respective shares of 25%, 25%, and 50% (no unity of interest); to vest upon their respective twenty-first birthdays (no unity of time).

Although the tenants in common hold in undivided shares and can enjoy the whole of the estate, their shares are a fixed amount of the undivided whole that can be conveyed *inter vivos* or at death. For example, at the death of one tenant, assuming an inheritable estate, her share passes by will or intestacy. This does not mean that the property is physically divided, but rather that heirs or devisees step into the shoes of the deceased tenant to become a co-owner with the survivors.

### (c) — Co-parcenary

At the time of primogeniture a problem arose if no male heirs were available. In these circumstances the common law provided that two or more daughters could take the property as one heir. Co-parcenary arose only with intestate succession, and although the four unities were usually present, there was no right of survivorship. Due to intestate succession legislation in Canada, co-parcenary is now of only historical interest.

### (d) — Tenancy by Entireties

Historically, a conveyance of land to a husband and wife created, unless specified otherwise, a tenancy by entireties. All rents and profits generated from the property while both parties were alive went to the husband. A tenancy by entireties was virtually impossible to sever short of ending the marriage. If both signatures were provided, the estate could be conveyed although a right of survivorship remained. The present status of tenancy by entireties in Canada is varied. Most provinces have abolished it, but a tenancy by entireties may still be specifically created in Saskatchewan (*Land Titles Act*, S.S. 2000, c. L-5.1, s. 245).

## 13.2 — Severance

Severance legally ends a joint tenancy during the lifetime of one of the tenants, changing the co-ownership relationship to a tenancy in common. Imagine a situation where B and C, two law school friends, purchase a house as joint tenants during their first year. By the time they reach third year, C no longer wishes to have the property pass to B by virtue of *jus accrescendi*. Rather, should anything happen to her, she wants her share of the property to go to D. Yet C and B would like to retain co-ownership, as the house provides a small source of revenue to help fund their education. Severance would end the joint tenancy and right of survivorship, creating a tenancy in common, but the co-ownership would remain.

There are four methods to sever a joint tenancy at common law:

- *Mutual Agreement* — A written agreement to change the tenancy signed by all parties.
- *Unity Disruption* — To end unity of possession would end the co-ownership relationship completely, but if a joint tenant either unilaterally or with agreement destroys one of the other unities (interest, time, or title), the joint tenancy is terminated. For example, a co-owner could sever a joint tenancy by conveying her interest to herself (thus destroying unity of time) without the others being aware.
- *Course of Dealing* — One of the tenants could sever her joint tenancy by dealing with her interest in such a manner as to sufficiently "intimate that the interests of all were mutually treated as constituting a tenancy in common" (*Sorenson v. Sorensen* (1977), 90 D.L.R. (3d) 26 (Alta. CA.); leave to appeal allowed (1977), 6 A.R. 540 (note) (S.C.C.)). The sufficiency of the action is a question of fact to be determined in each case (*Flannigan v. Wotherspoon* (1952), [1953] 1 D.L.R. 768 (B.C. S.C.), and the onus rests upon the party claiming severance (*Negrey*).
- *Other Means* — There are other methods of severance based on limited factual circumstances such as bankruptcy, execution proceedings, court order, or the murder of one joint tenant by the other (*Novak v. Gatien* (1975), 25 R.F.L. 397 (Man. Q.B.)).

If there are more than two joint tenants, the severing party will become a tenant in common, while the remaining joint tenants will retain the right of survivorship. Provincial statutes provide specific rules for severing joint tenancies. In Saskatchewan, severance requires the consent of all joint tenants in properly executed documents (*Land Titles Act*, S.S. 2000, c. L-5.1, s. 156). In Manitoba, a tenant may unilaterally sever provided that written notice of the instrument is given to the co-owners (*Real Property Act*, R.S.M. 1987, c. R-30, s. 79(1)(c)). However, legislation does not bar a claim that the co-tenancy has been equitably severed.

## 13.3 — Partition

At common law, in the absence of mutual agreement, there was no right to force partition, i.e., physical division or sale of property held in co-ownership. The theory was that parties could always turn a joint tenancy into a tenancy in common, and thereby gain control of their shares to alienate or devise as they wished. This situation was changed by three statutes — *Partition Act, 1539*, (31 Hen. VIII, c. 1); *Partition Act, 1540*, (32 Hen. VIII, c. 32); *Partition Act, 1868*, (31 & 32 Vict., c. 40), which permitted parties to apply to courts for a physical partition of the property or sale in lieu of partition. These statutes leave to judicial discretion whether the property should be divided physically or sold with the proceeds divided. They do not, however, allow a court to refuse a partition application altogether.

This English legislation remains the underlying basis for partition applications in Canada, although most provinces have modernized the statutes. Any co-owner has a right to make application for partition, and judicial discretion extends to whether the property should be divided or whether it should be sold.

Courts may consider such factors as the nature of the property, the number, relationship, and contribution of the parties (*Miller v. Walker*, 2006 ABQB 424 (Alta. Q.B.)), the absence or disability of any of the parties, as well as any other circumstances relevant to the consideration of what is just and fair. For example, a court could hardly divide physically a single-family residence on a city lot among several children. A sale would be necessary, either to an outside party or to some of the co-owners, with the proceeds divided among the children. In each jurisdiction both the case law and legislation should be examined to determine the nuances.

In a suit for partition, a court will attempt to make all equitable allowances as between the parties. These include not only consideration of the property itself, if physical partition is contemplated, but also accounting and, if necessary, the set-off of appropriate costs among the parties.

Once completed, the divided real property (or monetary equivalent) is held in several, meaning that each former tenant in common individually owns her respective share.

## 13.4 — Accounting

In co-ownership, each of the co-owners is entitled to use, enjoyment, and possession of the common property. In the absence of exclusion or a specific agreement, any profits a co-tenant in possession gleans from her own industry need not be divided among the co-owners. She is entitled to the *fructus industriales* (fruits of her labour) generated from the productive use of the property. For example, should one co-owner decide to live at the cottage for the summer while her co-owners tour Europe, she will be entitled to rent-free accommodation and the profits made from the roadside blueberry stand she sets up to sell berries harvested on the property. However, a co-owner profiting from her own *fructus industriales* is singularly responsible for losses for such enterprises. In the absence of an agreement to the contrary, the losses associated with a failed crop are the debt of the farming co-tenant only (*Henderson v. Eason* (1851), 117 E.R. 1451 (Eng. Q.B.)).

Accounting among co-owners was enshrined in the *Statute of Anne, 1705*, (4 & 5 Anne, c. 3). This statute permitted courts, upon the request of a co-owner, to examine the co-owners concerning their respective contribution and benefits associated with the property, and "for their pains and trouble in auditing and taking such account, have such allowance as the court shall adjudge to be reasonable". Now, as then, in order to be fair, courts consider the nature of the expenditure, the time of the claim (i.e., during the course of the co-ownership or at partition), and whether one of the tenants has had exclusive possession during the period covered by the requested accounting.

### (a) — Exclusive Possession

A tenant enjoying sole possession cannot be required to account as long as she does not exclude her co-owner(s) from any part of the property (*Dacyshyn v. Semeniuk*, 2007 BCSC 71 (B.C. S.C.)). Should one co-owner deprive another of the right to possession (a situation known as ouster), or otherwise be in receipt of rents or profits beyond a just share, he can be called to account to his co-owners either during the co-ownership or at partition. In these circumstances the co-owner has benefited, not because of any risk taken or labour extended, but at the expense of his co-tenants.

Parties may agree to exclusive possession by one co-tenant, either in advance or retroactively. Such an agreement does not constitute a break in the unity of possession. In the absence of such an agreement, where a tenant either actively or constructively ousts his co-owners, a rental payment may be demanded by the co-owners through an accounting. When such a demand is made, the co-owner in possession may bring forth evidence of disbursements in relation to the property for which a leasehold tenant would not be responsible.

### (b) — Third Party Rents and Profits

A co-owner is accountable for rents and profits accruing from his status as a co-owner as opposed to his own labour. For example, if no co-owner is in possession, and an enterprising co-owner rents the property to an outside party, that co-owner must account to the other co-owners for the monies received and distribute the profits proportionally (*Allen v. Henzi*, 2002 BCSC 474 (B.C. S.C.)). Monies received from exploitation of natural resources by a third party are similarly divisible among the co-owners. For example, the profits from granting a profit à prendre (Chapter 15) for gravel on the property will be shared by all.

### (c) — Expenditures

A co-owner who voluntarily undertakes repairs cannot, with some exceptions, turn to his co-owners for compensation. One such exception, e.g., a tenant who is paying occupation rent as a lessee of the co-owners, has rights commensurate with a leasehold tenant. Similarly, repairs necessary to prevent ruin may be apportioned among the co-owners (*Leigh v. Dickson* (1884), 15 Q.B.D. 60 (Eng. Q.B.)).

Improvements to the property may be considered at partition. The value of improvements is assessed according to the lesser of the cost of such efforts, or the extent to which they have increased the value of the property. Co-owners are well advised to agree on improvements in advance.

Charges on the property of an ongoing nature such as taxes, mortgage payments (both principal and interest), and utilities are recoverable in proportion to the share of the estate held by each of the co-tenants (*Dacyshy*).

### (d) — Waste

Co-owners are accountable for waste (spoilage or destruction) in the same manner as life estate holders (*Sheffield Welding & Fabricating Ltd. v. 958760 Alberta Ltd.*, 2003 ABQB 181 (Alta. Q.B.)) (Chapter 14).

### (e) — Renewable and Non-Renewable Resources

Renewable resources are not the subject of an accounting should one co-owner exploit the resource through her own labour, provided she engages in good resource management practices and does not exclude her co-owners should they wish to engage in similar activities. She is, however, subject to the doctrine of waste. For example, she may manage a timber lot, but not clear cut. In the case of non-renewable resources, the industrious co-owner can enjoy the profits from his labour provided he does so with prudence. He can work an existing mine, but cannot open a new one without the agreement of his co-owners.

American precedents adopt an alternative approach, holding that there must be an accounting in relation to non-renewable resources. The theory is that exploitation diminishes the value of the estate. These cases make a distinction in non-renewable resources between those that are visible and easily quantified, and those that are not visible, such as oil and gas or minerals. Some American courts have held that profits derived from non-renewable visible resources need not be shared as long as a co-owner obtains the consent of his co-tenants to exploit (*Threatt v. Rushing*, 361 So. 2d 329 (Miss., 1978)). Profits derived from non-renewable, non-visible resources are shared among the co-owners even if exploited only by one (*White v. Smyth*, 214 S.W. 2d 967 (Tex., 1948)).

## 13.5 — Statutory Regimes of Co-ownership: Matrimonial, Condominium, and Co-operative Property

In addition to common law forms of co-ownership, all Canadian provinces have provided for new forms of co-ownership through statute — most notably matrimonial property, condominiums, and co-operatives. While the mechanics and nuances of these statutes differ from province to province, they share a conceptual similarity.

### (a) — Matrimonial Property Legislation

Historically in English land law, upon marriage a husband gained an immediate right to management and profits of any real property held by his wife (the doctrine of coverture). In most Canadian provinces, *Married Women's Property Acts* at the end of the nineteenth century permitted women to acquire and hold property in their own right. Because conventional roles mitigated against a woman actually purchasing property in her own name, separating the property of the husband and wife often meant hardship. At marriage breakdown, a wife was often left with no property while the titled husband took all. Similarly, a common law spouse who assisted her partner in acquiring property in his name was sometimes left destitute.

Courts attempted to address the inequities through the doctrine of resulting trust. However, this doctrine required a common intention (express or implied) that the property was to be shared, and often no such intent could be found. A common law partner might well receive nothing because of a lack of proof of the other partner's intention to share (e.g., *Murdoch v. Murdoch*

(1973), [1975] 1 S.C.R. 423 (S.C.C.)).

In *Pettkus v. Becker*, [1980] 2 S.C.R. 834 (S.C.C.), the Supreme Court responded by adopting the constructive trust as a remedy for unjust enrichment. In a constructive trust, if equity so demands, a court deems a trust for the partners, giving them shares in the property according to their contribution. Courts continue to apply this doctrine in the context of alternative family relationships in jurisdictions where statutes have not yet addressed such living arrangements.

The requirements for constructive trust based upon unjust enrichment are:

- an enrichment;
- a corresponding deprivation (contributions may constitute such a deprivation);
- a lack of a juristic reason (a reason recognized at law) for the enrichment; and
- a sufficient nexus (causal connection) between the deprivation and the enrichment (*Peter v. Beblow*, [1993] 1 S.C.R. 980 (S.C.C.)).

The legal device of constructive trust to assist spouses who would otherwise be left without property was largely replaced in the 1970s through matrimonial property legislation passed in all common law provinces. This legislation views marriage as an economic partnership requiring an orderly dissolution at breakdown, assumes both spouses have contributed equally to the acquisition of family property, and declares that such property should be divided equally. The definition of family property varies by province.

Spouses retain separate property during the course of the marriage and deal with it autonomously. When divorce, separation, or nullification occurs, an application is made for a division of property. Courts may depart from the presumption of equal division on the basis of a list of factors specific to each statute. Factors include individual inheritances and gifts, length of the marriage, personal injury damages, and property brought into the marriage. The matrimonial home is subject to particular possessory rights outlined in each jurisdiction. It is often the family asset of greatest financial value and the locus of family life. The matrimonial home may or may not be divided depending on the family's best interests (*Elliott v. Elliott*, 2007 BCSC 98 (B.C. S.C.)).

### (b) — Condominium Legislation

The condominium creates both private and common ownership of real property. Generally, a condominium divides land and a portion of its airspace into strata that may be held individually as units. The existence of shared areas such as hallways, staircases, parking lots, heating, and recreational areas necessitates a form of common ownership. In these areas, common property is held by the unit-holders as tenants in common, sharing proportionally to each unit-holder's share of total private ownership.

All common law provinces have legislation governing the formation, registration, administration, and termination of condominiums. Upon construction of the physical structure and the sale of units to individual purchasers, title to the property as a whole is cancelled. Title to the units passes to the purchasers, as well as an undivided share in the common property. The unit-holder is responsible for maintenance of, and repairs to, his private unit, as well as a share of the costs of maintaining the common property. Financing the latter necessitates the payment of monthly condominium fees. Each unit-holder retains the right to use and enjoyment of all common property to the extent that that use does not interfere with the use and enjoyment of other unit-holders.

A condominium corporation is created which is responsible for administering the condominium and its day-to-day operations. Unit-holders elect representatives to the condominium corporation's board of directors. Provinces differ regarding formation and administration of the corporation. For example, an Alberta condominium is grounded in bylaws and a condominium plan. Ontario employs a declaration, the contents of which are prescribed by the Act, read in association with the legislation, as the basis for the constitution of the corporation (e.g., *Condominium Property Act*, R.S.A. 2000, c. C-22; *Condominium Act*, R.S.O. 1998, c. C-19).

### (c) — Co-operative Legislation

A co-operative also provides individual members with exclusive use and possession of a unit of commonly held real property. Although each province has its own co-operative legislation, there are two methods through which this form of common ownership operates (e.g., *Co-operative Association Act*, R.S.A. 2001, c. C-28.1; *The Co-operatives Act, 1996*, S.S. 1996, c. C-37.3).

- The first method occurs where title to the property may be collectively held by the members of the co-operative as tenants in common. That tenancy in common issues each tenant a lease, providing the member with exclusive use and enjoyment of a portion of the whole.
- The second method is to create a co-operative corporation in which members purchase shares. The co-operative corporation holds title to the property. Each member has one share and one vote in the co-operative corporation. The co-operative corporation leases units to its members.

In both structures, membership carries with it the opportunity to participate in the governance of the co-op and a responsibility for a portion of the mortgage and operating costs. Unlike a condominium, a co-operative owner does not buy and sell title to their private unit, but instead would convey their share or their tenancy in common, as well as the lease.

# CHAPTER 14 — RIGHTS AND OBLIGATIONS OF THE FREEHOLD ESTATE HOLDER



## 14.1 — Extent of the Fee Simple

As the holder of the largest possible estate in the land, a fee simple holder enjoys considerable powers relating to the use and enjoyment of property. The Latin maxim is *cujus est solum ejus est usque ad coelum et ad inferos* — he who owns the soil owns from the centre of the earth to the heavens above. This was more accurate at common law than it is today where the realities of modern society have tempered the rights considerably.

### (a) — Mines and Minerals

At common law, the Crown laid claim to gold and silver beneath the surface of land as well as any treasure trove. In addition, it was within the power of the Crown to withhold any other mineral from a grant to the fee simple holder.

The opening of Western Canada and the granting of land throughout the settlement period illustrate the changing approach of the Crown vis-à-vis mineral rights. Early in the course of westward expansion certain grants, including land granted to the Canadian Pacific Railway and the Hudson's Bay Company, included subsurface minerals. This property became known as freehold land. In the late nineteenth century, the government recognized the potential revenue from subsurface mineral development. Subsequent grants reserved to the government gold and precious metals, then coal, and finally, "all minerals unto the Crown". A review of Crown grants through the West indicates that, with the exception of the early CPR and Hudson's Bay Company grants, one is likely to find a full reservation of minerals to the Crown. It is important to check the original grant for reservations (*Anderson v. Amoco Canada Oil and Gas*, 2004 SCC 49 (S.C.C.)). When the Crown has reserved subsurface minerals, the rights to explore, exploit, and convey are the subject of extensive statutory regulation. These outline not only the subsurface rights, but also the interests of surface rights holders in relation to those who may gain rights to exploit subsurface resources (*The Surface Rights Acquisition and Compensation Act*, R.S.S. 1978, c. S-65).

## (b) — Support

The landholder has the right to lateral and subjacent support of the land. Property holders may not deal with their own land in a manner that damages the support of neighbouring properties (lateral support). Those who gain subsurface rights (e.g., mining companies) must not exercise their rights in a manner that causes subsidence of the surface (subjacent support).

The right to subjacent support is absolute in the sense that damage to buildings on the property is recoverable (providing the subsidence caused the damage). The right to lateral support does not automatically include support for buildings. If the plaintiff can show that there would have been subsidence with or without the weight of the building, then any damage to the building is consequential to the damage to the land and is recoverable, though one should check recent case law in the jurisdiction for what courts will and will not include in damages (*Gallant v. F.W. Woolworth Co.* (1970), 15 D.L.R. (3d) 248 (Sask. C.A.); *Bullock Holdings v. Jerema* (1998), 15 R.P.R. (3d) 185 (B.C. S.C. [in Chambers])). If the building's weight contributed to the subsidence then a plaintiff seeking recovery for damages to the building must establish negligence on the part of a neighbour.

### (c) — Airspace

The maxim suggesting ownership to the heavens above was limited at common law by a recognition of airspace as a *res communis* — a thing common to all — that could not be the subject of ownership. The difficulty has been to determine where in law the fee simple holder's rights to the heavens above end, and the common public right to use and enjoyment begins. In Canada, the public right to airspace is claimed through legislation for such matters as utility rights-of-way (e.g., *The Power Corporation Act*, R.S.S. 1978, c. P-19, s. 33(2)).

The landholder retains certain rights to the airspace above her property. Although there are differing views as to the physical reach of the right, Canadian precedent seems to provide protection for as much of the airspace as is reasonably necessary for enjoyment of the surface (*Didow v. Alberta Power Ltd.*, [1988] 5 W.W.R. 606 (Alta. CA.); leave to appeal refused (1989), 94 A.R. 320 (note) (S.C.C.)). This position does not necessitate the actual occupation of that airspace but contemplates protection commensurate with enjoyment of the land and buildings on the land. Any direct invasion of the landholder's established airspace will constitute a trespass and is actionable *per se* (*Ford v. Zelman*, 2005 BCPC 344 (B.C. Prov. Ct.)). However, the landholder often brings an action in nuisance on the basis that the defendant's behaviour constitutes an unreasonable interference with the landholder's use and enjoyment of property (*Sutherland v. Canada (Attorney General)*, 2002 BCCA 416 (B.C. C.A.); additional reasons at (2003), 2003 CarswellBC 288 (B.C. C.A.); leave to appeal refused (2003), 2003 CarswellBC 1102 (S.C.C.)).

Condominium statutes provide for a flying fee that may occupy a stratum many stories above ground level (e.g., a condominium on the twentieth floor). Some provinces also have legislation dealing with the registration of airspace plans and parcels (*Air Space Act*, S.N.B. 1982, c. A-7.01).

### (d) — Water Rights

At common law, water was *res communis* (common to all) until captured. The common law position reflected the situation in England and eastern Canada where water was plentiful. In contrast, settlement on the Western prairies was often dependent on the availability of scarce water. To ensure the equitable distribution of water, Parliament vested the Crown with property in all water in the Northwest Territories (*The Northwest Irrigation Act, 1898*, S.C. 1898, 61 V., c. 35, s. 4). Water became property. The federal government then fashioned a scheme for water rights distribution in the West. Although the federal government still retains a role in water management, property in water now vests in the provincial Crowns (The Natural

Resources Transfer Agreement, *Constitution Act, 1930, 20-21, George V, c. 26 (U.K.); Saskatchewan Watershed Authority Act, 2005*, S.S. 2005, c. S-35.03). Statutes modify the common law dealing with water rights, particularly in relation to water use, water quality protection, and riparian rights.

Although landholders did not own the water, the common law provided for riparian rights — rights for those whose land came into contact with water flowing in a defined course. The extent of the right was partially dependent on whether the water was surface water, ground water, or flowed in a defined course. While the following outlines the common law, statutes must be consulted to determine the extent to which these rights have been abrogated.

With respect to water flowing in a defined water course, riparians held significant rights to use and enjoy both surface and subsurface waters substantially undiminished in quality and quantity. Each riparian could use unlimited quantities of water for reasonable ordinary purposes even if the use resulted in a diminished flow for downstream riparians. Ordinary purposes included domestic uses such as household needs, watering of domestic stock, and maintaining a produce garden for family use. Riparians who extended water use to non-domestic extraordinary purposes (often commercial) could not substantially diminish the quality or quantity of the flow to downstream riparians without risk of liability (*Miner v. Gilmour* (1859), 14 E.R. 861 (Lower Canada P.C.)).

Other surface riparian rights included a right of natural drainage into the flowing water course, a right of access to flowing water, and title to land by virtue of accretion (*McKie v. K.V.P. Co.* (1948), [1949] 1 D.L.R. 39 (Ont. C.A.)). Riparian rights survive unless specifically abrogated by statute (*Neuman v. Parkland (County)*, 2004 ABPC 58 (Alta. Prov. Ct.)).

In some cases, an estate owner may have title to the bed of a body of water. Ownership depended on a combination of factors including whether the body of water was navigable, whether it was tidal or freshwater, and whether the bed had been specifically granted or reserved by the Crown. Rights to the bed included exclusive fishing rights in the column of water above. The riparian could also erect structures on his segment of the bed as long as they did not have the potential to interfere with the rights of others. If water was navigable, all members of the public had the paramount right to navigate on the water (*Graham v. Andrusyk*, 2006 BCSC 1614 (B.C. S.C.)). The public also had the right to fish except where the bed was privately owned.

Surface or underground water in undefined courses, although not subject to riparian rights, was subject to a landholder's usufructuary right to capture and use as much of the subsurface or surface water as she could recover. No right of action in negligence or nuisance existed even if the capture resulted in neighbouring wells running dry; the purpose for the extraction was irrelevant (*Langbrook Properties Ltd. v. Surrey County Council*, [1969] 3 All E.R. 1424 (Eng. Ch. Div.)).

Water flowing over land in an undefined course is called surface water. Landholders were entitled to contain and capture surface waters that flowed over their property even if natural drainage patterns would result in neighbouring properties receiving the flow. Catch ponds, sloughs, or diversion systems created by landholders to contain water were legally acceptable. Conversely, in those situations where excessive surface water was a problem, there was no obligation to receive such water, and landholders could repel it at their boundaries by using earthworks or other methods (*McLennan v. Meyer* (2005), 203 O.A.C. 274 (Ont. C.A.)). There was also no obligation to prevent natural drainage onto adjoining properties even if the result was flooding on those properties. However, once the water was on a landholder's property, he could not take steps to divert it onto the land of another. Again, statutes in many jurisdictions have changed the common law rights relating to surface waters. Similarly, legislation has been introduced which substantially alters rights relating to drainage in order to provide systematic flood control, particularly in agricultural and recreational areas.

### (e) — Wild Animals

Under the common law, the fee simple landholder could claim the right to hunt, capture, and kill the wild animals that cross or inhabit the real property (*ratione soli*). This right did not give title to the animals, only a right to possession. Wild animals *per se* were not the subject of ownership. In Canada, legislation creates property rights in wildlife, vests them in the Crown, and outlines wildlife management policies (*Species at Risk Act*, S.C. 2002, c. 29; *Wildlife Act*, R.S.N.S. 1989, c. 504).

## 14.2 — The Extent of the Life Estate

Because the life estate would revert to the holder of the fee simple at the end of the measuring life, the life tenant's use and enjoyment was tempered at common law by the requirement to preserve the estate for that future interest. Although a grantor could specifically outline other terms, the common law developed a number of presumptions concerning the scope of the life tenant's rights.

### (a) — Rents, Profits, and Emblements

The holder of a life estate is entitled to the rents and other profits from the land over the duration of his interest. These include the right to harvest annual crops produced by his own effort (*fructus industriales*). In the case of crops that naturally regenerate such as fruits or nuts, the life estate holder is entitled to the fruit of the tree, but must not harm the tree from whence comes the fruit. Should the life estate be terminated by death before the life tenant reaps a crop he planted, his heir, or the tenant himself in an estate *pur autre vie*, has the right to emblements, i.e., the annual crop return.

In estates where the value of the property lies in the exploitation of renewable and non-renewable resources such as a timber estate, the line between the life estate holder's right to rents and profits and his duty to preserve the estate for the next interest holder is generally governed by the law of waste. Unless the grant otherwise specifies, a life estate holder may not open a mine, but can prudently manage an existing mine and enjoy all profits. Where the main purpose of the estate is to produce and sell timber (a timber estate) the life estate holder may exploit the trees in a manner consistent with good resource management practices (*Hiltz v. Langille* (1959), 18 D.L.R. (2d) 464 (N.S. CA.)). Disputes are determined according to whether the practices of the life estate holder are consistent with customary management standards.

### (b) — Ongoing Fees and Disbursements

The life estate holder in possession is responsible for annual taxes and expenses on the theory that she should not receive rents and profits from property while at the same time allowing taxes to accumulate (*Waldie v. Denison* (1893), 24 O.R. 197 (Ont. Ch.)). This is a burden on the life estate holder to preserve the estate for the reversion or remainder. However, if the taxes are greater than the revenues from the property, the life estate holder is not obliged to make up the difference. Alternatively, a grantor may specifically charge the remainder-person with the responsibility for taxes in the grant.

A similar approach applies to any mortgage payments due on the property. Although the life estate holder is expected to shoulder the periodic costs of remaining on the land, mortgage costs are divided between remainder and reversionary interest holders and life tenant. The life tenant is burdened only with the interest on the debt, while the other interest holder pays the capital.

Unless specifically directed in the grant, there is no obligation on the life tenant to repair or maintain the tenement. Thus, short of a positive act of waste, the life estate holder is within her rights to allow the property to degenerate. Should she choose to make repairs, the rule of thumb is that major undertakings to prevent ruin of the estate are the responsibility of the reversion or remainder-person (*Buhr Estate v. Bohr* (1993), 90 Man. R. (2d) 118 (Man. Q.B.)). Voluntary day-to-day repairs are the responsibility of the life estate holder and no reimbursement should be expected.

There is no obligation at common law on either the life estate holder or other interest holders to insure the property, although each is entitled to do so. In practice, life estate holders tend to insure their interest.

### (c) — Waste

Waste is defined as an act that alters the nature of the real property to the prejudice of the reversion or remainder. A creation of the Courts of Equity, the law relating to waste has been supplemented by the common law and statute. At common law, there are four varieties of waste.

- *Ameliorating Waste* — alterations that improve the value of the land. In days when land was described by its physical appearance, any change to the character of the property could be problematic. Today, such concerns are largely irrelevant, and the potential liability for ameliorating waste can retard development and impose economic hardship on the life estate holder. An action for ameliorating waste is unlikely to succeed as improvements generally advantage the property, unless the life tenant has completely changed its character.
- *Permissive Waste* — an omission on the part of the life estate holder rather than a positive act. Although the life tenant may have no duty to repair or maintain the property, a failure to undertake day-to-day repairs, household maintenance, or even cultivation can result in major hardship. Statute law often imposes minimum standards of care on all landholders that can minimize the hardship. For example, provincial statutes address nuisance and public health issues relating to real property (*Cities Act*, S.S. 2002, c. C-11.1) and noxious weeds statutes hold rural landholders to a minimum level of stewardship (*Noxious Weeds Act*, C.C.S.M. c. N110).
- *Voluntary Waste* — the commission of any spoilage or destruction that negatively impacts on the value of the property. A life estate holder will be responsible for positive acts of voluntary waste unless declared unimpeachable for waste in the grant. Examples of voluntary waste include opening a mine and imprudent exploitation of resources (i.e., failure to exercise good resource management practices). In determining whether voluntary waste has occurred, courts will examine such factors as the nature of the land, past use, injury to the remainder or reversion (including diminished monetary value), and the locale.

- *Equitable Waste* — an act of wanton destruction. Even if a tenant was unimpeachable for waste, the Courts of Equity protected the property when a life tenant committed an act of severe destruction — an act that a prudent man would not do to his own property. Only an explicit waiver of equitable waste in the grant would excuse actions such as house stripping or the cutting down of shade trees.

### (d) — The Trust Alternative

As an alternative to relying on the common law to protect the remainder or reversion, a settlor may establish a trust charging a trustee with property management responsibilities while passing the use and enjoyment of the land to an equitable life estate holder. For example, a trust document may make provision for a trustee to pay taxes, distribute revenue, and insure the property, thus preserving the fee simple while the beneficiary remains in possession. The possibilities can vary according to the needs of the parties and the nature of the real property (*Hawkins Estate, Re*, 2006 BCSC 1374 (B.C. S.C. [in Chambers])).

## 14.3 — Limitations Upon the Exercise of Proprietary Rights

Although the holder of an estate in possession is entitled to use and enjoyment, the right is not unfettered. Common law restrictions on use and enjoyment can give rise to tort actions. The Latin maxim is *sic utere tuo ut alienum non laedas* — use your own property so as not to injure that of your neighbours. These tort actions include trespass, negligence, strict liability, and nuisance. The following provides a brief outline, but specific tort law texts should be consulted. Further federal, provincial, and municipal land use regulation may impact individual rights to use and enjoyment.

### (a) — Trespass

Trespass is a physical invasion of property. Once direct entry is established, the tort is the physical invasion itself. No damage need be proven and intent is irrelevant (*Entick v. Carrington* (1765), 95 E.R. 807 (Eng. K.B.)). Walking across another's property without permission is a trespass, as is the continuing encroachment of a misplaced fence or building. In either case, the one in lawful possession of the land may sue for damages and, if the activity is likely to reoccur, an injunction (*Filliol v. Kozlowski*, 2002 ABQB 767 (Alta. Master)). There may also be recourse to public welfare statutes dealing with trespass (e.g., *Petty Trespasses Act*, C.C.S.M, c. P-50).

Historically, case law held that an occupier of land had a duty to a trespasser only to the extent of avoiding reckless disregard or willful attempts to injure unwanted guests. In 1975, the Supreme Court of Canada adopted a standard mandating that occupiers treat trespassers with common humanity (*Veinot v. Kerr-Addison Mines Ltd.* (1974), [1975] 2 S.C.R. 311 (S.C.C.)). A failure to meet this standard opens the occupier to liability for injuries sustained by a trespasser. Factors relevant to whether an occupier has satisfied this standard include the gravity and likelihood of harm, the condition of the land, the nature of the intrusion, the cost of eliminating the danger, and the likelihood of trespassers entering the property. Some provinces have varied the common law standard through occupier's liability legislation.

### (b) — Negligence

A landholder does not have a right to engage in activities on her land in such a manner as to cause damage to the property of others. The landholder has a duty of care to avoid causing reasonably foreseeable harm. This does not bar the landholder from engaging in the full use and enjoyment of her property, but introduces the requirement of reasonable care into the exercise of those rights (*Neuman v. Parkland County*).

### (c) — Strict Liability

In certain limited circumstances, a landholder is liable for damages to another's property even if he has exercised reasonable care. The doctrine of strict liability, often called the Rule in *Rylands v. Fletcher* (1866), [1861–73] All E.R. Rep. I (Eng. Exch.); affirmed (1868), [1861–73] All E.R. Rep. 1 (U.K. H.L.), at 12, holds that where an individual, for his own purposes, brings something onto his land likely to do mischief if it escapes, and it does escape and does damage, he is responsible for all damages that are the natural consequences of the escape. On appeal, Lord Cairns introduced a "gloss on the rule" providing that the defendant landholder will be liable only if the circumstances originated in a "non-natural use of the land", namely, a special use that brings with it some increased danger to others or is unusual and out of the ordinary. For example, the British Columbia Court of Appeal held that large quantities of fill that had been spread on a residential property, and that escaped after a heavy rainfall onto neighbouring lands constituted a non-natural use of the land. It was not the substance itself (in this case earth) but the volume and location of the substance that constituted a non-natural use of the land (*Chu v. Dawson* (1984), 18 D.L.R. (4th) 520 (B.C. CA.)). Alternatively, the escaping substance itself can be dangerous despite its customary use, as in the case of aerial chemical spraying (*Cruise v. Niessen*, [1977] 2 W.W.R. 481 (Man. Q.B.); reversed (1977), [1978] 1 W.W.R. 688 (Man. C.A.)).

The doctrine of strict liability is under scrutiny in the courts. On the one hand are moves to draw this tort closer to the tort of negligence by introducing requirements of forseeability (*Cambridge Water Co. v. Eastern Counties Leather Plc* (1993), [1994] 1 All E.R. 53 (U.K. H.L.)). On the other hand are American trends toward the creation of a super-tort that goes beyond strict liability to absolute liability for those engaged in ultra-hazardous and abnormally dangerous activities upon their properties. The debate has yet to be definitively addressed by the courts in this country.

### (d) — Nuisance

The law of nuisance attempts to balance the rights of landholders by providing that no one may use his land in such a manner as to unreasonably interfere with his neighbour's use of property or physical well-being. Unreasonableness is the key concept, with the focus on the unreasonableness of the harm rather than the unreasonableness of the conduct of the defendant.

In a private nuisance, the onus will be on the plaintiff to establish unreasonable interference by highlighting such factors as the nature of the harm to person or property, the duration of the nuisance (although a one-time nuisance is actionable), and the character of the neighbourhood. The defendant may counter such arguments with claims of the social utility of his own actions. Courts have arbitrated such disputes by asking whether the harm was more than a landholder should be required to bear in a modern complex society. Nonetheless the establishment of substantial physical damage to property or persons assures recovery in nuisance (*Scheneck v. Ontario* (1981), 131 D.L.R. (3d) 310 (Ont. H.C.); additional reasons at (1982), 1982 CarswellOnt 530 (Ont. H.C.); affirmed (1984), 15 D.L.R. (4th) 320 (Ont. CA.); affirmed (1984), 1984 CarswellOnt 1424 (Ont. C.A.); affirmed [1987] 2 S.C.R. 289 (S.C.C.)).

Nuisance has been found in cases dealing with noxious fumes, airborne pollution (*Walker v. McKinnon Industries Ltd.*, [1949] 4 D.L.R. 739 (Ont. H.C.); varied (1950), 1950 CarswellOnt 200 (Ont. C.A.); affirmed (1951), [1951] 3 D.L.R. 577 (Ontario P.C.)), smoke, vibration, noise (*Epstein v. Reymes* (1972), 29 D.L.R. (3d) 1 (S.C.C.), *Sutherland v. Vancouver Airport Authority*) and even interference with communications signals (*Nor-Video Services Ltd. v. Ontario Hydro* (1978), 4 C.C.L.T. 244 (Ont. H.C.)). To date, nuisance has not yet extended to include unreasonable interference with aesthetics (*St. Pierre v. Ontario (Minister of Transportation & Communications)* (1987), 39 D.L.R. (4th) 10 (S.C.C.)), but the maxim "the doors of nuisance are never closed" applies.

Public nuisance is an unreasonable interference so widespread in its effects that it impacts upon a class of Her Majesty's subjects. In these situations, the action is most often brought by the Attorney General on behalf of the citizenry. A private action for a public nuisance is possible provided that the plaintiff has special damage that differs in kind, rather than degree, from that suffered by the public at large (*Hickey v. Electric Reduction Co.* (1971), 21 D.L.R. (3d) 368 (Nfld. S.C.); *Gleneagles Concerned Parents Committee Society v. British Columbia Ferry Corp.* (2001), 37 C.E.L.R. (N.S.) 212 (B.C. S.C.)). Because each parcel of private property is unique, interference with a real property interest constitutes special damage.

# CHAPTER 15 — INTERESTS IN LAND OTHER THAN ESTATES



## 15.0 — Introduction

Valuable legal and equitable property rights exist that are less than estates. These are called incorporeal hereditaments or servitudes — inheritable non-possessory rights relating to land possessed by another. For example, X may have an easement to cross Y's property to reach a nearby river. Y has a fee simple and is in possession of the land while X enjoys a defined non-possessory right in the same land providing lawful access for the stated purpose.

Common law rights in land held by another include easements, rent charges, and profits à prendre. Equity also recognizes additional interests in land that have no parallel or equivalent at common law, including restrictive covenants, equitable mortgages, and agreements of purchase and sale. Each are addressed in turn.

## 15.1 — Easements

An easement attaches to property to permit the utilization of land possessed by another. It may be either positive in the sense of granting the right to enter onto the land for a particular purpose (although it cannot include the right to take anything off the real property) or negative in the sense of limiting the use of land by the estate holder.

### (a) — Requirements

The common law requires four elements for a valid easement — a dominant and servient tenement, an accommodation of the dominant tenement, that the tenements be held by separate holders, and the subject matter of the easement must be acceptable (*Ellenborough Park, Re* (1955), [1956] Ch. 153 (Eng. C.A.)).

- *Dominant and Servient Tenement* — An easement requires a dominant tenement (land that is accommodated, serviced, or supported), and a servient tenement (land over which the right is exercised). The focus is on the property rather than the present benefit to any individual. In the United States, an easement can be in gross, i.e., without a dominant tenement, but such is not the case in England or Canada, unless specifically provided by statute (e.g., *Land Titles Act*, R.S.O. 1990, c. L-5, s.39).

- *Accommodation of the Dominant Tenement* — A connection must exist between the dominant and servient tenements such that the dominant tenement receives a practical benefit. Although the properties need not be adjacent, a sufficient nexus must exist to enhance the normal use and enjoyment of the dominant property regardless of who holds the dominant tenement (*Dukart v. Surrey (District)*, [1978] 2 S.C.R. 1039 (S.C.C.)).

- *Separate Tenement Holders* — The dominant and servient tenements must be held by different parties. At common law, a fee simple holder cannot hold an easement over her own property because she already has the full bundle of rights in relation to the land. Should the holder of a dominant tenement acquire the servient tenement, the easement disappears under a common law rule known as the doctrine of merger. Some land conveyancing legislation provides that merger does not take place and a fee simple holder may register an easement against her own property (e.g., *Land Titles Act*, R.S.A. 2000, c. L-4, s. 68).

- *Capable of Being the Subject Matter of an Easement* — This requirement is defined in *Shelf Holdings Ltd. v. Husky Oil Operations Ltd.*,

[1989] 3 W.W.R. 692 (Alta. CA.); leave to appeal refused [1989] 4 W.W.R. lxxi (note) (S.C.C.):

- The grant cannot confer a right inconsistent with the proprietorship or possession of the servient owners;
- The right granted cannot be too wide or vague;
- The right must be more than a mere right of recreation without utility or benefit to the dominant tenement;
- The easement cannot place a positive obligation on the servient tenement (*Nordon v. Faridi*, [1996] 5 W.W.R. 242) (B.C. C.A.); and
- The subject of the easement must be acceptable to the courts. Among others, easements for light, passage (right of way), solar access, and beach use (*Dukart v. Surrey*) have been recognized at common law. Although the class of easements is not closed (*Clos Farming Estates v. Easton*, [2002] NSWCA 389), courts have resisted new forms of easements on the grounds that "to allow a multiplication of the species of legal right would render the law uncertain to the great harm of the public welfare" (*Keppell v. Bailey* (1834), 39 E.R. 1042 (U.K. Ch.)).

An easement runs with the land. Once established, an easement becomes an interest in land. It runs with the property and is enforceable by subsequent holders of the dominant tenement against subsequent holders of the servient tenement, subject to conditions imposed by the relevant land conveyancing systems.

### (b) — Creation of an Easement

An easement can be created by one of four methods: expressly (by grant or reservation), by implication, by statute, or by prescription.

- *Express* — An express easement requires the owner of the servient tenement to execute an instrument that outlines the nature and extent of the right granted in favour of the named dominant tenement. The courts will also recognize an easement when the owner of the dominant tenement reserves an interest in a servient tenement at the time she conveys the servient property. Express easements may be registered as interests under the Torrens systems on the certificates of title of both the dominant and servient tenements (e.g., *Land Titles Act*, R.S.A., 2000, c. L-4, s. 67).
- *Implied* — A landholder may claim an easement by implication. When the holder of two tenements conveys a dominant or servient tenement,

the grant of an easement will be implied in relation to any necessary or continuous easements exercised on the servient tenement. The maxim is that one cannot derogate from her own grant (*Wheeldon v. Burrows* (1879), 12 Ch. D. 31 (Eng. C.A.)). If access to the now dominant tenement requires passage over the servient, the grantor of the now dominant tenement cannot refuse to give access over the now servient tenement to her purchaser. If the land holder retains the dominant tenement without reserving an easement over the servient tenement, the courts will be less sympathetic and will, as a rule of construction, support an implied easement only where the common intention of the parties demands such an implication, or where the easement is by necessity (*Babine Investments Ltd. v. Prince George Shopping Centre Ltd.*, 2002 BCCA 289 (B.C. C.A.); additional reasons at (2002), 2002 CarswellBC 2217 (B.C. C.A.)). Necessity is present if the property could not otherwise be enjoyed without implying such an easement (e.g., a right of way is necessary over the servient tenement to access a public highway).

- *Statutory* — Various federal and provincial statutes provide for the acquisition of easements by public or private authorities. These easements do not meet the requirements of common law easements but rather those of specific statutes. They often exist and bind landholders by operation of law without appearing on a certificate of title or on the land registry ledgers. Respective statutes in each jurisdiction must be consulted to ascertain the number and reach of such easements.
- *Prescriptive* — Prescription is a right to an easement or servitude over another's land gained by long use. The Latin maxim *nec vi, nec clam, nec precari* requires that the use of the land contrary to the initial title holder must have been without violence, without secrecy, and without permission (*Mason v. Partridge*, 2005 NSCA 144 (N.S. C.A.)). The subservient land owner must be aware of the use, but must not have acquiesced. Knowledge of the use without active attempts to stop the use may constitute acquiescence, but is not generally interpreted as permission sufficient to defeat a prescriptive claim. The use must also be uninterrupted for the period of time required by the common law or specified in the legislation of the relevant jurisdiction. If the fee simple holder actively stops the use, the time period required for uninterrupted use begins anew.

  Historically, the common law required a prescriptive right claimant to show continuous use since time immemorial (set at 1189). The difficulty of such proof led English judges to develop an easier way to claim prescriptive rights — the fiction of a lost modern grant. If a user was able to establish peaceful, open, uninterrupted use for a period of twenty years, courts would deem that there must have been a grant giving express permission to undertake the particular practice, but that the grant had been lost.

In Canada, most provinces have specific statutory provisions dealing with prescription. The majority of Torrens jurisdictions prohibit property interests gained by prescription (e.g., *Land Titles Act, 2000*, S.S., 2000, c. L-5.1, s. 150). In provinces with both Torrens and deed registry systems (Chapter 16), prescription is usually abolished with respect to land once brought under the Torrens system. For land held under deed registry systems, it is important to check prescriptive rights on a province-by-province basis.

### (c) — Licence

A licence is not an interest in land, but rather is a personal right granted to particular persons for a particular time with respect to real property. A licence is permission to do that which would otherwise be a trespass. There is no requirement for a dominant and servient tenement. A licence is revocable and does not pass to subsequent holders of the land. There are fewer formal requirements to establish a licence as compared to an easement, and greater flexibility in the scope of the right that may be granted (*Gypsum Carrier Inc. v. R.* (1977), [1978] 1 F.C. 147 (Fed. T.D.)).

## 15.2 — Profits à Prendre

A profit à prendre is the right to enter onto the land of another to take some product of the land or profit from the soil. Profits include plants, minerals, timber, wild animals, fish, oil, and gas, or even the soil itself. The holder of a profit à prendre does not own the subject of the profit *in situ* (in the ground). Rather he has a right to sever or capture the named resource in accordance with the grant, and thereby acquire ownership of it (*British Columbia v. Tener* (1985), 17 D.L.R. (4th) 1 (S.C.C.)). Until severance, the holder of the profit holds a mere right to exploit. The grant may be in several — subject to the grantee's exclusive enjoyment (e.g., mineral rights are often held in several), or in common — others, often including the owner of the fee simple, share the right (e.g., animal grazing rights are often held in common).

Profits à prendre may be held in gross; there need not be a dominant and servient tenement. Profits à prendre may exist independently of other estates or interests. They may run with the land, either at common law or for a time specified in the grant. Profits can be created expressly by either grant or reservation, and in some provinces by statute or by prescription. Special attention should be paid to resource management legislation and the case law in each province (*Bank of Montreal v. Dynex Petroleum Ltd.*, 2002 SCC 7 (S.C.C.)).

## 15.3 — Rent Charges

A rent charge is a periodic payment in relation to land where the recipient holds no reversionary interest in the land. There is no relationship of landlord and tenant between the parties. A legal rent charge, created by deed, will, or statute is an incorporeal hereditament. A rent charge runs with the land and thus binds subsequent land owners. It is also possible to create an equitable rent charge.

## 15.4 — Restrictive Covenants

Restrictive covenants arose in the Courts of Equity. A restrictive covenant is an agreement restricting the use of real property that benefits one party (the covenantee) and burdens the other (the covenantor). The promise can be positive, requiring the holder of the burdened property to do something (e.g., promise to maintain a fence that separates the two properties), or negative — to refrain from a particular activity on the property (e.g., not to use the property for commercial purposes). As with an easement, there must be a dominant and servient tenement, and although the properties need not be contiguous, there must be a nexus between the benefit to the dominant tenement and the burden upon the servient. There can be no restrictive covenants in gross, unless by statute.

A covenant is not a grant of an interest in land nor does a covenant permit physical access to the servient tenement. It is a promise given respecting the use of land that may or may not run with the land. The wider scope of restrictive covenants permits a broader range of controls over a neighbour's land use than would be possible with an easement. However, this does not imply carte blanche; some restrictive covenants have been struck down as contrary to public policy such as those that incorporate NIMBY (Not In My Backyard).

A, the owner of a cottage property, negotiates a restrictive covenant with her neighbour B, who owns the adjacent property. In return for a lump sum payment, B agrees in writing that he will not use his property as "an inn, bed and breakfast, hotel or other accommodation for the travelling public or transient paying guests". A believes this will ensure her privacy and the quiet use and enjoyment of her property. As between A and B, the restrictive covenant is enforceable. The question is whether successors in title can enforce the covenant. The answer is sometimes. The maxim is that benefits run at law while burdens run in equity.

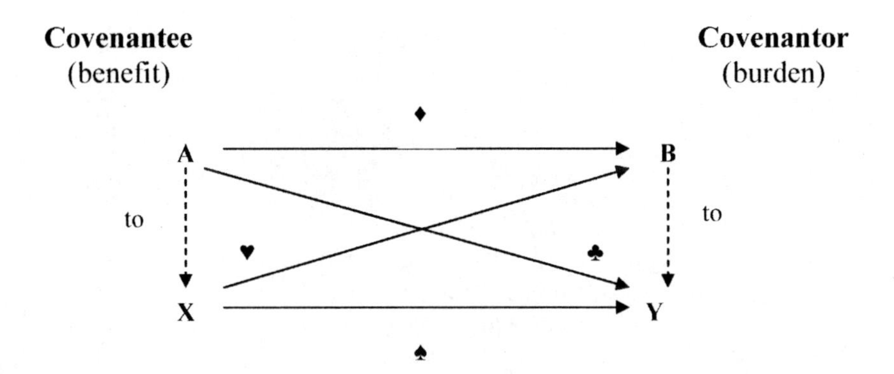


♦*Covenantee/Covenantor* — Should B open a bed and breakfast in his home, A may enforce the convenant against him by way of an action for breach of contract. She may request specific performance in Equity.

♥*Successor Covenantee/Original Covenantor* — Assume that A sells her property to X. X also wishes the protection of the covenant. X may enforce the covenant against B if:

- the covenant touches and concerns the land of the covenantee A (i.e., directly affects the value of the land or actual land use);
- the original covenantee A, has a legal estate at the time the agreement is made;
- the assignee X, holds the same legal estate as the covenantee A; and,
- the covenant is clearly intended to automatically run with the land.

This is called the benefit running at law, meaning that it was enforceable in the Courts of Common Law.

♠*Original Covenantee/Successor Covenantor or* ♣ *Successor Covenantee/Successor Covenantor* — Assume that B sells the burdened property to Y. Y decides she would like to convert the century home to a country inn. Prior to the nineteenth century in England, the burden associated with a restrictive covenant would not bind successor covenantors at law unless there was privity of contract or estate, i.e., the successor covenantor Y, was in a contractual or estate relationship with the successor covenantee X. This was the case even if the successor covenantor had notice of the restriction. However, the case of *Tulk. v. Moxhay* (1848), 41 E.R. 1143 (Eng. Ch. Div.) held that the burden could run in equity if four requirements were met. These requirements remain in place today in order to have a restrictive covenant run with the land:

- The covenant is negative i.e., the holder of the servient tenement agrees to not do something as opposed to agreeing to do some positive act. The courts look at the substance of the covenant as well as the form. A negative covenant can be fulfilled by the covenantor doing nothing and should not require any financial expenditure; covenantors do not have to put their hands in their pockets (*Parkinson v. Reid*, [1966] S.C.R. 162 (S.C.C.); *Amberwood Investments Ltd. v. Durham Condominium Corp. No. 123* (2002), 211 D.L.R. (4th) 1 (Ont. C.A.); additional reasons at (2002), 2002 CarswellOnt 1201 (Ont. C.A.)). In the above example, B agreed not to enter the accommodation business — a negative covenant.

- The covenant must touch and concern the land such that not only the covenantee, but also the dominant tenement benefits. Moreover, the intention must be clear that the burden is intended to run with the land. A's intention was to provide for the use and enjoyment of the property as a quiet retreat. Although this benefits her personally, the covenant is tied to the long term value and use of her property by restricting land use on the neighbouring property.

- The properties, both burdened and benefited, must be sufficiently described in the transfer documents to permit the holder of the burdened lands to ascertain the extent and scope of the commitment (*Galbraith v. Madawaska Club Ltd.*, [1961] S.C.R. 639 (S.C.C.)).

- The successor, if a *bona fide* purchaser of the legal estate for value, must have notice of the covenant. This notice may be either actual or constructive (Chapter 16)).

Equity requires the covenantee A, or her successor X, to establish the right to the benefit before it will be enforced against the burdened covenantor, B or Y. In order to do this, the covenantee or her assignee, A or X, must adduce evidence that he/she has retained some land that the covenant was intended to benefit. The assignee must further establish that the covenant was attached to the dominant tenement and passed with the conveyance of the land (annexation), was expressly assigned (assignment), or that the dominant and servient tenements were both included in a building scheme (development scheme). Assuming that A transfers all the real property to X and that the covenant was expressly assigned, X should be able to enforce the covenant against B or Y.

## 15.5 — Mortgages

Under ecclesiastical (canon) law, usury was a sin. Entrepreneurs searched for a way to use land as security for a loan while staying within the law. The solution derived was a process known as live-gage, where the debtor would transfer the land to the creditor by livery of seisin. This required the debtor to go to the property and pledge it as security for the loan. Once the loan was repaid, the land was redelivered to the debtor. This process was both inconvenient and impractical. Lenders were not interested in physical possession of the land, and the debtor often needed to remain in possession to earn the funds to repay the debt. This gave rise to the mort-gage, where the debtor would stay in possession of the land unless he defaulted on payments. Only then would the creditor take possession.

A mortgage is the conveyance of real property as security for a debt. There are two types of mortgages — legal and equitable.

### (a) — Legal Mortgages

In a conventional legal mortgage, the debtor transfers legal title to the mortgagee who is the creditor. As long as the mortgagor made regular repayments, he was entitled to remain in possession of the property. Courts of Common Law held that the title transfer to the mortgagee was subject to a condition requiring a reconveyance of title at the agreed repayment date if all conditions of the contract were met. If a debtor defaulted on payments the creditor took absolute title and could take possession, sell the property, and retain the proceeds.

Courts of Equity took a different approach. If a debtor had not paid all the debt by the date agreed in the contract, but was able to make the last payments within a reasonable time, for example a day or a week later, the Courts of Equity said that in conscience, a debtor should not lose the property. They were prepared to give the mortgagor the right to redeem the property for a reasonable time after the debt was due. This became an equitable right of redemption — an interest in the real property.

The equitable right of redemption did not permit a perpetual delay of repayment. The Courts of Equity recognized the need to, at some point, permit the mortgagee to realize upon his security. Equity ruled that after a reasonable time, the mortgagee could apply to the Court to foreclose (bring to an end) a mortgagor's equitable right of redemption. If the mortgagor did not pay the debt by the foreclosure date specified by the Equity court, the mortgagee could seize the mortgagor's property. This became known as the equitable right of foreclosure.

In Torrens registration systems and Ontario (under the *Land Registration Reform Act*, R.S.O., 1990, c. L-4), mortgages fall within the definition of a charge. Charge in this context is not the same as a rent charge. If a title is charged with a mortgage, it means that the mortgage is registered against the title. The title is not transferred to the mortgagee, but the mortgagor still has a right of redemption, and the mortgagee has a right of foreclosure to gain title to the property. In contrast, a rent charge does not provide the recipient of the charge with any legal estate in the property itself.

All Canadian land conveyancing statutes have extensive mortgage provisions. For example, Saskatchewan has numerous statutory provisions that address the creation, registration, and discharge of a mortgage as well as the rights of mortgagors and mortgagees (*Land Titles Act*, 2000, S.S. 2000, c. L-5.1, ss. 123–160).

### (b) — Equitable Mortgages

In an equitable mortgage, the legal estate is not transferred to the mortgagee, but the mortgagee has the same rights to recover the property as if the title had in fact been transferred. Subject to the specific provisions in each province, an equitable mortgage may arise in several ways:

- *From an equity of redemption* — A mortgagor may give a second mortgage using his equity of redemption as security. Since the mortgagor himself has only an equitable right of redemption, this is the extent of the interest he can encumber. In those provinces where a mortgage is a charge on the title, a second mortgage would be a legal interest entitling the second mortgagee to recover the property by redeeming the debt (realizing the equity of redemption), subject to the rights of the first mortgagee.

- *From an equitable interest* — A mortgagor may mortgage a beneficial interest, such as interest held as beneficiary under a trust. The mortgagee receives an interest in the same beneficial title, and because of *nemo dat*, a mortgagor can pass no greater title than she holds.

- *By deposit of deed* — A mortgagor may deposit title deeds with a mortgagee. In return for funds and a written agreement, the mortgagor delivers the property deed to the mortgagee as security without formal transfer of the title. Although this is not a legal mortgage, Equity will deem to be done that which ought to have been done, and will protect the mortgagee's right to seize the property and order the legal title transferred to the mortgagee if the mortgagor does not pay the debt.

- *By virtue of failed legal mortgage* — If a legal mortgage fails for want of certain formalities, it may nonetheless be enforceable in Equity provided the court can establish that the substance of the transaction supports the finding of an equitable mortgage. For example, an agreement to enter a legal mortgage coupled with an advance of funds may create an equitable mortgage.

## 15.6 — Agreements of Purchase and Sale

The *Statute of Frauds, 1677* ((U.K.), 29 Cha. 2, c. 3), requires that the contract for the sale of real property be in writing and signed by the identified buyer and seller of the land. In addition, the document must include a description of the property, price, closing date, and other essential terms and conditions. Once the agreement is in place, Equity deems to be done that which ought to have been done and considers the purchaser of the property as the holder of equitable title. The seller continues to hold legal title for the buyer until the closing date. Once the agreed price is paid, the legal title to the land is passed to the purchaser. The seller retains possession of the land until legal title passes and can enjoy the rents and profits generated from the property until that date.

Equity deems the vendor to be a constructive trustee, obliging him to maintain the property for the purchaser. However, the doctrine of equitable conversion provides that the buyer assumes the risk of damage to the property until closing. Most standard agreements of purchase and sale contractually reverse this burden, assigning the risk of loss to the vendor until the closing date.

An agreement of purchase and sale is distinct from an agreement for sale. Both arise when the parties (a vendor and purchaser) agree to transfer real property for a set price. Equitable title passes to the purchaser at the time the agreement is signed. However, with an agreement for sale, the vendor also vacates the property and allows the purchaser to take possession. In return, the purchaser makes periodic payments to the vendor at a set rate of interest. Over time, the purchaser acquires an equitable title proportional to the amount of the purchase price paid. Upon complete payment (including interest) by the purchaser, the vendor is obliged to transfer the legal title to the purchaser — a right enforceable by specific performance — should the need arise.

In deed registration systems, both agreements for sale, and agreements of purchase and sale can be protected by registration. In Torrens systems, statutes must be consulted to see whether these agreements are registerable interests or whether they can be filed as caveats.

# CHAPTER 16 — LAND CONVEYANCING SYSTEMS

## 16.0 — Introduction

The English common law system of land conveyancing was imported into Canada. Statutes have built upon that foundation leading to two major conveyancing systems — deed registration and title registration. Deed registration applies in the four Atlantic provinces, Ontario, and parts of Manitoba. Title registration, otherwise known as the Torrens system, applies in Alberta, Saskatchewan, British Columbia and parts of Manitoba. In Ontario and those parts of Manitoba where deed registration is the background system, legislation has been introduced to enable conversion to title registration.

## 16.1 — Common Law

The common law system of land conveyancing was largely reflective of the underlying principles of the doctrine of tenures and estates. Land conveyancing was open and public with livery of seisin to inform feudal lords and tenants to whom, and from whom, services were due. As interests in land came to be transferable by written instrument (e.g., leases, uses, wills), it became necessary for the transferee at each land transaction to assure himself that he was receiving the full interest claimed. Was one taking a fee simple subject to any other interests? Was there a pre-existing leasehold, mortgage, easement, or an equitable interest?

Despite the increasing complexity of land interests, the common law system continued to promote private responsibility for conveyancing. Establishing the legitimacy of someone's claim required a search of the documents to establish a chain of title, back through each predecessor to (hopefully) the Crown grant. Vendors were required to offer documents supporting title, while purchasers had the burden of assessing the quality of those documents in relation to the title.

The role of the state was limited to arbitrating disputes over title as they arose in the courts. Land could be conveyed or otherwise fettered on numerous occasions over extended periods of time without involvement of the state. There was no state-regulated system of conveyancing. The result was that a transferee was responsible to seek out not only documents in the transferor's actual possession, but also those in the possession of other solicitors, churches, and governments. The system was expensive, complex, and uncertain. Eventually, statutes imposed forty or sixty years as the rule to establish a good root of title.

Although all provinces in Canada have developed conveyancing statutes overriding the common law, rules that developed as courts arbitrated title disputes under the common law system are still relevant today as background rules of interpretation. If a conveyancing statute does not specifically override the common law rules of priority in a particular situation, those rules still apply. Thus it is necessary to be aware of the rules developed at common law for priority among interests, particularly unregistered interests.

In analyzing two or more competing interests within a common law conveyancing regime, three questions are asked to determine priority:

- Is each interest legal or equitable?
- Does notice or lack of notice change the priority in any way?
- Are there other relevant considerations that would impact on the priorities?

Rules developed to reflect the priority of competing claims.

### (a) — Pre-Existing Legal Interests

- *Followed by a Legal Interest* — As between two competing legal interests, the rule is first in time, first in right. The legal interest is enforceable, whether or not the subsequent legal interest holder has notice of the existing right. Even in those circumstances where every effort is made to learn of such rights and the error arises through no fault of the subsequent legal interest holder, the earlier legal right prevails. If a vendor sold a legal title that was invalid because of a pre-existing title, the purchaser would lose his title to the pre-existing legal title holder, even if neither the vendor nor the purchaser knew of the defect in the vendor's title.
- *Followed by an Equitable Interest* — A legal interest has priority over a equitable interest in all but the rare circumstances where the holder of the legal interest is by his conduct estopped from claiming his interest.

### (b) — Pre-Existing Equitable Interests

- *Followed by an Equitable Interest* — As between two competing equitable interests, the general rule of first in time, first in right is repeated but qualified. All other equities being equal, first in time, first in right. The issue becomes, in what circumstances are the equities unequal? Guided by the principle of equity that he who seeks equity must come with clean hands, the court will consider the conduct of the parties and all the circumstances to determine the better equity (*Rice v. Rice* (1854), 61 E.R. 646 (Eng. Ch. Div.)).

- *Followed by a Legal Interest* — Historically, equitable interests were not protected by the Courts of Common Law. This meant that the holder of an equitable interest in land could initiate an action in contract against the party who conveyed the legal estate without honouring his equitable interest, but he had no way to recover the property itself because the Courts of Common Law recognized only the legal title holder.

  Slowly the Courts of Equity extended the number of persons against whom they would enforce equitable property rights on the grounds that conscience required imposing the equitable interest upon subsequent legal interest holders. For example, in 1465, the purchaser of a legal estate who had notice of an existing equitable interest was bound by that interest (Y.B. 5 Edw. 4, Mich. pl.16). In 1522, successors of a trustee were bound by the beneficial interest pursuant to that trust, even if the trust was unknown at the time of transfer (Y.B. 14 Hen. 8, Mich. pl.5, fo.7). In 1595, those in receipt of a legal interest by way of gift were bound (*Chudleigh's Case* (1595), 76 E.R. 260 (K.B.)).

  In 1761, the rule was expressed in a form that still applies today: the holder of an equitable interest can enforce that interest against all who obtain a subsequent legal interest with the exception of a *bona fide* purchaser for value of a legal estate who is without notice of the equitable interest (*Stanhope v. Earl of Verney* (1761), 2 Eden 81 (Ch.)). This principle is known as the polar star of equity.

  Considerable case law has developed to clarify each element of the polar star rule. The purchaser for value includes someone who pays with money or non-monetary consideration (money's worth). *Bona fide* necessitates good faith and the absence of any evidence of sharp practice. The most extensive judicial discussion has surrounded the term "without notice". Case law recognizes three categories of notice that may be ascribed to the purchaser claiming the protection of the polar star of equity.

  - *Actual Notice* — A purchaser of a legal interest has actual notice if the legal right (though not necessarily the instrument containing the right) is brought home to him. This is established by either his own admission, or evidence from witnesses to establish that he was made aware of the legal right. Information that would, if pursued, lead to discovery of that legal right is not sufficient to constitute actual notice, although this may constitute constructive notice (*Mayer v. Brüning*, 2001 NSSC 35 (N.S. S.C.); *cf. Canadian Imperial Bank of Commerce v. Rockway Holdings Ltd.* (1998), 108 O.A.C. 231 (Ont. C.A.); affirming (1996), 29 O.R. 350 (Ont. Gen.

Div.)). The facts need not be formally brought to the attention of the purchaser, but rather he can have learned them in casual conversation.

- *Constructive Notice* — This is notice attributed to a purchaser based on what a reasonable or prudent individual would discover in the course of investigating title. Should the purchaser choose not to make reasonable inquiries as to the state of the vendor's title, the courts will assume such knowledge as would have come to the purchaser's actual notice had she been duly diligent. In order to satisfy the requirement of reasonable investigation, the purchaser would inspect the appropriate documentation relating to land and assess the chain of title. She would also inspect the real property itself to gain knowledge of possible interests from evidence of, for example, physical occupation or the physical evidence of the exercise of a profit à prendre. If a purchaser learned information sufficient to raise her suspicions by making inquiries, the standard of reasonableness would require that she investigate fully (*Jared v. Clements*, [1901] L.J. 137; *Ramlal v. Chaital*, [2004] 1 P. & C.R. (P.C.)). The test of what constitutes reasonable enquiries has at times been subjective (*Corkum v. Dagley*, 2007 NSCA 9 (N.S. C.A.)).
- *Implied Notice* — also known as imputed notice — ascribes information to the purchaser that has come to the attention of an agent, such as a solicitor, acting on her behalf. Implied notice can be based upon the actual or constructive knowledge of the agent. In short, the action or omissions of the agent are imputed to the purchaser.

### (c) — Deficiencies of Common Law Conveyancing

Even if an individual could satisfy herself of her position relative to competing interests in the particular real property, several problems remained with common law conveyancing. First, conveyancing was not only complex but also inefficient. Assuming a search was successfully completed prior to the establishment of one interest in land, the entire process would have to be repeated before completing the conveyance.

Second, there was an unavoidable lack of certainty in the process. In spite of the best efforts of a prudent purchaser who could claim sufficient expertise to undertake the task, she could never be sure that there was not a preceding interest that she had missed, or in the case of a competing equitable interest, that a subsequent interest might not usurp her own priority.

Third, a purchaser of an interest in land, who was held to a fairly high standard of diligence in searching the title, still had to rely largely on the vendor as the source of information on the state of the title. This vendor was the individual most likely to withhold prejudicial information.

Fourth, the purchaser was required to somehow determine not only the overall validity of the chain, but also the legal validity of every document relevant to the title. Challenging a document resulted in a challenge to the chain of title. Issues included capacity of the parties, incorrect description of the interest, mistake, and forgery.

Searching and verifying title became a profitable undertaking for many solicitors who acted as agents of the purchaser and warranted clear title. Solicitors guaranteed that they had done everything a reasonable agent would do in the circumstances, and if any competing interests came to light subsequent to the completion of the purchase, the purchaser could legitimately claim to be without notice and maintain her priority. The agent warranted that there would be no claim of constructive notice ascribed to the agent and imputed to the purchaser, and further guaranteed the legal value of each of the documents in the chain of title. These assurances gave the purchaser a contractual right to recover from the title searcher for damages if the searcher had failed to properly assess the state of the title. For this service, the purchaser paid a considerable fee.

Despite the deficiencies, the common law system was sufficiently entrenched to make any attempt at introducing alternative systems of land conveyancing difficult. Although there was an initial attempt in England in the sixteenth century (*Statute of Enrolments*, 1535 (U.K.), 27 Hen. VIII, c. 16), it was two hundred years before an alternative regime was introduced and successfully implemented.

## 16.2 — Deed Registration

Inspired by the New England registry, Nova Scotia adopted deed registration in 1752. The regime quickly spread, gathering momentum with the arrival of the United Empire Loyalists after the American Revolution. The objectives of deed registration are to remedy the deficiencies of common law conveyancing, specifically, to simplify title searches, to facilitate and expedite real property conveyancing, and to provide a greater degree of certainty of title.

The role of the state remains largely passive, although the system provides local, centralized facilities for registration and storage of documents affecting title to real property. These registry offices have a legislated mandate to record and catalogue transactions so that interest holders may investigate the current state of the title and trace the chain to ensure its adequacy. Deed registration statutes facilitate certainty of title by setting out a specific number of years beyond which it is not necessary to trace the chain to prove a good root. The length of time varies from province to province (*Registry Act*, R.S.O. 1990, c. R. 20, s. 112).

Research through a central location makes the deed registration system more efficient and less time consuming than its common law predecessor. However, the potential purchaser must still look beyond the registry office for interests that may affect title by operation of law, for example, property tax. Deed registration searches are less cumbersome and arguably more reliable than the common law dependence upon the vendor; nonetheless, searches are still only as good as the searcher, and documents may be missed.

The state provides a depository for documents and makes them available for inspection by interested parties. It does not guarantee the documents' legal value. As a result, such defects as forgery, incapacity of the parties, and incorrect description of the property are left to the purchaser's judgment. Private companies offer title insurance, whereby the purchaser may pay a premium for a guarantee of compensation in the event of an undiscovered defect.

Deed registration statutes qualify common law rules of priority. Statutes include the rule, first registered in time, first in right, but modify the rule depending upon three factors:

- order of registration,
- timing of notice, and
- standard of notice.

### (a) — Order of Registration

The simplest system is based on the running shoe rule, under which registration of either a legal or an equitable interest constitutes actual notice. Any notice outside the register is irrelevant. Assuming for the moment that an instrument is executed first in time, priority can be preserved by registering the document first. It is incumbent upon a potential interest holder to examine the register immediately prior to closing the deal to ensure that no interests have been registered since her initial search. Such mini-searches are often undertaken literally minutes before the transfer of an interest. Once the documents are properly executed, it is in the best interests of the new interest holder to register as quickly as possible to establish her priority.

The running shoe rule permits the possibility of leaping priorities. Even if an interest (legal or beneficial) would not have priority at common law, if it is registered first, it may gain priority and leap over unregistered interests executed earlier in time. Strictly applied, this occurs even in those situations where the subsequent interest holder is aware of an unregistered interest. Only registration constitutes notice and establishes priority.

### (b) — Timing of Notice

In some jurisdictions, the question of when notice of the unregistered interest was given is relevant in determining priorities. This modification of the running shoe rule addresses the question of when the notice of the unregistered interest arises.

If a subsequent interest holder has no actual notice nor imputed actual notice of an unregistered interest, completes the transaction, registers her interest, and then learns of the unregistered interest that was executed but unregistered earlier in time, her registered interest will prevail provided she is otherwise *bona fide* and for value.

If notice is provided prior to execution and registration, then the unregistered transaction that was executed earlier in time will prevail. Depending on the governing statute, the earlier executed transaction may also prevail in those circumstances where the notice is provided after execution, but before registration of the second interest (e.g., *Registry Act*, R.S.O. 1990, c. R. 20, s. 71).

### (c) — Standard of Notice

The third variable that affects priority of interest is the standard of notice. Deed registration statutes may qualify the running shoe rule to provide that first registered in time, first in right applies only if the registrant of the new interest is *bona fide*, for value, and without notice of the unregistered interest. Notice includes not only the notice provided by the registration, but also notice of an unregistered interest in the common law sense. The particular statute will specify whether the standard of notice required is actual, constructive, or imputed.

For example, should an individual (or her agent) searching a title, fortuitously learn of an existing unregistered interest (say, in conversation with a fellow title searcher in the registry office), she may be bound to recognize the priority of that interest. A situation where the holder of a pre-existing interest might claim that the holder of the subsequent interest had constructive notice is more difficult to imagine. Under a deed registration system, a reasonable and prudent purchaser would be expected to make inquiries at the registry office and other locations to learn of interests that exist by operation of law, but a search in the common law sense, including the inspection of property, would no longer be expected. Any registry office inquiry would provide notice of registered interests and would meet the common law standard for constructive notice expected of the subsequent interest holder, though she still must check for taxes and other interests recorded elsewhere. Since a purchaser is deemed to have notice of the register whether she chooses to examine it or not, it is a situation of constructive notice.

### (d) — Deficiencies of Deed Registration Systems

Deed registration thus facilitates the searching and proving of title, sets parameters for the time beyond which one need not trace title, and by statutorily altering common law priorities provides a greater degree of certainty of title to interest holders. Problems remain related to the legal value of the relevant documents, the level of expertise required for a search, and costs associated with searching, evaluating, and completing a land transaction. Errors, though infrequent, are still possible. Although there is greater security than at common law for a registered interest holder, there remain problems associated with the adequacy of a private search, and depending on the particular permutation of the running shoe rule, there are possible complications arising from notice of unregistered interests.

## 16.3 — Title Registration and the Doctrine of Indefeasibility

Title registration was developed by Robert Torrens, a collector of customs in South Australia during the mid-nineteenth century. He believed that a system of land conveyancing could be modeled on shipping legislation which permitted the conveyancing of personal property by registration in a publicly-administered record. In 1858, the first title registration system was legislated in South Australia, with Torrens himself as the first Master of Titles. The Canadian Parliament adopted the system for the Northwest Territories in 1868, believing such a system would expedite western settlement as an efficient and straightforward method of conveying title to real property that had not yet been granted by the Crown.

The statutes provide for unpatented land (unregistered land such as Crown land) to be brought into the system and a certificate of title issued (*The Land Titles Act*, R.S.S. 2000, c. L-51, ss. 75-76; *Land Titles Act*, R.S.A. 2000, c. L-4, s. 36). The Crown grant and the certificate of title are stored at a land titles office. Other than certain statutory exceptions, from that time forward interests related to the land must be registered on the certificate to be effective. When the property is transferred from the original grantee, the previous certificate of title is cancelled and a new certificate of title is issued in the name of the transferee. Interests that continue appear on the transferee's new certificate.

Land titles registration is not a complete code in that it does not affect inter-party dealings relating to unpatented land, nor does it affect unregistered interests in registered lands. Interests that are outside the system are governed by common law rules unless another statute addresses those interests, such as natural resources management schemes. For example, in Saskatchewan, Crown land situated in the Northern half of the province not yet brought into the Torrens registration system would be subject to common law rules of priority unless overridden by particular natural resource statutes.

The Torrens system of title registration simplifies and expedites land conveyancing and provides certainty of title through a state-operated system. It is based on three principles: the mirror principle, the curtain principle, and the insurance principle.

### (a) — Mirror Principle

As with deed registration, the state provides a central location where documents relevant to title are stored and recorded. A certificate of title is issued, and interests that burden that title are noted on the certificate as an accurate reflection of interests claimed in relation to the real property. The state guarantees the certificate of title in terms of the description of the estate and the title holder. Torrens system statutes provide that only those interests endorsed on the certificate of title, or otherwise specifically provided for in legislation, bind subsequent interest holders. Moreover, until it is registered, any transaction relating to the real properly does not create an interest in the land enforceable against a third party transferee, whether or not he is aware of the unregistered interest. It is unnecessary to look beyond the information presented on a certificate of title to learn the property description and holder with certainty. As to interests that might burden that title, it is necessary to look at the statutes, as well as the details of the interests on the back of the certificate of title.

As between competing registered interests, the priority of interest is according to the time of registration rather than date of execution of the instrument, and there is no need to search prior to the issuance of the existing certificate.

### (b) — Curtain Principle

With the issuance of a certificate of title comes a state guarantee that the holder of that title is the holder of the estate named in the certificate, and that those investigating title need look no further than interests registered thereon or those implied by statute. A metaphoric curtain or wall shields subsequent interest holders from interests that may have existed prior to the date of issuance of the certificate of title.

### (c) — Insurance Principle

Should a mistake occur in the certificate of title, the state provides compensation from a fund known as the assurance fund.

### (d) — Doctrine of Indefeasibility

When taken together, the mirror principle, the curtain principle, and the insurance principle constitute the underlying doctrine of indefeasibility of title. An indefeasible title is one in which should a defect in title appear, the indefeasible title holder will retain the land and the party whose interest was defeated will only receive damages.

Once a title is registered, any *bona fide* purchaser of land for value who acquires that property from a registered owner will hold indefeasible title notwithstanding that third parties might have invalidated the transferor's title (*Turta v. Canadian Pacific Railway*, [1954] S.C.R. 427 (S.C.C.)).

In relying on the register, the purchaser is not affected by actual, implied or constructive notice of unregistered interests and is protected against ejectment. To claim the benefits of an indefeasible title, a certificate holder must be a purchaser for valuable consideration. The purchaser need not examine the previous certificate of title in order to claim to have relied on the faith of the register or to have acted in reliance upon the title. A purchaser is deemed to have actual notice of the contents of the certificate of title.

If an error is discovered in a certificate of title, the Registrar is empowered to correct such errors as long as rights conferred for value are not prejudiced. The Registrar may correct mistakes in two situations: if there is an error in the certificate such that it is not reflective of the instrument of transfer between the two parties; or if a transferee has not paid value for the interest. In neither case would rights acquired for value be prejudiced by the change. In the first, the certificate is simply corrected to reflect the understanding of the parties to the transaction. In the second, no value was given for the interest.

The doctrine of indefeasibility is subject to certain exceptions.

## 16.4 — Exceptions to Indefeasibility

The exceptions to indefeasibility include: statutorily implied exceptions, prior certificate of title, misdescription, adverse possession, and fraud. Each of these requires examination.

### (a) — Statutorily-Implied Interests

Within Torrens legislation, stated exceptions to the mirror principle bind subsequent purchasers even though they are not individually noted on the certificate of title. Often these exceptions are incorporated into one section of the legislation and appear as a list. Among the more common exceptions are short term residential leases, utility, highway and other public easements, unpaid taxes, statutory rights of expropriation, and decrees, orders, or executions against or affecting the interest of the landowner. Other exceptions are specific to the jurisdiction. Many of the interests are included for practical reasons. For example, it would be difficult to expect all short term leases to be registered on title. It is also impractical for utility companies to register statutory easements provided in legislation on all individual titles that lie in their path.

### (b) — Prior Certificate of Title

It is possible to defeat a certificate of title with a prior certificate of title. A prior certificate is not a certificate issued at an earlier point in time, then cancelled, but rather is a certificate in contemporaneous existence with another for the same piece of land (*Turta v. Canadian Pacific Railway*, [1954] S.C.R. 427 (S.C.C.)). In order for two such certificates to exist, there must have been an error at the Land Titles Office. Even though the holder of the later certificate is a *bona fide* purchaser for value, he loses to the prior certificate holder. Although this is an exception to indefeasibility, the plea of prior certificate is sufficiently rare that it does not undermine the fundamental certainty of the system. Further, the assurance fund is available to compensate the holder of the later certificate.

### (c) — Misdescription

Misdescription occurs when a certificate of title describes boundaries or parcels that properly fall within the certificate of other land. Two competing land holders contest which piece of land has a misdescription in its certificate. Once there is an adjudication of the respective rights, the correction of the title may, to the extent necessary to rectify the misdescription, deprive a *bona fide* purchaser for value of her interest.

### (d) — Adverse Possession

Adverse possession is an acquisition of title to land based on longstanding occupation (informally called squatter's rights). The effect of adverse possession on title varies across Canadian Torrens jurisdictions. Although some provinces have abolished adverse possession, others accommodated it to varying degrees. For example, in Manitoba the title of an individual in actual occupation claiming rights by virtue of adverse possession is preserved in land being brought into the Act. Once the land is within the Act, no such rights may be acquired (*Real Property Act*, R.S.M. 1988, c. R-30, s. 58(1)(i)).

### (e) — Fraud

Torrens systems continue to struggle with the relationship between fraud and indefeasibility. The dilemma is that it is not possible to give the land both to the original registered owner who has no role in the fraud, and to the *bona fide* purchaser or third party interest holder for value without notice who has taken from a fraudster. Legislatures have struggled with the wording of fraud provisions to draw the line between protected and unprotected parties in a way that allows the system to function fairly and effectively. Wherever that line is drawn, only one party can hold the land. The other innocent party must accept damages from the legislated safety net of the assurance fund.

In some provinces, the legislation states that knowledge of another's unregistered interest alone is not fraud, (*Land Titles Act*, R.S.A. 2000, c. L-4, s. 203(3); *The Land Titles Act*, R.S.S. 2000, c. L-51, ss. 23(2)) but the legislation does not define what constitutes fraud.

## 16.5 — The Challenge of Fraud as an Exception to Indefeasibility

The courts have struggled to interpret the legislative provisions relating to fraud within real world fact situations. Allegations of fraud may be assessed on three criteria to determine defeasibility:

- *Fraud and the volunteer* — Has value been given?
- *Fraud by the registrant or a participating or colluding party* — Are the parties *bona fide*?
- *Fraud and the subsequent* bona fide *registrant* — If the parties are *bona fide* have given value, does immediate or deferred indefeasibility apply?

### (a) — Fraud and the Volunteer

A registered *bona fide* interest holder may find that her interest is defeasible if she did not acquire it for value and the grantor has been fraudulent. For example, if a property interest is inherited from an individual who acquired title by fraud, the subsequent title will be defeasible. Courts have interpreted value to include not only money but also non-monetary consideration (money's worth). Although full market value is not necessarily required, the courts may closely examine payments that are substantially below the actual value of the property. Impeachment of the interest of a volunteer also applies if the transaction is gratuitous, such as a gift or inheritance.

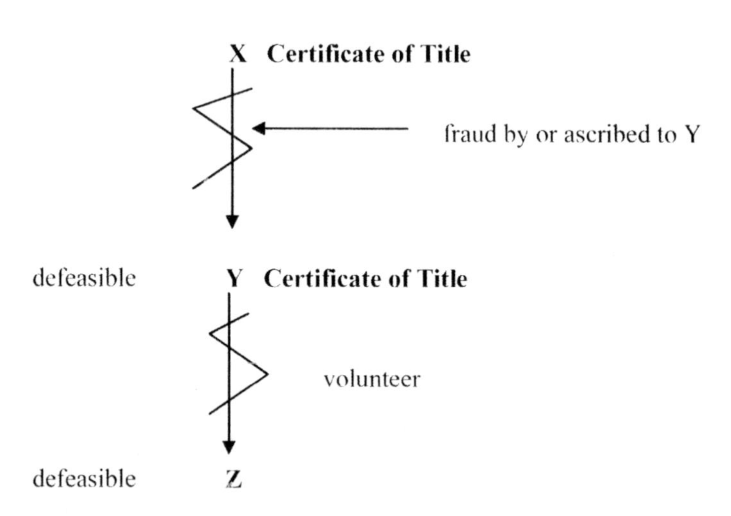


## (b) — Fraud by the Registrant or a Participating or Colluding Party

Fraud by the registrant or another party who has participated or colluded in fraud, including a subsequent registrant with knowledge of, or acquiescence to, an existing fraud can destroy *bona fide* and therefore defeat title. Dishonest actions by the registrant such as deceit or misrepresentation do not receive the protection of indefeasibility. Any dishonest or deliberate trick to prevent an individual from registering her interest will constitute fraud. Similarly, exploitation of a known mistake to further a purchaser's own ends constitutes fraud. Courts ascribe fraud not only to a party who directly participates in the action, but also to one who colludes or acquiesces in the fraud.

However, knowledge alone of an unregistered interest is not sufficient to constitute fraud (*The Land Titles Act*, R.S.S. 2000, c. L-51, s. 23(2); *Land Titles Act*, R.S.A. 2000, c. L-4, s. 203(3)). For example, if a purchaser is aware that an unregistered agreement of purchase and sale exists with regard to a property but proceeds with her own purchase of the same property, she has not, without more, committed fraud under the legislation. Fraud arises only when the purchaser is aware of dishonest activity and willfully ignores it or actively participates in it (*Hackworth v. Baker*, [1936] 1 W.W.R. 321 (Sask. Q.B.); leave to appeal refused (1936), 1936 CarswellSask 46 (Sask. C.A.)).

Even where the purchaser has a strong suspicion of a fraud, there may be no legal duty to conduct a full inquiry. While case law from New Zealand has suggested that a purchaser can be tainted with passive fraud (*Assets Co. v. Roihi*, [1905] A.C. 176 (New Zealand P.C.)), the majority in the above Saskatchewan Court of Appeal decision upheld the right of a purchaser to rely on the faith of the register providing that she had no actual knowledge of the fraud nor behaved dishonestly (*Hackworth v. Baker*).

The distinction between these two cases arguably illustrates the boundaries of fraud. In the New Zealand case a forged — and thus void — document was successfully registered. The purchaser had suspicions about this document but took no further steps to confirm those suspicions, leading the Court to ascribe fraud to the purchaser. In contrast, the interest in the Saskatchewan case was unregistered and was defeated not by any trickery on the part of the purchaser, but rather by his reliance on the statutory provision that knowledge of an unregistered interest does not constitute fraud. In the New Zealand case, the purchaser was willfully blind to a possible fraud, whereas in the Saskatchewan case there was no fraud but rather an unregistered interest that a purchaser was legally entitled to ignore. Reliance on the rights afforded by the *Land Titles Act*, even if prejudicial to another's interests, does not constitute fraud.

If an individual commits a fraud and obtains a certificate of title as a result, an obvious question arises concerning the rights of those who follow. If the subsequent registrant has knowledge of, or acquiesced in, the fraud, even if that person is the holder of a new certificate of title, their interest is subject to defeasance. This is because the interest holder lacks the *bona fide* necessary to claim protection of the act. *Bona fide* requires coming to the table with clean hands. Knowledge of (including willful blindness), or acquiescence to, fraud negates clean hands.

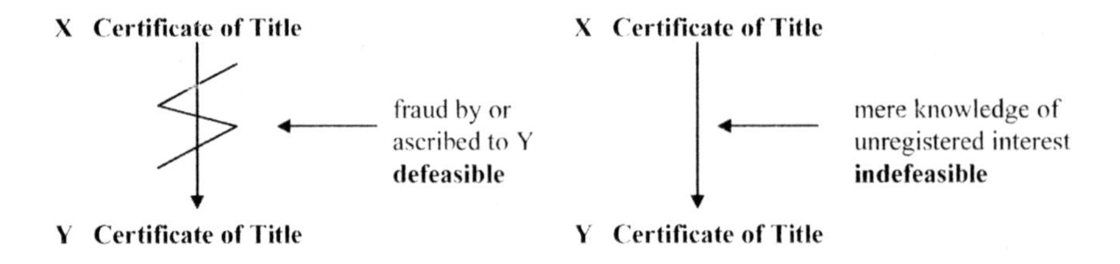


### (c) — Fraud and the Subsequent *Bona Fide* Registrant

Courts continue to struggle as between two theories of the relationship between fraud and a subsequent *bona fide* registrant: immediate and deferred indefeasibility.

Under immediate indefeasibility, a *bona fide* purchaser for value who obtains a certificate of title without knowledge that the certificate of title was obtained by fraud will receive the protection of the land titles legislation. The curtain will fall behind her certificate, thereby giving her an indefeasible title.

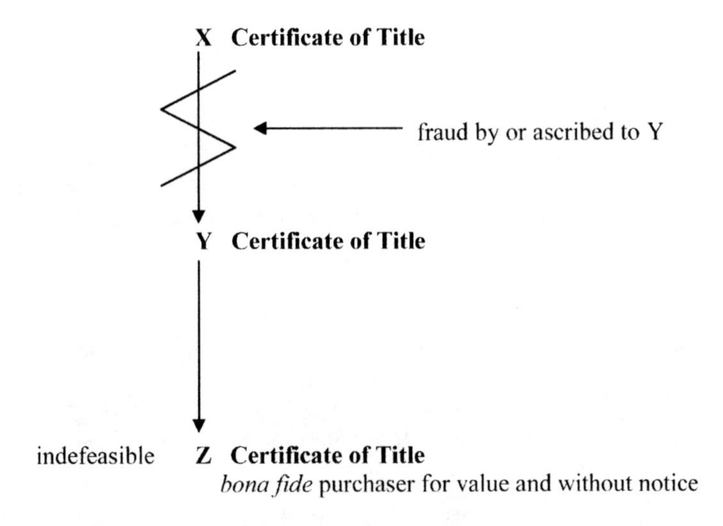


The case of *Hermanson v. Martin* (1986), 33 D.L.R. (4th) 12 (Sask. C.A.); additional reasons at [1987] 4 W.W.R. 94 (Sask. C.A.) addressed this question in a situation where a vendor forged the signature of his wife (who held as joint tenant) in order to sell property to an innocent purchaser. After the issuance of the new certificate of title to the purchaser, the forger's wife learned of the transaction. She alleged that the purchaser's title was defeasible because of fraud. But for the fraud, the purchaser would not have gained title. Nonetheless, the purchaser was innocent of wrongdoing and was able to rely on the legislation for the protection of his new title. The forger's wife could recover only damages from the assurance fund. The title of the *bona fide* purchaser for value and without notice became indefeasible as soon as it was issued.

Under deferred indefeasibility, the *bona fide* purchaser for value who obtains a certificate without knowledge that the previous certificate of title was obtained by fraud does not receive the protection of the land titles legislation, and loses her certificate of title to the original owner. The rationale is that the title is defective, similar to the reasoning of *nemo dat*. Consider the *bona fide* holder of a certificate of title, completely unaware of a fraudster who has successfully transferred title to a subsequent *bona fide* purchaser for value and without notice of the fraud. Under the principle of immediate indefeasibility, through no fault of her own, the original owner would lose the property to that subsequent *bona fide* purchaser who now holds the existing certificate of title and would be forced to vacate the land. Deferred indefeasibility, however, would recognize that the latter title rests upon a fraudulent foundation and would support the claim of the original owner. Although there is a possible remedy through the assurance fund, the property itself is lost to the subsequent *bona fide* purchaser who may have no desire to vacate the land. Under deferred indefeasibility, there must be one clean step before subsequent title is protected.

The issue in cases of immediate versus deferred indefeasibility is whether the curtain falls immediately behind each new certificate of title innocently obtained, or whether the certificate of title from which a new title is derived also has to be innocently obtained. The argument in favour of immediate indefeasibility is that the incidences of fraud remain so few in number, relative to the number of land transactions per year, that adopting deferred indefeasibility is not justified, considering the cost of such an approach in terms of loss of certainty of title. Recent Canadian case law has supported both positions (*CIBC Mortgages Inc. v. Saskatchewan (Registrar of Titles)*, 2005 SKQB 470 (Sask. Q.B.); *c.f. CIBC Mortgages Inc. v. Chan* (2005), (sub nom. *Household Realty Corp. v. Liu)* 205 O.A.C. 141 (Ont. C.A.); *c.f. Rabi v. Rosu* (2006), 277 D.L.R. (4th) 544 (Ont. S.C.J.)), and the debate continues.

## 16.6 — Caveats

Caveats are mechanisms provided in Torrens systems to give notice of a claim of an interest in land without that claim being verified or guaranteed by the land titles system. A person believing she has a claim in land may take a document evidencing that claim to the land titles office. As long as the document supports a potential interest in land, the land titles office will file a caveat against the land in which the interest is claimed. The caveat gives notice to subsequent purchasers that the caveator claims an interest in the land. The land titles system does not vouch for the validity of the claim. To determine the validity of the claim, an interested party may examine the underlying document filed in the land titles office and make his own assessment of its legal merit. If an interested party wishes to dispute the claim, he may ask a court to arbitrate its validity. If a court rules the caveated interest valid, all registrations subsequent to the date of the registration of the caveat take subject to that interest. If a court rules a caveated interest invalid, the caveat is struck from the certificate of title.

Interests protected by the system are "registered" on proper forms specified in the legislation. Caveats, which give notice to subsequent purchasers but do not receive the protection of the system without being first proven in a court, are "lodged" or "filed".

In Saskatchewan, caveats have been removed from the land titles legislation (*The Land Titles Act*, R.S.S. 2000, c. L-51). Rather all claimed interests may be registered and may be challenged when the certificate of title is examined.

# Part IV

# Aboriginal Title

# CHAPTER 17 — ABORIGINAL TITLE AND THE COMMON LAW



## 17.0 — Introduction

Before Europeans came to Canada, the Aboriginal inhabitants had pre-existing systems of land-holding. These systems were conceptually very different from European legal systems. In *First Nations Jurisprudence and Aboriginal Rights* at 130, Professor James Youngblood Henderson describes something of the orientation of these systems in general terms:

> The Creator's covenants make First Nations people responsible for care of the land and resources; every kinship and person has a significant role in caring for the land. These covenants establish the gifted land as sacred and holy, while these responsibilities create a territorial jurisdiction and jurisprudence. Most First Nation Elders express the covenantal relationship to the land as being "on loan" from the Great Spirit, a concept that embodies the responsibilities of steward-

> ship. The Elders maintain both that the land belongs to their people and that the people belong to the land.

Canada has many different Aboriginal nations, and some of the details of traditional land-holding differed from community to community. Volume 1 of the Royal Commission on Aboriginal Peoples, *Looking Forward, Looking Back*, at 47–75, tries to describe some of these differences between several Aboriginal nations' frameworks. This report suggests that amongst the M'kmaq, for example, land was assigned to particular families for planting grounds in the summer, fishing stations in the spring and autumn, and hunting grounds in the winter. Once particular land had been managed by a family for seven generations, it was considered inviolable. Amongst the Blackfoot, by contrast, all land was seen as collectively owned by the community, although there was individual ownership of property other than land and a system for transfer of such individual property. Fully understanding the different systems of land ownership is difficult outside the complex spiritual frameworks of Canada's Aboriginal peoples, but we can at least note that Canada's various Aboriginal peoples had legal circumstances attuned to their own contexts and frameworks.

These details aside, the fundamental point about Aboriginal systems of land-holding is that they remain, in important ways, part of the present-day Canadian legal order. Aboriginal tenure is a property regime that is very different from common law tenure. Though there remain many complex questions about the interaction of different concepts of property, today, along with the common law and civil law, Aboriginal tenure is a recognized legal property regime in Canada. This chapter examines the doctrine of Aboriginal title as recognized by the common law, and the next chapter examines the doctrine of Aboriginal title as recognized by Canada's Constitution.

## 17.1 — The Principle of Continuity

Prior to European contact and the assertion of European sovereignty, Aboriginal nations had legal systems. Very shortly after Canadian Confederation in 1867, Justice Munk of the Quebec Superior Court was called to decide a case that involved the implications of Cree law on the prairies. Justice Munk wrote in *Connolly v. Woolrich* (1867), 17 R.J.R.Q. 75 at 79 (Que. S.C.); aff'd *Johnstone v. Connelly* (1869), 17 R.J.R.Q. 266 (Que. Q.B.) as follows:

> Will it be contended that the territorial rights, political organization such as it was, or the laws and usages of Indian tribes were abrogated — that they ceased to exist when these two European nations began to trade with aboriginal occupants? In my opinion it is beyond

> controversy that they did not — that so far from being abolished, they were left in full force, and were not even modified in the slightest degree.

This doctrine of continuity was far from universally recognized in early Canadian case law, but as scholars like Kent McNeil and John Borrows have shown, the stronger interpretation of the common law both in Canada and elsewhere is that it accepts the continuing force of norms from prior legal systems and recognizes them as rights.

Chief Justice McLachlin refers to this doctrine of continuity in *Mitchell v. Minister of National Revenue*, [2001] 1 S.C.R. 911, 2001 SCC 33 (S.C.C.), at para. 62, as "govern[ing] the absorption of aboriginal laws and customs into the new legal regime upon the assertion of Crown sovereignty over the region". Chief Justice McLachlin cites to Brian Slattery's seminal article, "Understanding Aboriginal Rights" (1987) 66 Can. Bar Rev. 727, where Slattery states at p. 738 that "[w]hen the Crown gained sovereignty over an American territory, colonial law dictated that the local customs of the native peoples would presumptively continue in force and be recognizable in the courts, except insofar as they were unconscionable or incompatible with the Crown's assertion of sovereignty."

In some cases, continuing Aboriginal rights were recognized through treaty relationships, and it is to these contexts that we first turn, before returning to the recognition of Aboriginal title by the common law itself.

## 17.2 — The Royal Proclamation, 1763 and the Treaty of Niagara

In 1763, to address problems that were arising and to protect Aboriginal nations, some of whom had supported the British in the North American components of the Seven Years' War, the King issued an Imperial Order known as the *Royal Proclamation, 1763*, directing his subjects in their relationship with Aboriginal nations.

Aboriginal scholar John Borrows reports that the Royal Proclamation, 1763 reflects terms assented to by Aboriginal nations in the Treaty of Niagara in 1764. Professor Borrows describes two thousand chiefs from Nova Scotia to the Mississippi to Hudson Bay travelling for weeks and months to arrive at a council with the Crown to negotiate a sacred agreement. At Niagara, the Aboriginal nations assented to the Royal Proclamation as they understood it. Based on records of the treaty in wampum belts and based on oral recollections of the treaty, many Aboriginal people have regarded the Proclamation and Treaty of Niagara as guaranteeing their ongoing sovereignty, living together but not merging with the settlers.

The preamble to the Proclamation includes reference to the prevention of frauds and abuses in relation to purchasing "Lands of the Indians":

> And whereas great Frauds and Abuses have been committed in purchasing Lands of the Indians, to the great Prejudice of our Interests, and to the great dissatisfaction of the said Indians; In order, therefore, to prevent such irregularities for the future, and to the end that the Indians may be convinced of our Justice and determined Resolution to remove all reasonable Cause of Discontent.

The Proclamation prohibited English governors from granting lands outside their commissions, prohibited English subjects from buying Aboriginal lands, and ordered any English subjects who had already bought or settled Aboriginal lands to leave the land:

> [N]o Governor. . .do presume, upon any Pretence whatever, to grant Warrants of Survey, or pass any Patents for Lands beyond the Bounds of their respective Governments, as described in their Commissions. . .or upon any Lands whatever, which, not having been ceded to or purchased by Us as aforesaid, are reserved to the said Indians, or any of them.
>
> And We do hereby strictly forbid, on Pain of our Displeasure, all our loving Subjects from making any Purchases or Settlements whatever, or taking Possession of any of the Lands above reserved.
>
> And We do further strictly enjoin and require all Persons whatever who have either willfully or inadvertently seated themselves upon any Lands .. which, not having been ceded to or purchased by Us, are still reserved to the said Indians as aforesaid, forthwith to remove themselves from such Settlements.

These prohibitions applied to any hunting grounds within the Thirteen Colonies, Quebec, Grenada, and Florida, as well as to "all the Lands and Territories lying to the westward of the Sources of the Rivers which fall into the Sea from the West and North." In English property terms, the Proclamation affirmed Aboriginal allodial ownership of any unpurchased land in the Americas.

The Proclamation ordered protection of all the Aboriginal lands from interference by Europeans:

> And whereas it is just and reasonable, and essential to our Interest, and the Security of our Colonies, that the several Nations or Tribes of Indians with whom we are connected, and who live under our Protection, should not be molested and disturbed in the Possession of such Parts of Our Dominions and Territories as, not having been ceded to or purchased by Us, are reserved to them, or any of them, as

their Hunting Grounds.

Aboriginal lands would only be brought into the English tenure system by transfer to the Crown after fair and honest purchase:

> If, at any Time any of the Said Indians should be inclined to dispose of the said Lands, the same shall be purchased only for Us, in our Name, at some public meeting, or Assembly of the said Indians, to be held for that purpose by the Governor or Commander in Chief of our colony respectively within which they lie.

Within the Thirteen Colonies, Quebec, Florida, and Grenada, the governors were given authority to settle and agree with Aboriginal nations concerning allodial lands within the colonies:

> We have also thought fit, with the advice of our Privy Council as aforesaid, to give unto the Governors and Councils of our said Three new Colonies, upon the Continent, full Power and Authority to settle and agree with the Inhabitants of our said new Colonies ... for such Lands, Tenements and Hereditaments, as are now or thereafter shall be in our Power to dispose of.

In sum, the Royal Proclamation, 1763 affirmed Aboriginal nations' allodial tenure in unpurchased lands under English protection in North America. The Crown prohibited subjects from directly purchasing such lands. The Crown declared itself protector over lands still under Aboriginal tenure to prevent any interference by Europeans on these lands. Additional land could only be brought into the English tenure system by sales made voluntarily by Aboriginal nations and in fair and honest purchase by the Crown.

## 17.3 — Treaty Relationships

### (a) — The *Nowegejick* Principle

From early European contact with the Aboriginal nations of what became Canada, British policy included signing treaties with Aboriginal nations to recognize and embody a relationship between the Crown and these Aboriginal nations.

Volume 1 of the Report of the Royal Commission on Aboriginal Peoples, *Looking Forward, Looking Back*, at p. 633-34, describes the way in which

> [a]ccording to oral tradition, treaties were entirely consistent with the Aboriginal relationship to the land, because they were instruments to include newcomers in the circle of relations with whom the original stewards were required to share life. The sacredness and durability of the historical agreements is beyond dispute for Aboriginal participants, observers and later historians of the oral tradition. The sacred

> pipe was smoked, the wampum belt was woven, the medicine bundles were opened, expanding the compacts beyond the people actually present at the ceremony, to include as witnesses and participants the grandparents who had already gone to the spirit world and the children not yet born, whose well-being would depend on the decisions taken.

Because the written texts of treaties represent only one form of the understanding reached in the treaty context and because of different kinds of power imbalances at the time of signature of the written texts, the Supreme Court of Canada has adopted a special principle for treaty interpretation. This principle suggests that treaties should be interpreted broadly and in the way that Aboriginal people would have understood them. This principle has come to be known by the name of the case in which it was succinctly articulated, *Nowegijick v. R.* (1983), 144 D.L.R. (3d) 193 at 198 (S.C.C.):

> [T]reaties and statutes relating to Indians should be liberally construed and doubtful expressions resolved in favour of the Indian. . .In *Jones v. Meehan*, 175 U.S. 1 (1899), it was held that "Indian treaties must be construed, not according to the technical meaning of their words, but in the sense in which they would naturally be understood by the Indians."

In *Mitchell v. Sandy Bay Indian Band*, [1990] 2 S.C.R. 85 (S.C.C.), Chief Justice Dickson expanded on the *Nowegejick* principle at 98:

> Two elements of liberal interpretation can be found in this passage: i) ambiguities in the interpretation of treaties and statutes relating to Indians are to be resolved in favour of the Indians, and ii) aboriginal understandings of words and corresponding legal concepts in Indian treaties are to be preferred over more legalistic and technical constructions. In some cases, the two elements are indistinguishable, but in other cases the interpreter will only be able to perceive that there is an ambiguity by first invoking the second element.

The *Nowegejick* principle has been affirmed as a foundational principle of treaty interpretation in subsequent Supreme Court of Canada cases dealing with Aboriginal rights, typically in the words: "Indian treaties should be liberally construed and uncertainties resolved in favour of the Indians." (*R. v. Simon* (1985), 24 D.L.R. (4th) 390 at 402 (S.C.C.)).

As the next chapter will discuss further, this method of construction requires an examination of history and evidence extrinsic to the treaty documents themselves, including, in a culture that passed its history from one generation to the next without the written word, oral history evidence.

### (b) — The M'kmaq Compacts

In Canada, the British Imperial Crown signed Peace and Friendship Compacts with the M'kmaq peoples over a period stretching from the late seventeenth century through much of the eighteenth century. Four of the major treaties were in 1725, 1749, 1752, and 1760-61, although, as detailed by works like William Wicken's *M'kmaq Treaties on Trial*, there were other treaties as well.

The M'kmaq Compacts were the context for the Supreme Court of Canada decision in *R. v. Simon, supra.* As noted earlier, that case affirmed the *Nowegejick* principle in the context of treaties. In responding to an argument by the federal government that the M'kmaq Compacts were not treaties because they did not include clear and defined land cessions, the Supreme Court held that they were solemn promises between the competent representatives of Aboriginal nations and the Crown outlining the terms of their relationship. That, the Court said, was a treaty.

The M'kmaq Compacts were also part of the context for Supreme Court of Canada decisions in later cases, including *R. v. Marshall*, [1999] 3 S.C.R. 456 (S.C.C.); reconsideration refused [1999] 3 S.C.R. 533 (S.C.C.), and, most recently, *R. v. Bernard*, (sub nom. *R. v. Marshall)* [2005] 2 S.C.R. 220, 2005 SCC 43 (S.C.C.). In the part of this most recent case concerned with these treaties, the Supreme Court had to interpret a clause in the Compacts related to rights to trade. Chief Justice McLachlin expressed at para. 25 something important about the interpretation of treaty rights: "[T]reaty rights are not frozen in time. Modern peoples do traditional things in modern ways. The question is whether the modern trading activity in question represents a logical evolution from the traditional trading activity at the time the treaty was made." On the particular facts of the case, certain commercial logging practices that were claimed as treaty rights were not accepted, but the case affirms the evolving nature of treaty rights and that historical terms can have modern force.

### (c) — The Robinson-Huron Treaty (1850)

The Robinson-Huron Treaty of 1850 is an early Canadian example of the typical form of more recent treaties. In it, the Aboriginal nations of northwest Ontario agree to cede their lands. The English text of the Robinson-Huron Treaty reads as a conveyance:

> That for, and in consideration of the sum of two thousand pounds of good and lawful money of Upper Canada, to them in hand paid, and for the further perpetual annuity of six hundred pounds of like money, the same to be paid and delivered to the said Chiefs and their Tribes at a convenient season of each year, of which due notice will

> be given, at such places as may be appointed for that purpose, they the said Chiefs and Principal men, on behalf of their respective Tribes of Bands, do hereby fully, freely, and voluntarily surrender, cede, grant, and convey unto her Majesty, her heirs and successors for ever, all their right, title, and interest to, and in the whole of, the territory above described, save and except the reservations set forth in the schedule hereunto annexed: which reservations shall be held and occupied by the said Chiefs and their Tribes in common, for their own use and benefit.

The words "in common" are words of Aboriginal tenure. Should the Aboriginal nations "desire to dispose of any part of such reservations or of any mineral or other valuable productions thereon," the Crown was to purchase such land in open meetings.

The text also provides that Aboriginal nations may carry out traditional practices on the ceded lands:

> And the said William Benjamin Robinson of the first part, on behalf of Her Majesty and the Government of this Province hereby promises and agrees. . .and further to allow the said Chiefs and their Tribes the full and free privilege to hunt over the Territory now ceded by them, and to fish in the waters thereof, as they have heretofore been in the habit of doing; saving and excepting such portions of the said Territory as may from time to time be sold or leased to individuals or companies of individuals, and occupied by them with the consent of the Provincial Government.

The English text records Aboriginal nations delegating certain administrative control of their lands to the Crown:

> The [First Nations] further promise and agree that they will not sell, lease or otherwise dispose of any portion of their Reservations without the consent of the Superintendent-General of Indian Affairs, or other officer of like authority, being first had and obtained.
>
> And should the said Chiefs and their respective Tribes at any time desire to dispose of any part of such reservations, or of any mineral or other valuable productions thereon, the same will he sold or leased at their request by the Superintendent-General of Indian Affairs for the time being, or other officer having authority so to do, for their sole benefit and to the best advantage.

"Sole benefit and to the best advantage" is language of fiduciary responsibility. The Crown would be under ongoing responsibilities to the Aboriginal nations with which it had entered into these relationships. The Robinson-Huron Treaty illustrates the complex agreements contained in treaties between the Crown and Aboriginal nations outlining the terms of the relationships between European and Aboriginal nations in Canada.

### (d) — The Victorian Treaties (1873–1921)

In eleven numbered treaties known as the Victorian treaties, the Aboriginal nations entered into a relationship with the imperial Crown concerning most of the regions of Western Canada, excluding British Columbia. These treaties are similar in format to each other. The English opening of the Victorian treaties establishes their purpose:

> And whereas the said Indians have been notified and informed. . .that it is the desire of Her Majesty to open up for settlement, immigration and such other purposes as to Her Majesty may seem meet, a tract of country, bounded and described as hereinafter mentioned.. . .The [Indians] do hereby cede, release, surrender and yield up. (Treaty 8).

Rather than having a consideration clause specifically tied to the ceding clause as in the Robinson-Huron Treaty, these treaties make different commitments. These treaties commit the Crown to the creation of reserves with a condition precedent: "after consulting with the Indians thereof as to the locality which may be found to be most suitable for them." The Crown makes promises in return for jurisdiction over the land that are summarized by Mr. Justice Cory in *R. v. Badger*, [1996] 4 W.W.R. 457, 195 N.R. 1 (S.C.C.), at 473 [W.W.R.]:

> In exchange the Imperial Crown made a number of commitments, for example, to provide the bands with reserves, education, annuities, farm equipment, ammunition and relief in times of famine or pestilence.

The Victorian treaties also continue the Aboriginal rights to hunt and fish over the ceded territory:

> Her Majesty further agrees with her said Indians that they, the said Indians, shall base the right to pursue their avocations of hunting and fishing throughout the tract surrendered as hereinbefore described, subject to such regulations as may from time to time be made by her Government of her Dominion of Canada, and saving and excepting such tracts as may from time to time be required or taken up for settlement, mining, lumbering or other purposes by her said Government of the Dominion of Canada, or by any of the subjects thereof, duly authorized therefore, by the said Government.

The Aboriginal nations agree to maintain peace and good order within the ceded areas within and among Aboriginal nations as well as between Aboriginal nations and white subjects:

> They promise. . .they will maintain peace and good order between

> each other, and also between themselves and other tribes of Indians, and between themselves and others of Her Majesty's subjects, whether Indians or whites now inhabiting or hereafter to inhabit any part of the said ceded tracts.

The modern implications of these treaties are a subject of ongoing discussion, and determining their modern implications is not an easy undertaking. Treaty references to a "medicine chest" being available at the home of an Indian agent are generally agreed to be subject to a modern reading that guarantees health care services in a modern sense, and references to "a school" would now support funding for postsecondary education. However, claims by some that the proper interpretation of the treaties granted tax exemptions for all descendants of the treaty First Nations were rejected in the Federal Court of Appeal, with the Supreme Court declining leave to appeal: *Benoit v. Canada* (2003), 228 D.L.R. (4th) 1, 2003 FCA 236 (Fed. C.A.); leave to appeal refused (2004), 2004 CarswellNat 1209 (S.C.C.). Working out the modern scope and meaning of historical treaty guarantees is an ongoing challenge.

### (e) — Canadian Responsibility for Treaties

In *R. v. Secretary of State for Foreign & Commonwealth Affairs* (1982), [1982] 2 All E.R. 118 (Eng. C.A.), Lord Denning held that Canadian Aboriginal nations signed treaties with the Imperial Crown but that the responsibility to fulfill the terms of these treaties had been delegated to Canada as Canada gained political independence. Some of those responsibilities had in turn been transferred from Parliament to the provinces. Both the federal government and the provincial governments were in ongoing relationships of responsibility to Aboriginal nations. It was now the responsibility, Lord Denning said at 129, of Canadian courts to ensure that the federal and provincial governments fulfilled their administrative responsibilities in the course of governing:

> There is nothing, so far as I can see, to warrant any distrust by the Indians of the government of Canada. But in case there should be, the discussion in this case will strengthen their hand so as to enable them to withstand the onslaught. They will be able to say that their rights and freedoms have been guaranteed to them by the Crown, originally by the Crown in respect of the United Kingdom, now by the Crown in respect of Canada, but, in any case, by the Crown. No parliament should do anything to lessen the worth of these guarantees. They should be honoured by the Crown in respect of Canada so long as the sun rises and the river flows. That promise must never be broken.

## 17.4 — Judicial Recognition of Common Law Aboriginal Title

The principle of continuity, discussed earlier, implies that Aboriginal rights continued to exist even in contexts where the Crown did not enter into specific treaty relationships with Aboriginal nations. The courts have recognized this over the years, though early cases struggled with how exactly to articulate the concept of Aboriginal rights. More recent cases have developed more precisely a doctrine of common law Aboriginal title.

### (a) — American Background

Courts have addressed interactions between the common law of the settlers and pre-existing indigenous legal systems over a long period of time. For example, beginning in the early eighteenth century, a series of legal arguments were made by the Mohegan Indians against the colony of Connecticut. The resulting judicial decisions stretched over a period from 1705 to 1773 and were mostly unreported, other than in a summary form in Joseph Henry Smith's *Appeals to the Privy Council from the American Plantations*. As described by Mark Walters in "*Mohegan Indians v. Connecticut* (1705–1773) and the Legal Status of Aboriginal Customary Laws and Government in British North America", the legal meaning today of some of these early cases is something that is still a subject of ongoing argument.

For Canadian purposes, the early American courts faced up to Aboriginal rights issues most famously in a set of three cases collectively called the "Marshall Trilogy": *Fletcher v. Peck* (1810), *Johnson v. M'Intosh* (1823), and *Worcester v. Georgia* (1832). These cases arose in the context of a series of complex disputes among private parties and governments, and no Aboriginal nations were represented in the courts even though their rights were at stake. In *Johnson v. M'Intosh*, 5 L. Ed. 681 (1823), Chief Justice Marshall at 692-693 described some complex matters in somewhat pragmatic terms:

> The title to a vast portion of the lands we now hold originates in them [the Indians]. It is not for the courts of this country to question the validity of this title, or to sustain one which is incompatible with it.. . .However extravagant the pretension of converting the discovery of an inhabited country into conquest may appear, if the principle has been asserted in the first instance, and afterwards sustained; if a country has been acquired and held under it; if the property of the great mass of the community originates in it, it becomes the law of the land, and cannot be questioned.

Nine years later, in *Worcester v. Georgia*, 31 U.S. 530, 8 L. Ed. 483 (U.S.

Ga., 1832), however, Chief Justice Marshall at 500-501 examined the jurisdictional role of Aboriginal communities on Aboriginal lands in these terms:

> The Indian nations had always been considered as distinct, independent, political communities, retaining their original natural rights, as the undisputed possessors of the soil, from time immemorial, with the single exception of that imposed by irresistible power, which excluded them from intercourse with any other European potentate than the first discoverer of the coast of the particular region claimed.. . .The king purchased their lands when they were willing to sell, at a price they were willing to take, but never coerced a surrender of them. . .[The King's role was to] forbear all encroachments on Indian land.

Chief Justice Marshall thus affirmed the substantial rights of the Aboriginal occupants.

Over time, the American case law continued to develop on its own path and through long struggle. One particularly important moment came in the 1941 case of *United States v. Santa Fe Pacific Railway*, 314 U.S. 339 (U.S. Ariz., 1941), which concerned the land rights of the Hualapai people in northwestern Arizona. As wonderfully detailed by Christian W. McMillen in *Making Indian Law: The Hualapai Land Case and the Birth of Ethnohistory*, the chance to put the case with sufficient evidence before the United States Supreme Court came about from long struggles by Hualapai activists like Fred Mahone and the work of a young American government lawyer named Felix Cohen. Felix Cohen's work within the American government reshaped the way the American government understood the rights of American Indian communities.

The United States Supreme Court's judgment in the *Santa Fe Pacific* case would go on to serve as an important precedent for common law recognition of the land rights of indigenous peoples. It would be an important precedent in Canada in Justice Hall's judgment in the *Calder* case, which we discuss below, as well as in other courts around the world, such as in the major Australian case of *Mabo v. Queensland (No. 2)* (1992), 175 C.L.R. 1 (Australia H.C.).

### (b) — *St Catherine's Milling*

In Canada, *St. Catherine's Milling & Lumber Co. v. R.* (1888), 14 App. Cas. 46 (P.C.) addressed a third party dispute to which Aboriginal nations were not a party in the province of Ontario. The federal and provincial governments were disputing the beneficial ownership of timber revenues in land sold to the Crown under a treaty by Aboriginal nations. Section 109 of the

*British North America Act* read:

> 109. All Lands, Mines, Minerals and Royalties belonging to the several Provinces of Canada, Nova Scotia, and New Brunswick at the Union, and all Sums then due or payable for such Lands, Mines, Minerals or Royalties shall belong to the several Provinces of Ontario, Quebec, Nova Scotia and New Brunswick in which the same are situate or arise, subject to any Trusts existing in respect thereof, and to any Interest other than that of the Province in the Same.

In the case, Lord Watson held that while the Canadian constitution had changed administrative authority with respect to matters concerning Aboriginal interests between federal and provincial governments, it had not changed the nature of Aboriginal interests. He held the beneficial interest in timber lands to be in the Province.

With respect to the nature of Aboriginal title as protected by the *Royal Proclamation, 1763*, Lord Watson said *in obiter* at 54-55:

> [T]he tenure of the Indians was a personal and usufructuary right, dependent upon the goodwill of the Sovereign. The lands reserved are expressly stated to be "parts of our dominions and territories;" and it is declared to be the will and the pleasure of the sovereign that, "for the present," they shall be reserved to the use of the Indians, as their hunting grounds, under his protection and dominion. There was a great deal of learned discussion at the Bar with respect to the precise quality of the Indian right, but their Lordships do not consider it necessary to express any opinion upon the point. It appears to them to be sufficient for the purposes of this estate, underlying the Indian title, which became a *plenum dominium* whenever that title was surrendered or otherwise extinguished.

Lord Watson's words describe Aboriginal land-holding as being a distinct system with unique features, with these early decisions still struggling to articulate the unique features of Aboriginal title. Lord Watson also refers to a special relationship with the Crown. In the American decisions, Chief Justice Marshall had hinted at the duties of the Crown to act honourably. By a fair and honest purchase, the Crown could acquire the allodial title, bringing the land into the English tenure system. Lord Watson's judgment in *St. Catherine's Milling* referred to Aboriginal title as being capable of either surrender to or extinguishment by the Crown, expressing a special relationship with the Crown but leaving much to be explained in later cases.

### (c) — *Calder*

*Calder v. British Columbia (Attorney General)*, [1973] 1 S.C.R. 313 (S.C.C.) marked the recognition in principle by the majority of the Supreme

Court of Canada of Aboriginal title having a place within the common law. The case concerned a claim by the Nisga'a nation in British Columbia for the recognition of its title to its traditional territories. Six members of the Court split equally on whether Aboriginal title had been extinguished by actions of the federal and provincial governments since the assertion of British sovereignty, and one judge decided against the Nisga'a on certain technical grounds, so the Nisga'a lost on their claim, but six of the seven judges hearing the case had affirmed in principle the existence of Aboriginal title.

As a result, the case ultimately took on results different than that of its holding. The recognition in principle of Aboriginal title encouraged governments to modify their negotiating positions. Justice Hall's dissenting opinion, which rejected the claim that Aboriginal title had been extinguished because there had been no clear and convincing evidence of extinguishment, would affect later cases. And, indeed, the Nisga'a claim to their territory would ultimately be resolved through a negotiation process, with the *Nisga'a Agreement* approved in 1999, as we will discuss further in Chapter 19.

### (d) — *Guerin*

*Guerin v. R.*, [1984] 2 S.C.R. 335 (S.C.C.) marked the reaffirmation by a unanimous Supreme Court of Canada of *Calder*'s recognition of Aboriginal title. *Guerin* was decided in 1984, after the new *Constitution Act, 1982*, but it was still a judgment based on common law principles, and it was only later cases that turned to flesh out the meaning of the constitutional recognition and affirmation of Aboriginal rights. The Court in *Guerin* was considering claims of the Musqueam after the Crown leased on the Musqueam's behalf some of their land in Vancouver in a manner less favourable than the Musqueam had approved at a surrender meeting.

Justice Wilson held that the Crown had breached a fiduciary obligation that "has its roots in the aboriginal title of Canada's Indians as discussed in *Calder v. Attorney General of British Columbia*, [1973] S.C.R. 313." Justice Dickson (as he then was) attempted to provide slightly more detail on the nature of Aboriginal title:

> Indians have a legal right to occupy and possess certain lands, the ultimate title to which is in the Crown. While their interest does not, strictly speaking, amount to beneficial ownership, neither is its nature completely exhausted by the concept of a personal right. It is true that the sui generis interest which the Indians have in the land is personal in the sense that it cannot be transferred to a grantee, but it is also true, as will presently appear, that the interest gives rise upon

> surrender to a distinctive fiduciary obligation on the part of the Crown to deal with the land for the benefit of the surrendering Indians.

The law has not always developed smoothly, but both treaties and case law show that Aboriginal rights to land continued to apply after European contact and the assertion of European sovereignty. In some instances, the Crown signed treaties with Aboriginal nations to describe the ongoing relationship. Even where no treaties were signed, pre-existing legal rights of Aboriginal nations continued in Canadian law and were recognized by the common law even prior to the *Constitution Act, 1982*. In both treaty and common law contexts, there were overriding responsibilities on the Canadian Crown.

# Chapter 18 — Constitutionally Recognized Aboriginal Title



## 18.0 — Introduction

As we saw in the last chapter, Aboriginal rights to land arose from indigenous legal systems that pre-dated European contact. Thus, from the very beginnings of Canada, the Canadian Crown has had responsibilities to Aboriginal nations. The recognition of Aboriginal rights in the *Constitution Act, 1982* was nonetheless very significant. The *Constitution Act, 1982* enshrines existing Aboriginal and treaty rights. Aboriginal and treaty rights include property rights. Neither Parliament nor provincial legislatures can pass laws that fail to respect these rights guarantees.

The enshrining of Aboriginal and treaty rights in the Constitution has led to new bodies of case law interpreting the implications of this constitutional recognition. All the more recent case law on Aboriginal title has been in the context of these constitutionally guaranteed rights.

## 18.1 — Aboriginal Rights Constitutionalized

Section 35 of the *Constitution Act, 1982* declares that Aboriginal and treaty rights are protected by the Constitution:

> (1) The existing aboriginal and treaty rights of the aboriginal peoples of Canada are hereby recognized and affirmed.
>
> (2) In this Act, "aboriginal peoples of Canada" includes the Indian, Inuit and Métis peoples of Canada.
>
> (3) For greater certainty, in subsection (1) "treaty rights" includes rights that now exist by way of land claims agreements or may be so acquired.
>
> (4) Notwithstanding any other provision of this Act, the aboriginal and treaty rights referred to in subsection (1) are guaranteed equally to male and female persons.

Section 52 enunciates constitutional supremacy, protecting constitutionalized rights from all other laws:

> The Constitution of Canada is the supreme law of Canada, and any law that is inconsistent with the provisions of the Constitution is, to the extent of the inconsistency, of no force or effect.

## 18.2 — Six Principles of Constitutionalized Aboriginal Title

Constitutionalized Aboriginal title carries forward some characteristics of common law Aboriginal title, and constitutionalization also has some new implications. The main characteristics of constitutionalized Aboriginal title can be summed up in six principles:

### (a) — *Sui Generis*

Aboriginal title, the Supreme Court has said, is *sui generis*: of its own kind. Aboriginal title cannot be described in the first instance in terms appropriate to English tenure systems. The attempt to do so, Justice Dickson (as he then was) explains in *Guerin v. R.*, [1984] 2 S.C.R. 335 at 382 (S.C.C.), has always failed:

> [I]n describing what constitutes a unique interest in land the courts

> have almost inevitably found themselves applying a somewhat inappropriate terminology drawn from general property law. . .[t]o the *sui generis* interest which the Indians have in the land.

Aboriginal systems of land-holding are connected with Aboriginal spiritualities and are best described by Aboriginal people. Professor Leroy Little Bear at 2-62 describes an Aboriginal perspective on land in the following way: "The Creator, in granting land, did not give the land to human beings only but gave it to all living beings. This includes plants, sometimes rocks, and all animals. In other words, deer have the same type of estate or interest as any human being."

In the Supreme Court of Canada's leading case on constitutionalized Aboriginal title, *Delgamuukw v. British Columbia*, [1997] 3 S.C.R. 1010 (S.C.C.), Chief Justice Lamer describes at para. 113 how "[t]he idea that aboriginal title is *sui generis* is the unifying principle underlying the various dimensions of that title." As Chief Justice explains at further length at paras. 113–15, these *sui generis* dimensions include that: (1) Aboriginal title is inalienable other than by way of transfer to the Crown; (2) Aboriginal title has its source in prior occupation of territory by Aboriginal societies, giving rise to claims of title both from the fact of occupancy and from the interaction of Aboriginal and common law norms; and (3) Aboriginal title is communally held, with decisions about the land being governed by an Aboriginal nation.

In its most recent case on Aboriginal title, *R. v. Bernard*, (sub nom. *R. v. Marshall)* [2005] 2 S.C.R. 220, 2005 SCC 43 (S.C.C.) the Supreme Court of Canada has suggested that the *sui generis* nature of Aboriginal title does not mean that it cannot have parallels within common law property concepts. Indeed, Chief Justice McLachlin refers at para. 69 to the notion that one can interpret past Aboriginal practices and legal norms into norms recognized within the common law system:

> The evidence, oral and documentary, must be evaluated from the aboriginal perspective. What would a certain practice or event have signified in their world and value system? Having evaluated the evidence, the final step is to translate the facts found and thus interpreted into a modern common law right. The right must be accurately delineated in a way that reflects common law traditions, while respecting the aboriginal perspective.

The use of the translation metaphor has been critiqued by some writers, like Professor Paul Chartrand and Professor Mark Walters, and it may have its limits. However, one can read it in part as an important statement that Aboriginal rights that look very different from common law property rights may nonetheless have very significant impacts within the common law property regime once one understands and applies them.

### (b) — Purposive Constitutional Interpretation

In *R. v. Sparrow*, [1990] 1 S.C.R. 1075 (S.C.C.), Chief Justice Dickson applies the standard constitutional interpretation principle of purposive interpretation to s. 35 Aboriginal rights: "The nature of s. 35(1) itself suggests that it be construed in a purposive way. When the purposes of the affirmation of aboriginal rights are considered, it is clear that a generous, liberal interpretation of the words in the constitutional provision is demanded."

Chief Justice Lamer offers a purposive interpretation of s. 35 in *R. v. Van der Peet*, [1996] 2 S.C.R. 507 (S.C.C.); reconsideration refused (January 16, 1997), Doc. 23803 (S.C.C.):

> [W]hat s. 35(1) does is provide the constitutional framework through which the fact that aboriginals lived on the land in distinctive societies, with their own practices, traditions and cultures, is acknowledged and reconciled with the sovereignty of the Crown. The substantive rights which fall within the provision must be defined in light of this purpose; the aboriginal rights recognized and affirmed by s. 35(1) must be directed towards the reconciliation of the pre-existence of aboriginal societies with the sovereignty of the Crown.

The conjoined purposive elements of prior occupation and reconciliation appear repeatedly in later Supreme Court cases and inform the Court's understanding of particular Aboriginal rights and Aboriginal title questions.

### (c) — Honour of the Crown

A third fundamental principle of Aboriginal rights in Canada identified in *Guerin* and repeated throughout subsequent cases is the fiduciary responsibility of the Crown in relation to Aboriginal nations. The fiduciary relationships arise from the fact that the Crown promised in all its treaties with Aboriginal nations to protect Aboriginal people from the frauds and abuses of European immigrants (*Royal Proclamation, 1763* (U.K.), R.S.C. 1985, Appendix 2, No. 1). In return Aboriginal nations agreed to deal only with the Crown in all affairs relating to land. Thus, all Canadian governments, delegated by the Crown as trustees of its responsibilities under the agreements, have a fiduciary responsibility in Aboriginal matters.

Since the Court's decision in *Sparrow*, these fiduciary responsibilities have been described in terms of the concept of the "honour of the Crown". This broad concept prohibits "sharp dealings" and provides a fundamental interpretive lens for any governmental actions that may infringe on Aboriginal rights. Prior to 1982, it was possible for the government to "extinguish" Aboriginal rights with a clear and plain intent to do so; since 1982, extinguishments are no longer possible, and any infringements can be permitted only if they are in keeping with the honour of the Crown.

### (d) — Rejection of Discriminatory Precedents

In *Sparrow*, Chief Justice Dickson made clear that precedents from an earlier day based on ethnic biases or prejudices are inappropriate. Most pre-1982 cases dealing with Aboriginal property came forward in the context of federal-provincial or commercial disputes over proceeds from land. Aboriginal nations were not parties to such cases, nor were their interests represented. Chief Justice Dickson wrote at 1103:

> For many years, the rights of the Indians to their aboriginal lands — certainly as legal rights — were virtually ignored. The leading cases were directed at claims supported by the *Royal Proclamation* or other legal instruments, and even these cases were essentially concerned with settling legislative jurisdiction or the rights of commercial enterprises. For fifty years after the publication of Clement's *The Law of the Canadian Constitution* (3rd ed. 1916), there was a virtual absence of discussion of any kind of Indian rights to land even in academic literature. By the late 1960s, aboriginal claims were not even recognized by the federal government as having any legal status.

In *R. v. Simon* (1985), 24 D.L.R. (4th) 390 (S.C.C.), Chief Justice Dickson at 400 openly stated that the Supreme Court would reject precedents based on the "biases or prejudices of another era. . .[T]he language. . .reflects the biases and prejudices of another era in our history. Such language is no longer acceptable in Canadian law, and indeed, is inconsistent with a growing sensitivity to native rights in Canada."

### (e) — Aboriginal perspectives and Aboriginal evidence

Aboriginal rights are a distinct body of rights. Indeed, Chief Justice Lamer states in *R. v. Van der Peet*, [1996] 2 S.C.R. 507 (S.C.C.); reconsideration refused (January 16, 1997), Doc. 23803 (S.C.C.) at para. 19 that "Aboriginal rights cannot, however, be defined on the basis of the philosophical precepts of the liberal enlightenment. Although equal in importance and significance to the rights enshrined in the *Charter*, aboriginal rights must be viewed differently from *Charter* rights because they are rights held only by aboriginal members of Canadian society. They arise from the fact that aboriginal people are aboriginal" [underlining in original].

The implication of the *sui generis* nature of Aboriginal rights becomes explicit in Chief Justice Lamer's judgment in *Delgamuukw* at para. 119:

> The starting point of the Canadian jurisprudence on aboriginal title is

the Privy Council's decision in *St. Catherine's Milling and Lumber Co. v. The Queen* (1888), 14 A.C. 46, which described aboriginal title as a "personal and usufructuary right" (at p. 54). The subsequent jurisprudence has attempted to grapple with this definition, and has in the process demonstrated that the Privy Council's choice of terminology is not particularly helpful to explain the various dimensions of aboriginal title. What the Privy Council sought to capture is that aboriginal title is a *sui generis* interest in land. Aboriginal title has been described as *sui generis* in order to distinguish it from "normal" proprietary interests, such as fee simple. However, as I will now develop, it is also *sui generis* in the sense that its characteristics cannot be completely explained by reference either to the common law rules of real property or to the rules of property found in aboriginal legal systems. As with other aboriginal rights, it must be understood by reference to both common law and aboriginal perspectives.

The Supreme Court has repeatedly emphasized the importance in the Aboriginal rights and Aboriginal title area of taking account of Aboriginal perspectives. This principle has a particular implication in the area of evidence law. The evidence relevant to the points within Aboriginal rights and Aboriginal title cases that describes Aboriginal perspectives may be found in the form of oral histories. The use of such oral histories challenges certain presuppositions within the Canadian legal system. As described in volume 1 of the Report of the Royal Commission on Aboriginal Peoples, *Looking Forward, Looking Back*, at p. 33,

> The Aboriginal tradition in the recording of history is neither linear nor steeped in the same notions of social progress and evolution [as in the non-Aboriginal tradition]. Nor is it usually human-centred in the same way as the western scientific tradition, for it does not assume that human beings are anything more than one — and not necessarily the most important — element of the natural order of the universe. Moreover, the Aboriginal historical tradition is an oral one, involving legends, stories and accounts handed down through the generations in oral form. It is less focused on establishing objective truth and assumes that the teller of the story is so much a part of the event being described that it would be arrogant to presume to classify or categorize the event exactly or for all time.
>
> In the Aboriginal tradition the purpose of repeating oral accounts from the past is broader than the role of written history in western societies. It may be to educate the listener, to communicate aspects of culture, to socialize people into a cultural tradition, or to validate the claims of a particular family to authority and prestige.

[

. . . . .

]

> Oral accounts of the past include a good deal of subjective experience. They are not simply a detached recounting of factual events but, rather, are "facts enmeshed in the stories of a lifetime". They are also likely to be rooted in particular locations, making reference to particular families and communities. This contributes to a sense that there are many histories, each characterized in part by how a people see themselves, how they define their identity in relation to their environment, and how they express their uniqueness as a people.

As affirmed by the judgment of Chief Justice Lamer in *Delgamuukw*, at para. 87,

> Notwithstanding the challenges created by the use of oral histories as proof of historical facts, the laws of evidence must be adapted in order that this type of evidence can be accommodated and placed on an equal footing with the types of historical evidence that courts are familiar with, which largely consists of historical documents.

Thus, attention to Aboriginal perspectives is both a general imperative and a principle that has specific implications for the use of evidence in Aboriginal rights and Aboriginal title cases.

### (f) — Negotiation, Consultation, and Accommodation

The Supreme Court of Canada has also recognized explicitly that the Canadian court system is not necessarily an ideal place to resolve disputes concerning Aboriginal rights and Aboriginal title. Indeed, in sending the matters at issue in *Delgamuukw* back to trial, Chief Justice Lamer concluded in these terms at para. 186:

> [T]his litigation has been both long and expensive, not only in economic but in human terms as well. By ordering a new trial, I do not necessarily encourage the parties to proceed to litigation and to settle their dispute through the courts. As was said in *Sparrow*, at p. 1105, s. 35(1) "provides a solid constitutional base upon which subsequent negotiations can take place". Those negotiations should also include other aboriginal nations which have a stake in the territory claimed. Moreover, the Crown is under a moral, if not a legal, duty to enter into and conduct those negotiations in good faith. Ultimately, it is through negotiated settlements, with good faith and give and take on all sides, reinforced by the judgments of this Court, that we will achieve what I stated in *Van der Peet*, *supra*, at para. 31, to be a

> basic purpose of s. 35(1) — "the reconciliation of the pre-existence of aboriginal societies with the sovereignty of the Crown". Let us face it, we are all here to stay.

The Court has thus tried to encourage negotiated settlements for several reasons. These include that they are more likely to address the complex multiparty interests at sake. They are also seen as more likely to promote the reconciliation of Aboriginal societies and Crown sovereignty.

Some justices of the Court have noted other reasons as well. For example, in a concurring opinion in *R. v. Marshall*; *R. v. Bernard*, Justice LeBel noted at paras. 142–44 his concern that many Aboriginal rights issues are litigated in the context of proceedings brought against specific Aboriginal individuals. What is at stake are the rights of Aboriginal communities and nations. One might infer that these are perhaps best addressed less as defences in particular cases and more through nation-to-nation dialogue.

In fact, there has been much effort at negotiation in the decade since the *Delgamuukw* judgment. The prolonged and ongoing negotiation processes in some cases have given rise to a new concern. If Aboriginal rights or Aboriginal title are affected during ongoing negotiation processes, they must not be affected in ways that risk harming ultimate outcomes. In several recent cases, beginning with *Haida Nation v. British Columbia (Minister of Forests)*, [2004] 3 S.C.R. 511, 2004 SCC 73 (S.C.C.), the Supreme Court has made clear that governments are under a "duty to consult" Aboriginal nations during negotiation processes.

Chief Justice McLachlin explains this concept at paras. 26-27 of the *Haida Nation* case:

> Honourable negotiation implies a duty to consult with Aboriginal claimants and conclude an honourable agreement reflecting the claimants' inherent rights. But proving rights may take time, sometimes a very long time. In the meantime, how are the interests under discussion to be treated? Underlying this question is the need to reconcile prior Aboriginal occupation of the land with the reality of Crown sovereignty. Is the Crown, under the aegis of its asserted sovereignty, entitled to use the resources at issue as it chooses, pending proof and resolution of the Aboriginal claim? Or must it adjust its conduct to reflect the as yet unresolved rights claimed by the Aboriginal claimants?
>
> The answer, once again, lies in the honour of the Crown. The Crown, acting honourably, cannot cavalierly run roughshod over Aboriginal interests where claims affecting these interests are being seriously pursued in the process of treaty negotiation and proof. It must respect these potential, but yet unproven, interests. The Crown is not ren-

> dered impotent. It may continue to manage the resource in question pending claims resolution. But, depending on the circumstances, discussed more fully below, the honour of the Crown may require it to consult with and reasonably accommodate Aboriginal interests pending resolution of the claim. To unilaterally exploit a claimed resource during the process of proving and resolving the Aboriginal claim to that resource, may be to deprive the Aboriginal claimants of some or all of the benefit of the resource. That is not honourable.

The Court thus mandates the appropriateness of negotiation processes in place of litigation over every point, but it also makes clear the implications of an honourable negotiation process.

## 18.3 — The Emerging Case Law of Aboriginal Rights and Aboriginal Title

Our constitutional Aboriginal title case law remains in its early days. The courts have still not held that Aboriginal title exists on the specific facts of any actual case that has come before the courts. However, the developing Supreme Court of Canada case law does establish principles on which an Aboriginal title claim could succeed in a future case, and it is well worth seeking to understand the Court's main Aboriginal title cases.

The Supreme Court of Canada's first consideration of a constitutional Aboriginal title case comes only in 1999 in the *Delgamuukw* decision, but the *Delgamuukw* decision makes clear that the Court's approach to Aboriginal title flows from its broader approach to Aboriginal rights. As stated by Chief Justice Lamer at para. 2 of the lead judgment in the case, Aboriginal title is "a distinct species of aboriginal right that was recognized and affirmed by s. 35(1)". Thus, we actually need to begin with the Supreme Court's foundational cases on Aboriginal rights.

### (a) — *R. v. Sparrow*

*R. v. Sparrow*, [1990] 1 S.C.R. 1075 (S.C.C.) was the first s. 35 Aboriginal rights case to come to the Supreme Court of Canada. The Court ultimately resolved the case without defining the content of s. 35 but while saying more about justified infringements on s. 35 rights. Sparrow, the defendant in the case, was a member of the Musqueam First Nation in British Columbia. He was charged with illegal fishing after he fished with a net longer than that permitted in the Musqueam First Nation's fishing licence as established under the federal *Fisheries Act*. His defence was that he was exercising an Aboriginal right protected by s. 35.

Chief Justice Dickson held that the term "existing" in s. 35 meant that s. 35

protected rights that had not been extinguished prior to 1982. This did not, however, mean that these rights were subject to whatever regulation may have existed in 1982. Only clear evidence of an intent to extinguish an Aboriginal right prior to 1982 would result in extinguishment.

That said, s. 35 also did not, according to the Court, guarantee an absolute set of rights. Government powers that might modify certain exercises of rights would continue. However, as Chief Justice Dickson puts it at p. 1077, "federal power must be reconciled with federal duty and the best way to achieve that reconciliation is to demand the justification of any government regulation that infringes upon or denies aboriginal rights." A justified infringement would need to be for a sufficiently important purpose and there would also be, as Chief Justice Dickson describes it at pp. 1079-80, questions of "whether there has been as little infringement as possible in order to effect the desired result; whether, in a situation of expropriation, fair compensation is available; and, whether the aboriginal group in question has been consulted with respect to the conservation measures being implemented." The Court thus sent the specific case back to the trial court to be considered in accordance with these principles.

### (b) — *R. v. Van der Peet*

*R. v. Van der Peet*, [1996] 2 S.C.R. 507 (S.C.C.); reconsideration refused (January 16, 1997), Doc. 23803 (S.C.C.) came to the courts as the case of an individual charged with illegally selling salmon caught under a food fishing licence, with Van der Peet arguing that she had an Aboriginal right to do so. The Supreme Court of Canada decided the case as part of a trilogy in which it explained its approach to the test for Aboriginal rights. *Van der Peet* is the lead case in which the Court explains most about its reasoning.

In *Van der Peet*, Chief Justice Lamer sets out a test for Aboriginal rights. At para. 46, he sets this out in brief form: "In light of the suggestion of *Sparrow, supra*, and the purposes underlying s. 35(1), the following test should be used to identify whether an applicant has established an aboriginal right protected by s. 35(1): in order to be an aboriginal right an activity must be an element of a practice, custom or tradition integral to the distinctive culture of the aboriginal group claiming the right."

In particular, an Aboriginal right today is a modern continuation of a precontact practice. Chief Justice Lamer makes clear at para. 64 that practices can evolve, and the Court is not trying to "freeze" Aboriginal rights in some traditional form:

> The concept of continuity is also the primary means through which the definition and identification of aboriginal rights will be consistent with the admonition in *Sparrow, supra*, at p. 1093, that "the phrase

> 'existing aboriginal rights' must be interpreted flexibly so as to permit their evolution over time". The concept of continuity is, in other words, the means by which a "frozen rights" approach to s. 35(1) will be avoided. Because the practices, customs and traditions protected by s. 35(1) are ones that exist today, subject only to the requirement that they be demonstrated to have continuity with the practices, customs and traditions which existed pre-contact, the definition of aboriginal rights will be one that, on its own terms, prevents those rights from being frozen in pre-contact times. The evolution of practices, customs and traditions into modern forms will not, provided that continuity with pre-contact practices, customs and traditions is demonstrated, prevent their protection as aboriginal rights.

In the case, Chief Justice Lamer concluded that there was not evidence that the commercial exchange of fish was a central part of Sto:lo culture and thus held that Van der Peet did not have an Aboriginal right to sell salmon. There would be much more one could say about the case, and there have been important critiques like that of Professors Barsh and Henderson, but this main test is what we need for present purposes. Indeed, the Supreme Court has more recently updated the *Van der Peet* test in some respects in light of some of the critiques in *R. v. Sappier*, [2006] 2 S.C.R. 686, 2006 SCC 54 (S.C.C.). However, it is the *Van der Peet* test that principally underpins later developments in Aboriginal title.

### (c) — *Delgamuukw v. British Columbia*

In *Delgamuukw v. British Columbia*, [1997] 3 S.C.R. 1010 (S.C.C.), the Court at last confronted directly the implications of s. 35 for common law Aboriginal title. The case came through the appeal chain from the British Columbia Supreme Court where Justice McEachern had rejected the claims put on behalf of the Gitksan and Wet'suwet'en peoples.

Section 35(1) constitutionalizes pre-existing common law Aboriginal title (para. 133). Chief Justice Lamer gives a succinct description of Aboriginal title at para. 110:

> Aboriginal title is a right in land and, as such, is more than the right to engage in specific activities which may be themselves aboriginal rights. Rather, it confers the right to use land for a variety of activities, not all of which need be aspects of practices, customs and traditions which are integral to the distinctive cultures of aboriginal societies. Those activities do not constitute the right *per se*; rather, they are parasitic on the underlying title. However, that range of uses is subject to the limitation that they must not be irreconcilable with the nature of the attachment to the land which forms the basis of the

> particular group's aboriginal title.

This description contains two key propositions. First, Aboriginal title is an Aboriginal right but it is a broad Aboriginal right that is not confined to specific activities but that encompasses a general right in respect of particular lands. Within a spectrum of Aboriginal rights, "What aboriginal title confers is the right to the land itself" (para. 138). Second, however, Aboriginal title is different from other land ownership partly because it is subject to a special limit that the uses it permits must be reconcilable with the bases on which it is claimed.

Chief Justice Lamer tries at para. 130 to explain this second point in a manner accessible to the common law-trained reader:

> I am cognizant that the *sui generis* nature of aboriginal title precludes the application of "traditional real property rules" to elucidate the content of that title (*St. Mary's Indian Band v. Cranbrook (City)*. . .). Nevertheless, a useful analogy can be drawn between the limit on aboriginal title and the concept of equitable waste at common law. Under that doctrine, persons who hold a life estate in real property cannot commit "wanton or extravagant acts of destruction". . .or "ruin the property" (Robert E. Megarry and H. W. R. Wade, *The Law of Real Property* (4th ed. 1975), at p. 105). This description of the limits imposed by the doctrine of equitable waste capture the kind of limit I have in mind here.

Aboriginal title thus has analogies to certain kinds of estates within real property law, although identifying possible analogies must never distract one from the *sui generis* nature of Aboriginal title.

Because Aboriginal title is an Aboriginal right, the legal test for Aboriginal title becomes an adaptation of the main test for Aboriginal rights. Chief Justice Lamer explains at para. 142:

> The adaptation of the test laid down in *Van der Peet* to suit claims to title must be understood as the recognition of the first aspect of that prior presence. However, as will now become apparent, the tests for the identification of aboriginal rights to engage in particular activities and for the identification of aboriginal title share broad similarities. The major distinctions are first, under the test for aboriginal title, the requirement that the land be integral to the distinctive culture of the claimants is subsumed by the requirement of occupancy, and second, whereas the time for the identification of aboriginal rights is the time of first contact, the time for the identification of aboriginal title is the time at which the Crown asserted sovereignty over the land.

The test for Aboriginal title is thus whether there was exclusive prior occupation of land by an Aboriginal nation, with the requirement of continuity with present occupation expressed as a substantially maintained connection between the people and the land (para. 153).

As outlined by Chief Justice Lamer at paras. 165–69, there can in some instances be justified infringements on Aboriginal title. However, building on the *Sparrow* requirements for justified infringement, these will need to involve deep consultation with the Aboriginal nation that has within Aboriginal title the right to choose the uses to which land under Aboriginal title is put. They will also generally need to involve compensation, because Aboriginal title has an inherently economic element.

The decision in *Delgamuukw* is also important for two other propositions. First, *Delgamuukw* discusses a Canadian constitutional division of powers question that is important in the Aboriginal title context. Because s. 91(24) of Canada's Constitution assigns legislative power in relation to "Indians, and Lands reserved for the Indians" to the federal government, provincial laws can never have extinguished Aboriginal title rights, as only the federal government can legislate in relation to Aboriginal lands.

Second, *Delgamuukw*, as noted earlier, has much to say about the use of oral history evidence. Within our space constraints here, we cannot address matters of evidence law at length, and there have been subsequent adaptations of the *Delgamuukw* approach to oral history evidence to try to make it clearer (Newman, "*Tsilhqot'in Nation v. British Columbia* and Civil Justice: Analysing the Procedural Interaction of Evidentiary Principles and Aboriginal Oral History"). However, there stands from the case the main principle of using Aboriginal oral history evidence along with the kind of documentary evidence the common law might traditionally have preferred.

The fact that the trial judge had not considered the evidence in accord with the imperative to consider oral history evidence from Aboriginal sources meant that the Supreme Court sent the matter back to trial. Nonetheless, the Supreme Court's account of Aboriginal title within the case is the leading Canadian account of this area of law.

### (d) — *Marshall & Bernard*

*R. v. Bernard, (*sub nom. *R. v. Marshall)* [2005] 2 S.C.R. 220, 2005 SCC 43 (S.C.C.) is the Supreme Court of Canada's most recent Aboriginal title case. Part of the case is about interpretation of treaties, and we discussed that part in the previous chapter. Another part of the case related to a claim put by the M'kmaq for Aboriginal title to the areas at issue; if this were the case, they would have authorization to log those areas deriving from their Aboriginal title rather than from a treaty right.

The Court emphasizes that an Aboriginal title claim must be made out as a claim for title. Following *Delgaumuukw*, this has implications for the nature of what one must prove. Chief Justice McLachlin states at paras. 53-54 of *Marshall & Bernard*:

> Different aboriginal practices correspond to different modern rights. This Court has rejected the view of a dominant right to title to the land, from which other rights, like the right to hunt or fish, flow.. . .It is more accurate to speak of a variety of independent aboriginal rights. One of these rights is aboriginal title to land. It is established by aboriginal practices that indicate possession similar to that associated with title at common law. In matching common law property rules to aboriginal practice we must be sensitive to the context-specific nature of common law title, as well as the aboriginal perspective. The common law recognizes that possession sufficient to ground title is a matter of fact, depending on all the circumstances, in particular the nature of the land and the manner in which the land is commonly enjoyed: *Powell v. McFarlane* (1977), 38 P. & C.R. 452 at p. 471 (Ch. D.). For example, where marshy land is virtually useless except for shooting, shooting over it may amount to adverse possession: *Red House Farms (Thorndon) Ltd. v. Catchpole*, [1977] E.G.D. 798 (Eng. C.A.). The common law also recognizes that a person with adequate possession for title may choose to use it intermittently or sporadically: *Keefer v. Arillotta* (1976), 13 O.R. (2d) 680 (C.A.), *per* Wilson J.A. Finally, the common law recognizes that exclusivity does not preclude consensual arrangements that recognize shared title to the same parcel of land: *Delgamuukw*, at para. 158.

The requirement of exclusive occupation for an Aboriginal title claim has certain specific implications. As Chief Justice McLachlin states at para. 58, "It follows from the requirement of exclusive occupation that exploiting the land, rivers or seaside for hunting, fishing or other resources may translate into aboriginal title to the land if the activity was sufficiently regular and exclusive to comport with title at common law. However, more typically, seasonal hunting and fishing rights exercised in a particular area will translate to a hunting or fishing right."

This approach frames the approach to the specific case at paras. 61-62:

> The common law, over the centuries, has formalized title through a complicated matrix of legal edicts and conventions. The search for aboriginal title, by contrast, takes us back to the beginnings of the notion of title. Unaided by formal legal documents and written edicts, we are required to consider whether the practices of aboriginal peoples at the time of sovereignty compare with the core notions of common law title to land. It would be wrong to look for indicia of aboriginal title in deeds or Euro-centric assertions of ownership.

> Rather, we must look for the equivalent in the aboriginal culture at issue.. . .Aboriginal societies were not strangers to the notions of exclusive physical possession equivalent to common law notions of title: *Delgamuukw*, at para. 156. They often exercised such control over their village sites and larger areas of land which they exploited for agriculture, hunting, fishing or gathering. The question is whether the evidence here establishes this sort of possession.

On the facts of the case, Chief Justice McLachlin concluded that there had not been a demonstration of exclusive occupation of specific sites. As a result, there could not be a successful claim for Aboriginal title.

This most recent case from the Supreme Court of Canada thus makes clear the strict legal standards to which the courts will put Aboriginal title claims. There must be proof of exclusive occupation of specific sites. That said, there is room for interpretation of the appropriate meaning of exclusive occupation in particular circumstances, and this exclusive occupation is potentially demonstrable through oral history evidence that meets the relevant evidence law standards. The Court's broader aspiration is to a reconciliation process, which it seeks to further through these tests.

### (e) — The Duty to Consult

As stated earlier, negotiation and litigation practices in keeping with the honour of the Crown imply that governments may not simply use as they see fit lands that are the subject of Aboriginal claims. Several recent cases have begun to examine the concept of the duty to consult. At its essence, as stated by Chief Justice McLachlin at para. 35 of *Haida Nation v. British Columbia (Minister of Forests)*, [2004] 3 S.C.R. 511, 2004 SCC 73 (S.C.C.), a duty to consult "arises when the Crown has knowledge, real or constructive, of the potential existence of the Aboriginal right or title and contemplates conduct that might adversely affect it". The duty depends on particular circumstances. Chief Justice McLachlin explains this at para. 39:

> The content of the duty to consult and accommodate varies with the circumstances. Precisely what duties arise in different situations will be defined as the case law in this emerging area develops. In general terms, however, it may be asserted that the scope of the duty is proportionate to a preliminary assessment of the strength of the case supporting the existence of the right or title, and to the seriousness of the potentially adverse effect upon the right or title claimed.

The *Haida Nation* case concerned authorization by the province of British Columbia of logging in Haida Gwaii, a region subject to a long-standing claim by the Haida people. The Court held that the Crown had acted wrongly in granting a logging licence without carrying out appropriate consultation and accommodation of the Aboriginal interest.

In a companion case, *Taku River Tlingit First Nation v. British Columbia (Project Assessment Director)*, [2004] 3 S.C.R. 550, 2004 SCC 74 (S.C.C.), issues arose concerning the provincial government's decision to permit the reopening of an old mine when the proposal included a road that was to pass through traditional territories of the Taku River Tlingit First Nation. The province had engaged in a three-year environmental assessment of the mine reopening, had invited Aboriginal participation in the process, and had modified some terms of how specific permits would later be granted so as to allow for ongoing consideration of impacts on the First Nation. In the circumstances, the Court held that these steps met the province's duty to consult and accommodate.

In *Mikisew Cree First Nation v. Canada (Minister of Canadian Heritage)*, [2005] 3 S.C.R. 388, 2005 SCC 69 (S.C.C.), the Court applied the duty to consult in the context of treaty rights. The case concerned construction of a winter road in Wood Buffalo National Park in the vicinity of traditional hunting grounds of the Mikisew Cree First Nation. The lands in question were part of Treaty 8, and the Crown had the right to build roads in the Treaty 8 areas; however, the Mikisew Cree retained their traditional hunting rights. Where road construction would affect the exercise of these traditional hunting rights, the duty to consult was triggered.

Case law on the duty to consult is in its early days. However, this application of the honour of the Crown may have very important implications for land use and must be considered carefully. Although the duty to consult does not apply directly to private individuals or companies, the duty to consult may still impact in some ways on private land use. There remains much to be determined in the years ahead.

## 18.4 — Application: *Tsilhqot'in Nation v. British Columbia*

The British Columbia Supreme Court was called upon to apply this emerging body of case law in *Williams v. British Columbia*, (sub nom. *Tsilhqot'in Nation v. British Columbia)* 2007 BCSC 1700 (B.C. S.C.), decided in November 2007. Justice Vickers heard 339 days of argument between 2002 and 2007 on the claims of the Tsilhqot'in Nation and came the closest any Canadian judge has to making a declaration of Aboriginal title. In the process, he attempts to follow carefully the directions offered by the Supreme Court of Canada's case law and to offer his interpretation of what these mean. His judgment is 473 pages long, and we will note just some key features of the judgment to show how it flows from the principles we have discussed and how it raises some new questions for the future.

After setting out a significant amount of historical context and other background material and explaining the trial process, Justice Vickers begins by noting his special responsibilities in relation to the evidence presented in the case. As he describes matters at para. 132 of the judgment, "In order to truly hear the oral history and oral tradition evidence presented in these cases, courts must undergo their own process of de-colonization." He refers to the guidance from *Delgamuukw* and other cases before turning to work by noted scholar Jan Vansina on oral history. He describes at para. 196 the challenge ultimately before him as trial judge:

> I propose to take this entire body of [oral history] evidence into account and to the extent that I am able, consider it from the Aboriginal perspective. If the oral history or oral tradition evidence is sufficient standing on its own to reach a conclusion of fact, I will not hesitate to make that finding. If it cannot be made in that manner, I will seek corroboration from the anthropological, archeological and historical records. I understand my task is to be fair and to try to avoid an ethnocentric view of the evidence.

In order to seek fairness, Justice Vickers is ready to take special steps. For example, where some elders took the view that certain stories could be told only at night, he arranged special evening sittings of the Court (para. 167)

Significant parts of the judgment, like of any trial judgment, are taken up with a detailed account of the evidence and explanation of fact-finding from this evidence. The judgment is fascinating in its rich account of Tsilqhot'in history and Aboriginal encounters with the emerging Canadian state.

After an overview of the relevant case law, Justice Vickers seeks to describe at para. 583 the test established by the Supreme Court of Canada cases for Aboriginal title:

> It appears to me that the Supreme Court of Canada has set a high standard, requiring "regular use or occupancy of definite tracts of land". The Supreme Court has now clearly stated that "[t]o say that title flows from occasional entry and use is inconsistent with.. . .the approach to aboriginal title which this Court has consistently maintained": *Marshall; Bernard*, at para. 59.

He thus seeks to apply the test of exclusive prior occupation to analyze whether the claimants made out their Aboriginal title claim. In applying this test, he analyzes the facts carefully to try to establish which areas were subject to exclusive prior occupation and which not. Ultimately, the sense at which he arrives is that a claim seems likely applicable in respect of some lands within the claim and some not yet claimed, although more evidence would assist the matter further. He thus offers an opinion as to where Aboriginal title may exist but not a definitive conclusion on the Aboriginal title claim. Thus, Justice Vickers endeavours to apply carefully the law as arising from the developing cases.

After addressing several other legal questions, Justice Vickers turns at the end of the judgment to the aim of promoting reconciliation. Expressing worries that extended litigation might actually discourage reconciliation, he notes at para. 1369 that "[t]he narrow role this court can play in defining Tsilhqot'in Aboriginal rights in the Claim Area lies in an application of the jurisprudence to the facts of this case."

Justice Vickers urges the parties to negotiate further and expresses at paras. 1376–78 what in his view these negotiations need to face:

> What is clear to me is that the impoverished view of Aboriginal title advanced by Canada and British Columbia, characterized by the plaintiff as a "postage stamp" approach to title, cannot be allowed to pervade and inhibit genuine negotiations. A tract of land is not just a hunting blind or a favourite fishing hole. Individual sites such as hunting blinds and fishing holes are but a part of the land that has provided "cultural security and continuity" to Tsilhqot'in people for better than two centuries.
>
> A tract of land is intended to describe land over which Indigenous people roamed on a regular basis; land that ultimately defined and sustained them as a people. The recognition of the long-standing presence of Tsilhqot'in people in the Claim Area is a simple, straightforward acknowledgement of an historical fact.
>
> Given this basic recognition, how are the needs of a modern, rural, Indigenous people to be met? How can their contemporary needs and interests be balanced with the needs and interests of the broader society? That is the challenge that lies in the immediate future for Tsilhqot'in people, Canada and British Columbia.

The judgment also opens at least two major new questions for discussion. First, it opens questions related to the rights holder in an Aboriginal title claim. Justice Vickers seeks ultimately to apply to these facts the emerging law of Aboriginal title. He notes at para. 437 that "Aboriginal rights are communal rights. They arise out of the existence and practices of a contemporary community with historical roots." This principle raises immediately an additional question of identifying the proper community that holds the rights at issue, which can be complex because as he notes at para. 446, "Aboriginal people, like people in societies everywhere, typically belong to more than one group that helps to define their identities." Although British Columbia's argument would have seen any rights at issue as connected to the Xeni Gwet'in band, Justice Vickers concludes on the best guidance he can find in the case law and on the facts of the case that the proper rights holder is the larger Tsilhqot'in Nation.

Second, the judgment awakens new issues concerning the interaction of Aboriginal title and private property. Consistently with the Supreme Court of Canada's decision in *Delgamuukw*, Justice Vickers considers that only the federal government has jurisdiction within the Canadian division of powers to legislate with respect to lands affected by Aboriginal title (para. 1039). He concludes at para. 998, then, that Aboriginal title has not been extinguished by provincial grants of land in fee simple or of any other interests in land. The implication is that there may be ongoing Aboriginal title interests in land previously thought to be held by private owners in accordance with the principles of real property law we discussed in earlier Parts.

As of this writing, all parties to this case have filed appeals, although they are also pursuing settlement negotiations. What the future holds for constitutional Aboriginal title case law will remain to be seen in the years ahead. However, already, in both Supreme Court of Canada precedents and in applications in the lower courts, we see the emergence of a set of principles for addressing Aboriginal title cases. Each case, however, remains immensely complex in light of its specific circumstances and the challenges before all of us.

# CHAPTER 19 — BEYOND ABORIGINAL TITLE



## 19.0 — Introduction

The legal recognition of common law Aboriginal title prior to 1982 and the recognition of constitutionalized Aboriginal title since 1982 has had a tremendous significance to Aboriginal cultural communities with special historical and spiritual connections to their traditional territories. However, the doctrine of Aboriginal title also recognizes Aboriginal interests in land in only limited ways, recognizing "ownership" in certain ways but not a jurisdiction to manage a territory. In a number of ways, law related to Canada's Aboriginal peoples and land is going beyond concepts of Aboriginal title.

## 19.1 — Rights of Self-Government

The Supreme Court of Canada has thus far not said much about arguments that Aboriginal nations have rights of self-government. The Court has had opportunities to comment on the issue in some cases, but it has thus far chosen to avoid it. In *R. v. Jones, (*sub nom. *R. v. Pamajewon)* [1996] 2 S.C.R. 821 (S.C.C.), the Shawanaga and Eagle Lake First Nations in Ontario asserted a right to regulate gambling activities on their reserve lands. The First Nations put the claim as a general claim to manage their reserve lands, but the Court was ready only to assume without deciding that there was an inherent right of self-government (para. 24). It applied the *Van der Peet* test to the specific claim of managing gambling and determined that there was insufficient evidence before it on this point, thus avoiding broader questions.

However, the Canadian government in a 1995 policy document (Minister of

Indian Affairs and Northern Development, *Aboriginal Self-Government: The Government of Canada's Approach to Implementation of the Inherent Right and the Negotiation of Aboriginal Self-Government*), recognized an inherent right of Aboriginal self-government. The federal and provincial governments have been involved since then in negotiations with various Aboriginal First Nations of the implementation of this principle.

One important agreement, signed in 1999, was the Nisga'a Agreement, agreed between the federal government, the British Columbia government, and the Nisga'a people of northern British Columbia. The Nisga'a people were the community who brought the *Calder* case to the Supreme Court of Canada in 1973, this already after decades of pursuing their claim, so this Agreement provides one example of how long some negotiation processes take. The Nisga'a Agreement resolves the outstanding land issues with the Nisga'a people and provides for Nisga'a jurisdiction in many areas of law, including property rights, culture and language, child and family services, administration of justice, and education.

Legal challenges were put against the Nisga'a agreement in *Campbell v. British Columbia (Attorney General)*. There, Justice Williamson examined a wide set of legal precedents, ranging from the Marshall Trilogy in the United States through Canadian constitutional law on the division of powers. He concluded that Aboriginal nations had self-government prior to the assertion of Canadian sovereignty and that Canadian sovereignty had not extinguished all self-government, and he upheld the validity of the Nisga'a Agreement as a modern treaty.

## 19.2 — Modern Self-Government Agreements

The Nisga'a Agreement is only the first in a long list of modern self-government treaties reached with different First Nations within Canada in recent years. Others bearing some similarities to the Nisga'a Agreement include the Tlicho Agreement, the Westbank First Nation Agreement, the Kluane First Nation Agreement, the Carcross/Tagish First Nation Agreement, and others. Many agreements have been reached in parts of the country where there had not previously been treaties, notably in British Columbia. Others have been reached to find ways to redefine existing treaty arrangements.

A distinctive development has of course also taken place in what used to be the eastern part of the Northwest Territories, where the territory of Nunavut was separated officially from the Northwest Territories in 1999. Nunavut was created in large part to establish a place where Canada's Inuit peoples would exercise governmental authority. The government of Nunavut can carry out governance of the territory, including property and resource management, in accordance with traditional Inuit values and law.

## 19.3 — Evolving Webs of Property Relationships

These kinds of self-government agreements are one context in which there is the possibility for property relationships of Aboriginal peoples to evolve in new ways in accordance with the modern needs of Aboriginal peoples. At the same time, there is a complex web of property relationships involving Aboriginal property beyond a single form of Aboriginal title, and these also have potential to continue to evolve to continue to meet modern needs.

Within lands held by Aboriginal communities, either as reserve lands under the *Indian Act*, R.S.C. 1985, c. I-5 and/or as lands held under Aboriginal title, Aboriginal communities themselves have ways of allocating property. Within some communities, there are customary rights of possession by particular individuals, and First Nations operating under the *Indian Act* also apply a set of legal norms related to individual certificates of possession.

In addition, some First Nations are opting out of the land-related provisions of the *Indian Act* under new federal legislation, the *First Nations Land Management Act*, S.C. 1999, c. 24. This legislation authorizes First Nations who opt for its system to adopt land codes and engage in certain forms of regulation. A number of First Nations sought this legislation to allow them to pursue economic development more effectively. Some of the provisions of this legislation allow land codes adopted by First Nations under the legislation to create greater certainty for the mortgageability of certain leasehold interests on reserves. Attempts to establish property regimes better enabling borrowing of funds for various purposes are an example of how webs of property relationships are evolving, with First Nations attempting to strike careful balances between traditional values and values related to economic development.

Some First Nations have also used the *First Nations Land Management Act* to enact matrimonial property regimes, and others will do so under self-government agreements. Because of the Canadian division of powers, provincial matrimonial property legislation does not apply to Aboriginal property in certain contexts (*Derrickson v. Derrickson*, [1986] 1 S.C.R. 285 (S.C.C.)). The result has been an absence of legal protection in this area for decades, although, at this writing, the federal government is again discussing legislation that might address this while leaving room for individual First Nations to adopt their own systems.

## 19.4 — Property and Identity

The examples in the last section are just some small illustrations of the ways in which property has so much to do with who we are as individuals and as communities. In legal regimes connected with Aboriginal property, as in property law generally, property law is not static. Property law connects in vital ways to economic development, to cultural modes of being, to spirituality, and to our identities.

Aboriginal nations within Canada are in many instances seeking ways of making property law work more effectively for economic development. At the same time, property law must work coherently with other values, with perpetuation of cultural frameworks that ground individuals and communities, and with spiritual relationships.

These challenging questions are not unique to Canadian contexts. Around the world, property law matters. Around the world, indigenous peoples are seeking ways of having their perspectives recognized, whether in areas related to real property law or in seeking protections within intellectual property law for indigenous knowledge. The challenges of finding harmonies between different values in a complex area like property law are challenges for us all, and each of us can play a part in working toward reconciliations.

# INDEX

# PART II AND PART III — FURTHER READING


Atiyah, P.S., *The Sale of Goods*, 11th ed. by J. N. Adams (London: Longman, 2005).

Brownlie, I., *Principles of Public International Law*, 6th ed. (Oxford: Oxford University Press, 2003).

Cuming, Ronald C.C., *Saskatchewan and Manitoba Personal Property Security Acts Handbook* (Calgary: Carswell, 1994).

Hargreaves, A.D., *An Introduction to the Principles of Land Law*, 4th ed. by George A. Grove and J.F. Garner (London: Sweet and Maxwell, 1963).

Hayton, David J., ed., *Megarry's Manual of the Law of Real Property*, 8th ed. (London, Sweet and Maxwell, 2002).

Hogg, P.W., *Constitutional Law of Canada*, student ed. (Toronto: Carswell, 2007).

Holdsworth, Sir William, *A History of English Law*, vols. 1 to 9 (London: Sweet and Maxwell, 1903).

La Forest, Anne Warner, *Anger and Honsberger Law of Real Property*, 3rd ed., vols. 1 and 2 (Aurora: Canada Law Book, 2006).

Linden, Allen M. & Bruce Feldthussen, *Canadian Tort Law*, 8th ed. (Toronto: Butterworths, 2006).

Maine, Sir Henry, *Ancient Law*, 5th ed. (London: John Murray, 1884).

Milsom, S.F.C., *Historical Foundations of the Common Law*, 2d ed. (Toronto: Butterworths, 1981)

Pollock, Sir Frederick & Frederic William Maitland, *The History of English Law Before the Time of Edward I*, 2nd ed. (Washington: Lawyers' Literary Club, 1959).

Salmond, John W., *Jurisprudence*, 5th ed. (London: Stevens and Haynes, 1916).

Simpson, A.W.B., *A History of the Land Law*, rev. ed. (Oxford: Clarendon Press).

Sinclair, Alan M. & Margaret McCallum, *Introduction to Real Property*, 5th ed. (Markham: Butterworths, 2005).

Tyler, E.L.G. & N.E. Palmer, eds., *Crossley Vaines' Personal Property*, 5th ed. (London:: Butterworths, 1973).

Waddams, S.M. *The Law of Contracts*, 5th ed. (Aurora: Canada Law Book, 2005).

Ziff, Bruce, *Principles of Property Law*, 4th ed. (Toronto: Carswell, 2006).

# PART IV — CITATIONS AND REFERENCES


Barsh, Russel L. & James Youngblood Henderson, "The Supreme Court's *van der Peet* Trilogy: Naïve Imperialism and Ropes of Sand" (1997) 42 McGill L.J. 994.

Borrows, John, "Constitutional Law from a First Nations Perspective: Self-Government and the Royal Proclamation" (1994) 20 U.B.C.L. Rev. 1.

Borrows, John, *Recovering Canada: The Resurgence of Indigenous Law* (Toronto: University of Toronto Press, 2007).

Brownlie, I., *Principles of Public International Law*, 6th ed. (Oxford: Oxford University Press, 2003).

Chartrand, Paul, "*R. v. Marshall; R. v. Bernard:* The Return of the Native", (2006) 55 U.N.B.L.J. 135.

Henderson, James Youngblood, *First Nations Jurisprudence and Aboriginal Rights: Defining the Just Society* (Saskatoon: University of Saskatchewan Native Law Centre, 2006).

Hogg, P.W., *Constitutional Law of Canada*, student ed. (Toronto: Carswell, 2007).

Little Bear, Leroy, "A Concept of Native Title" (Dec. 1976) CASNP Bulletin 2-58.

McMillen, Christian W., *Making Indian Law: The Hualapai Land Case and the Birth of Ethnohistory* (New Haven, Yale University Press, 2007).

McNeil, Kent, *Common Law Aboriginal Title* (Oxford: Clarendon Press, 1989).

Morse, Bradford W., ed., *Aboriginal Peoples and the Law: Indian, Métis and Inuit Rights in Canada*, rev. 1st ed. (Ottawa: Carleton University Press, 1989).

Newman, Dwight G., "*Tsilhqot'in Nation v. British Columbia* and Civil Justice: Analyzing the Procedural Interaction of Evidentiary Principles and Aboriginal Oral History" (2005) 43 Alberta L. Rev. 423.

Royal Commission on Aboriginal Peoples, *Report of the Royal Commission on Aboriginal Peoples*, vols. 1 to 5 (Ottawa: Canadian Communication Group, 1996).

Slattery, Brian, "Understanding Aboriginal Rights" (1987) 66 Can. Bar Rev. 727.

Smith, J.H., *Appeals to the Privy Council from the American Plantations* (New York: Columbia University Press, 1950).

Vansina, Jan, *Oral Tradition as History* (Madison: University of Wisconsin Press, 1985).

Walters, Mark, "The Morality of Aboriginal Law" (2006) 31 Queen's L.J. 470.

Wicken, William, *M'kmaq Treaties on Trial: History, Land and Donald Marshall Junior* (Toronto: University of Toronto Press, 2002).